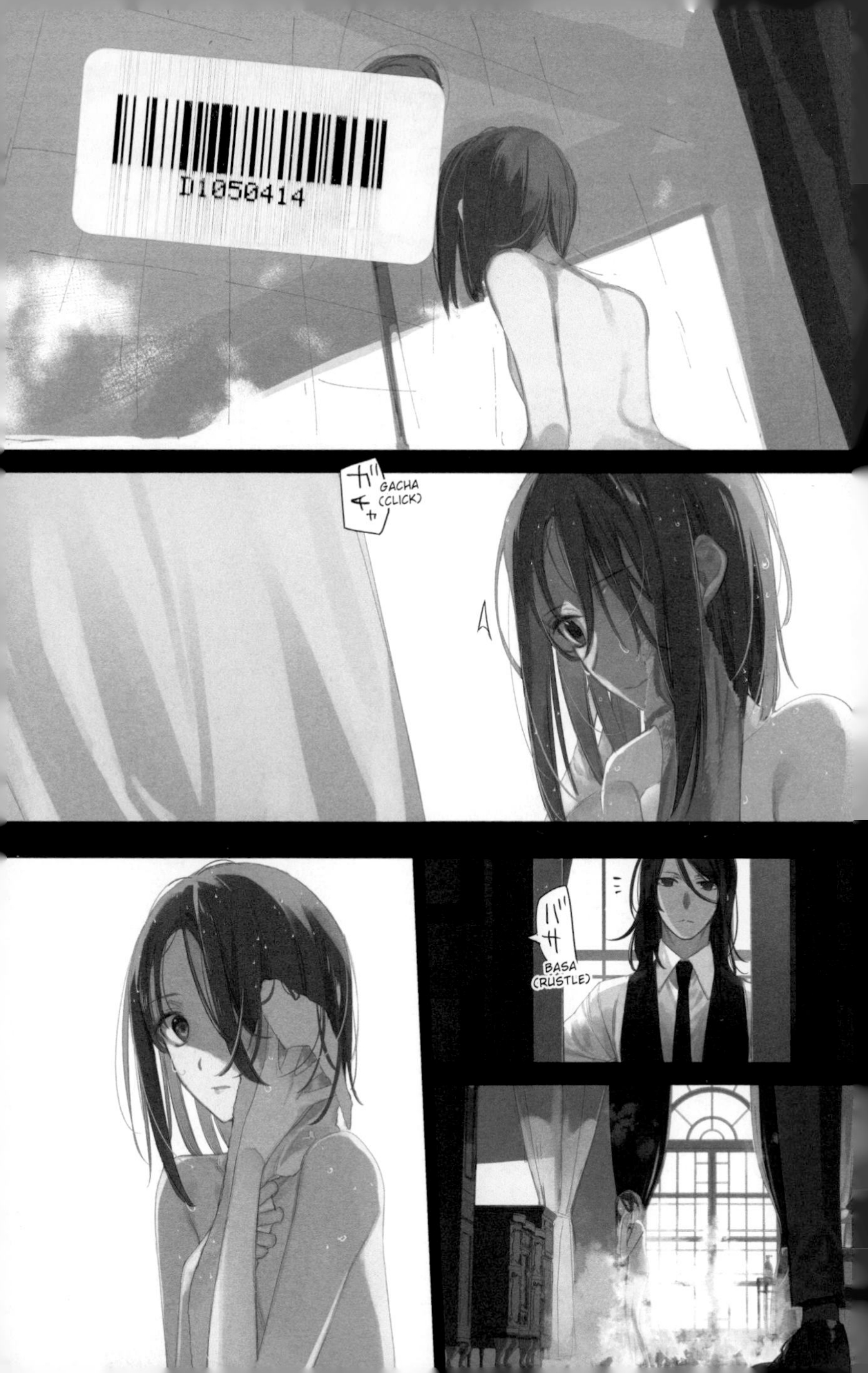
ガチャ
GACHA (CLICK)
バサ
BASA (RUSTLE)

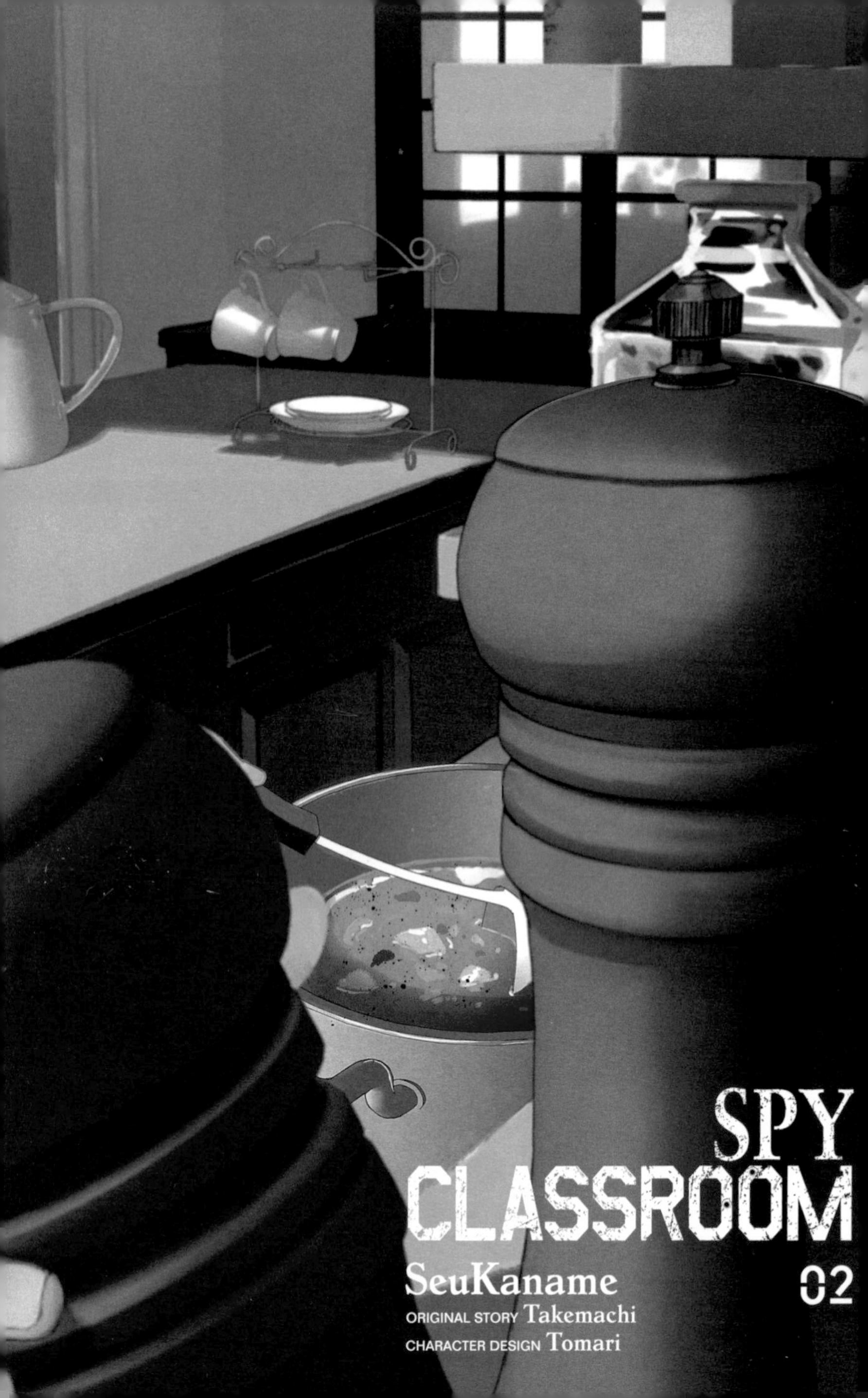
SPY
CLASSROOM
02
SeuKaname
ORIGINAL STORY Takemachi
CHARACTER DESIGN Tomari

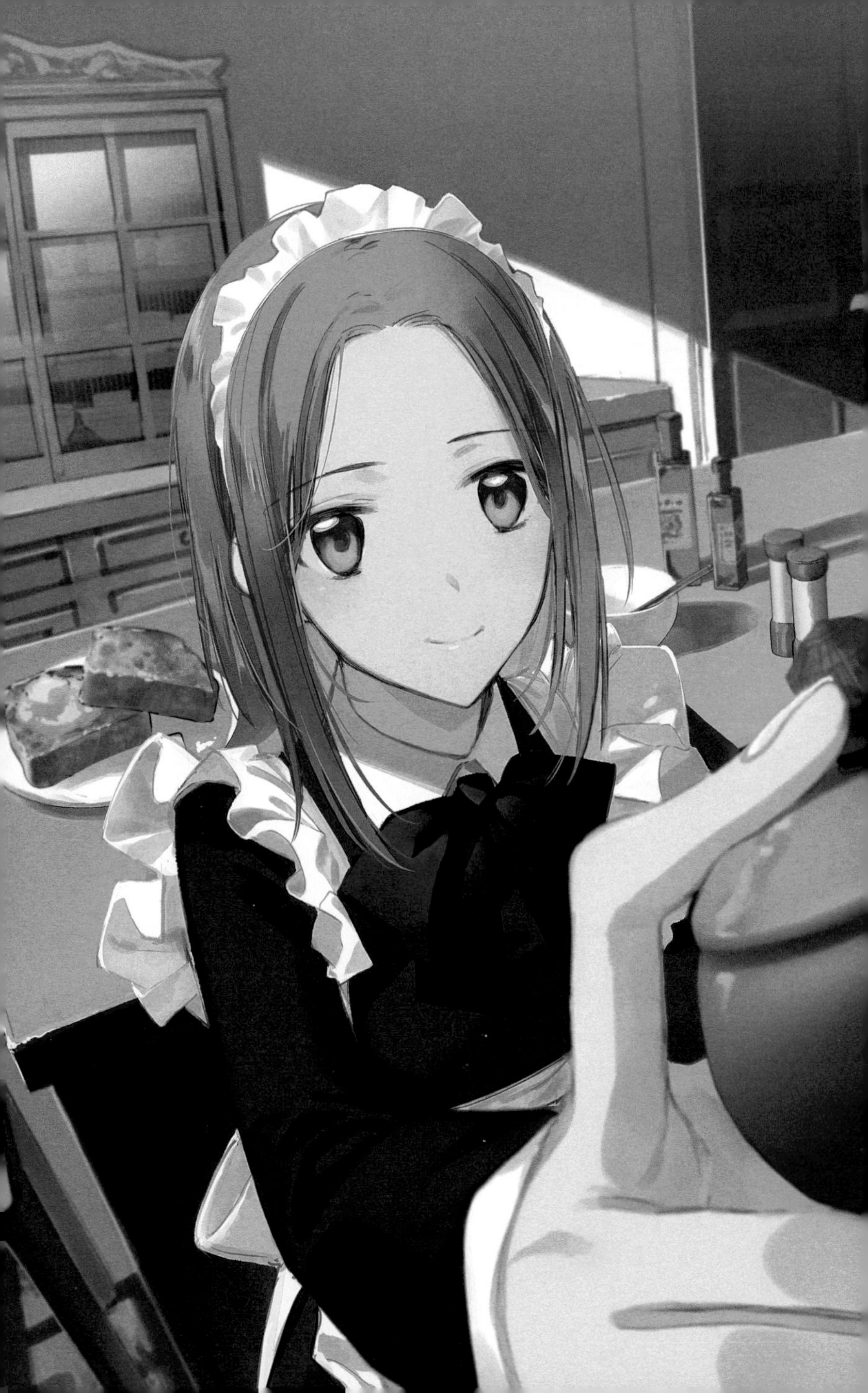

CONTENTS

SPY CLASSROOM
Specialized lessons for an Impossible Mission
Code name Daughter Dearest

Chapter 6 — Seduction

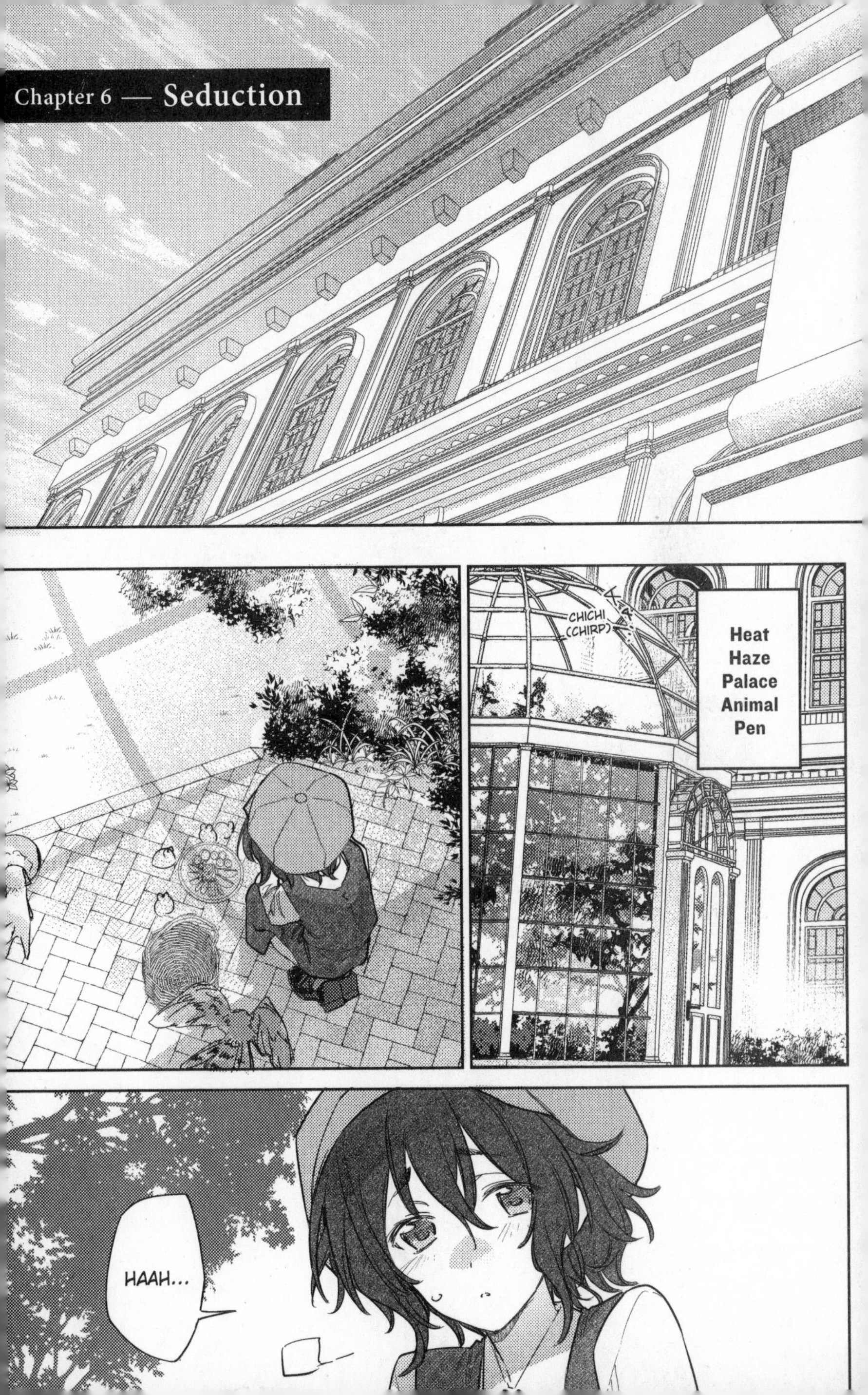
CHICHI (CHIRP)
Heat Haze Palace Animal Pen
HAAH...

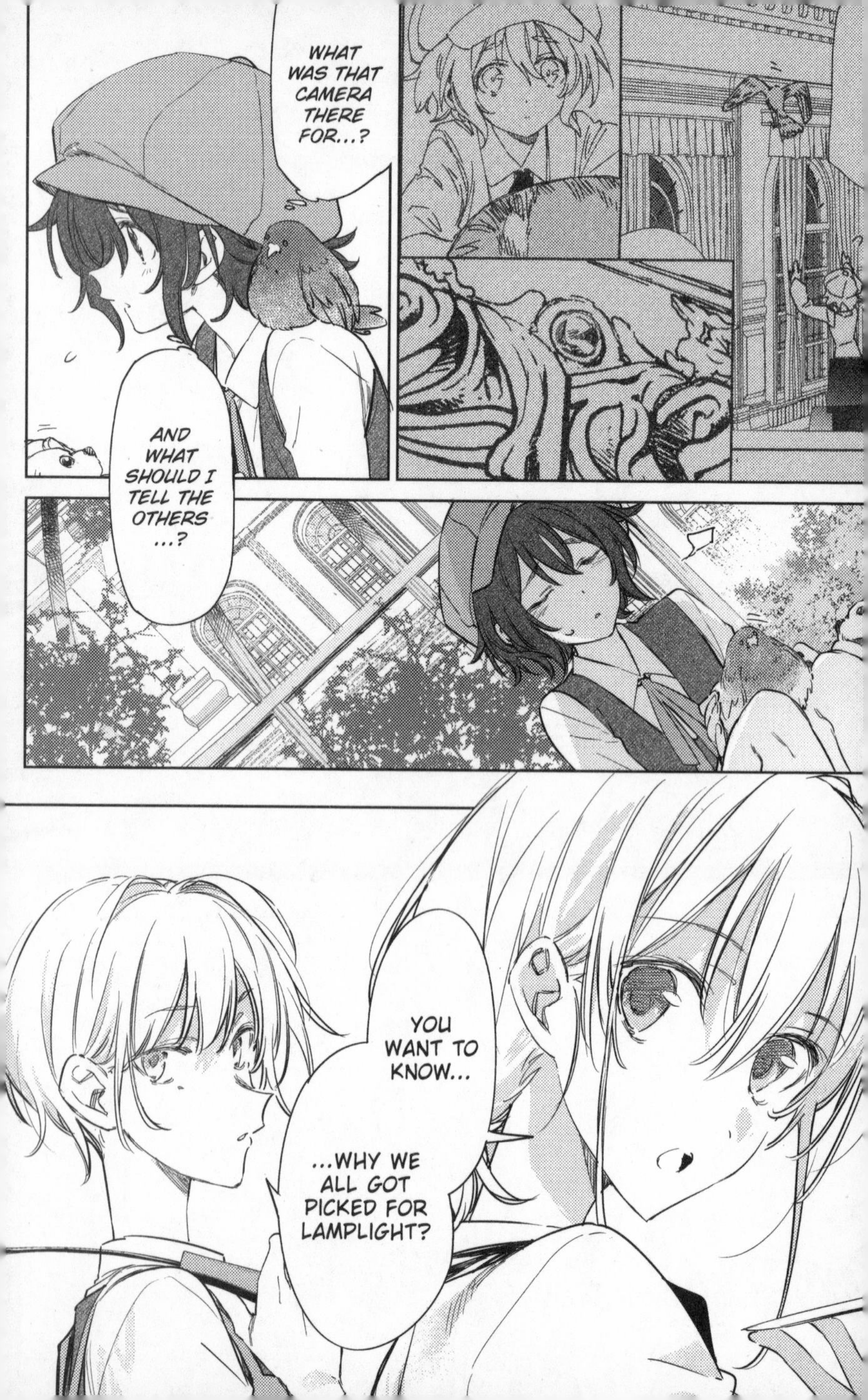
WHAT WAS THAT CAMERA THERE FOR...?
AND WHAT SHOULD I TELL THE OTHERS ...?
YOU WANT TO KNOW...
...WHY WE ALL GOT PICKED FOR LAMPLIGHT?

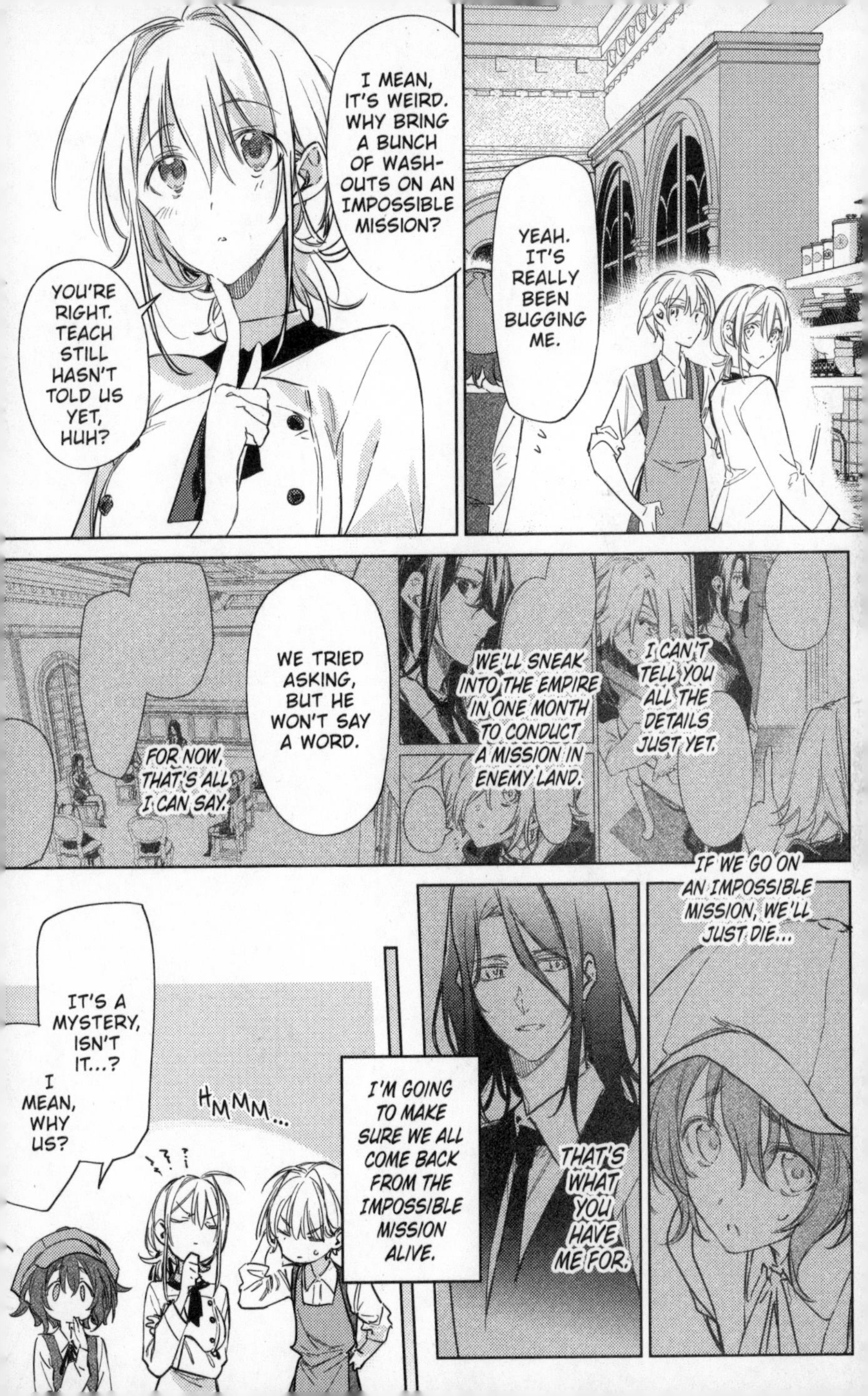
YEAH. IT'S REALLY BEEN BUGGING ME.
I MEAN, IT'S WEIRD. WHY BRING A BUNCH OF WASH-OUTS ON AN IMPOSSIBLE MISSION?
YOU'RE RIGHT. TEACH STILL HASN'T TOLD US YET, HUH?
I CAN'T TELL YOU ALL THE DETAILS JUST YET.
WE'LL SNEAK INTO THE EMPIRE IN ONE MONTH TO CONDUCT A MISSION IN ENEMY LAND.
WE TRIED ASKING, BUT HE WON'T SAY A WORD.
FOR NOW, THAT'S ALL I CAN SAY.
IF WE GO ON AN IMPOSSIBLE MISSION, WE'LL JUST DIE...
THAT'S WHAT YOU HAVE ME FOR.
I'M GOING TO MAKE SURE WE ALL COME BACK FROM THE IMPOSSIBLE MISSION ALIVE.
IT'S A MYSTERY, ISN'T IT...?
I MEAN, WHY US?
HMMM...

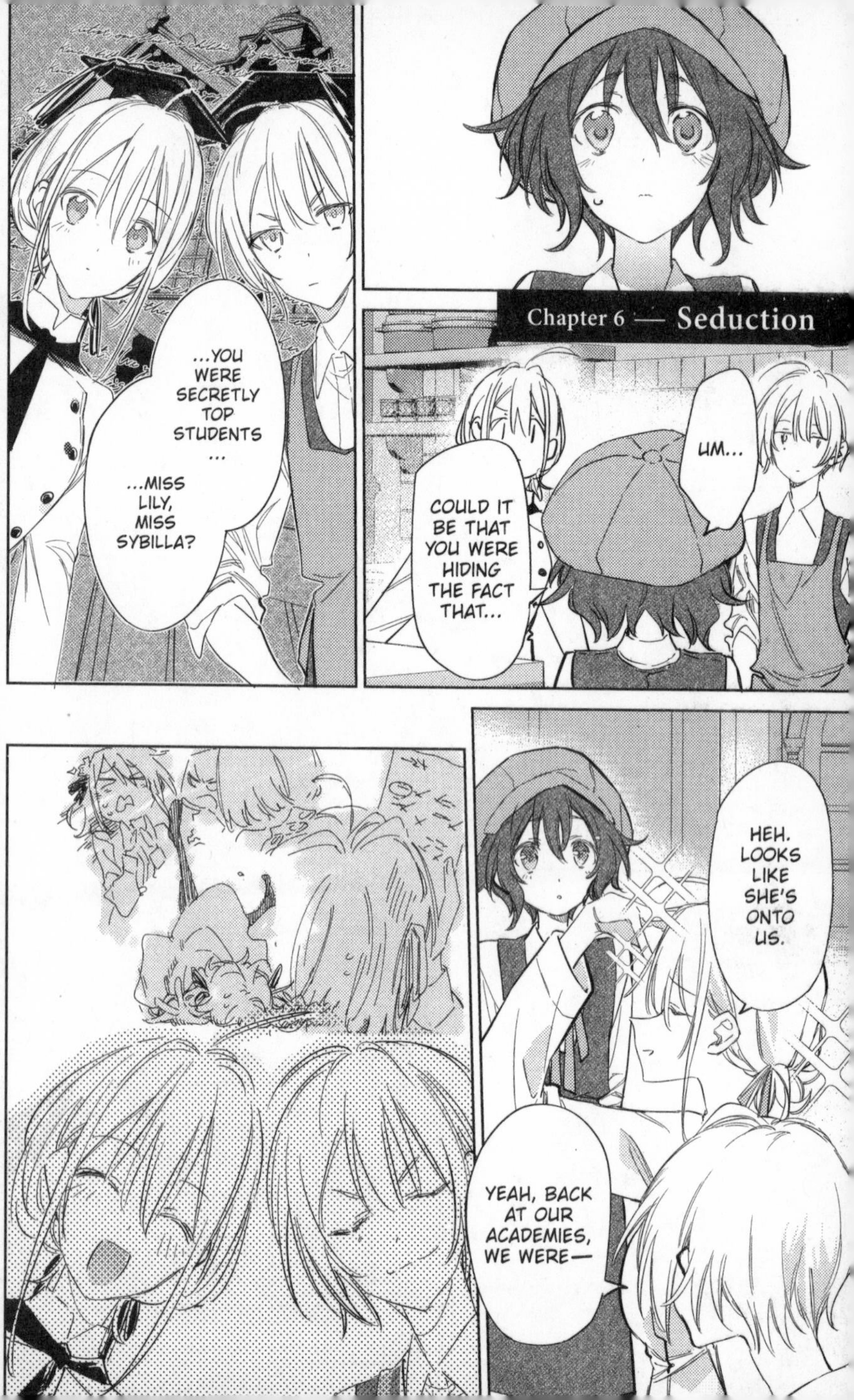
Chapter 6 — Seduction
UM...
COULD IT BE THAT YOU WERE HIDING THE FACT THAT...
...YOU WERE SECRETLY TOP STUDENTS ...
...MISS LILY, MISS SYBILLA?
HEH. LOOKS LIKE SHE'S ONTO US.
YEAH, BACK AT OUR ACADEMIES, WE WERE—

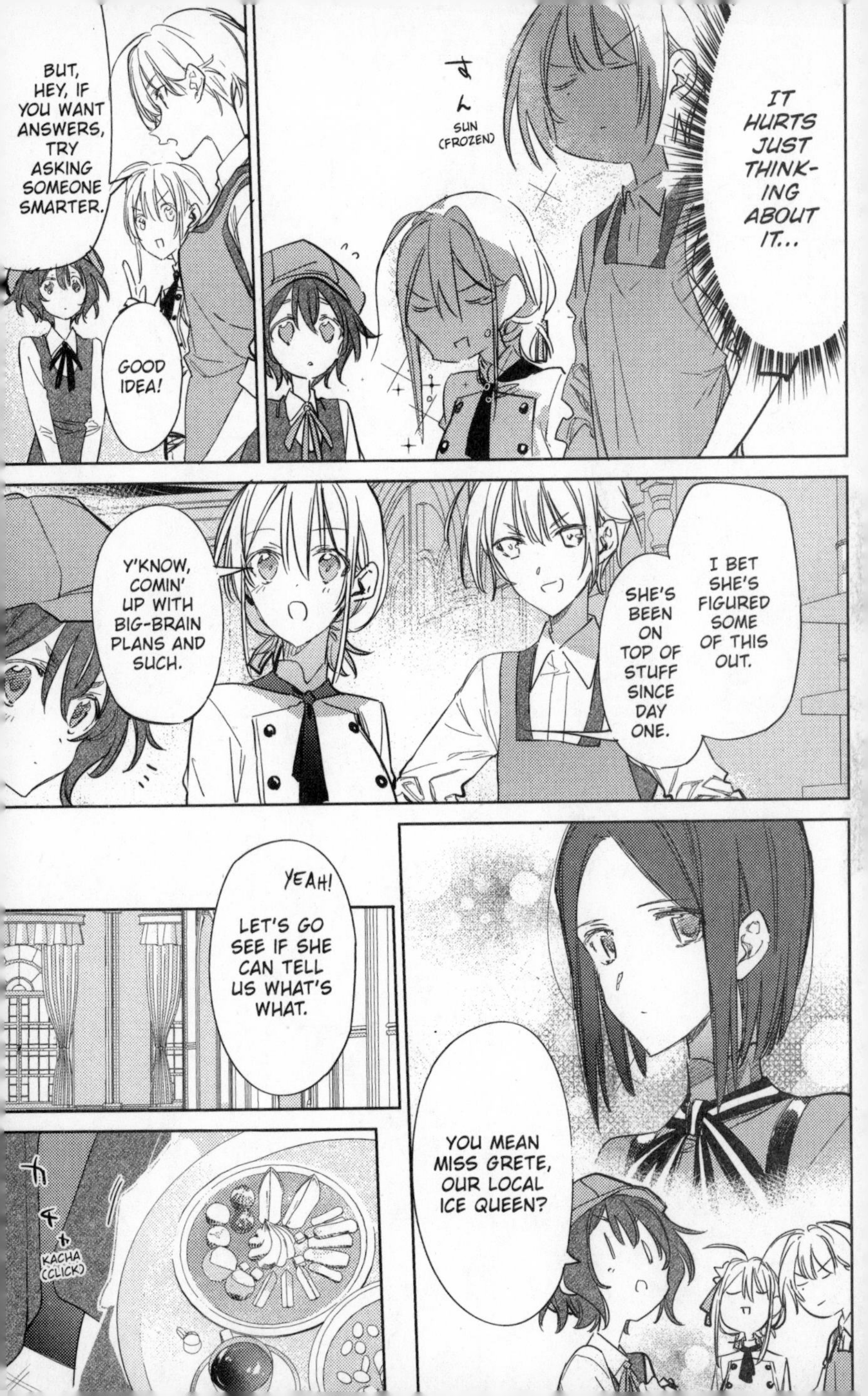
IT HURTS JUST THINKING ABOUT IT...
すん
SUN (FROZEN)
BUT, HEY, IF YOU WANT ANSWERS, TRY ASKING SOMEONE SMARTER.
GOOD IDEA!
I BET SHE'S FIGURED SOME OF THIS OUT.
SHE'S BEEN ON TOP OF STUFF SINCE DAY ONE.
Y'KNOW, COMIN' UP WITH BIG-BRAIN PLANS AND SUCH.
YOU MEAN MISS GRETE, OUR LOCAL ICE QUEEN?
YEAH!
LET'S GO SEE IF SHE CAN TELL US WHAT'S WHAT.
カチャ
KACHA (CLICK)

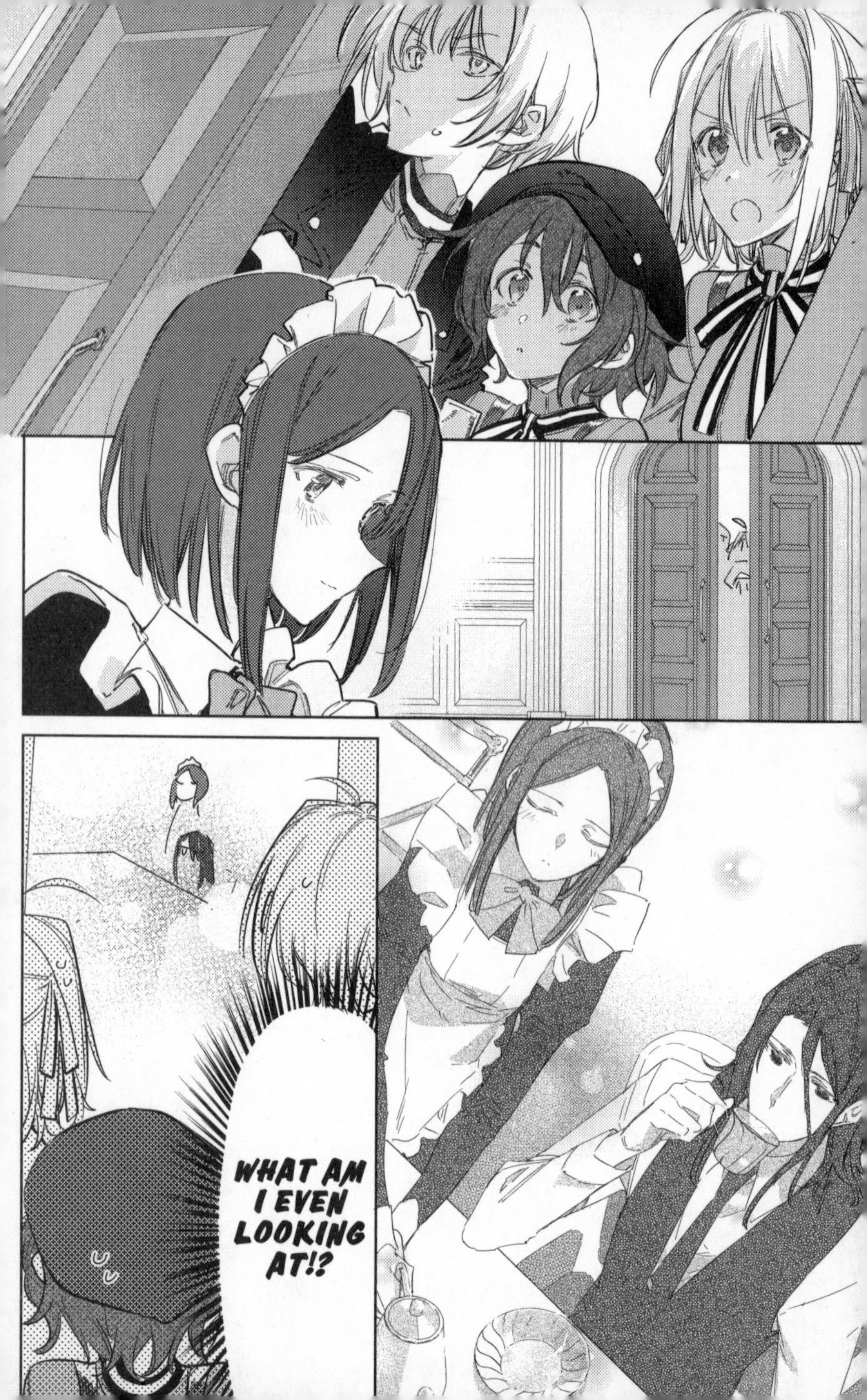
WHAT AM I EVEN LOOKING AT!?

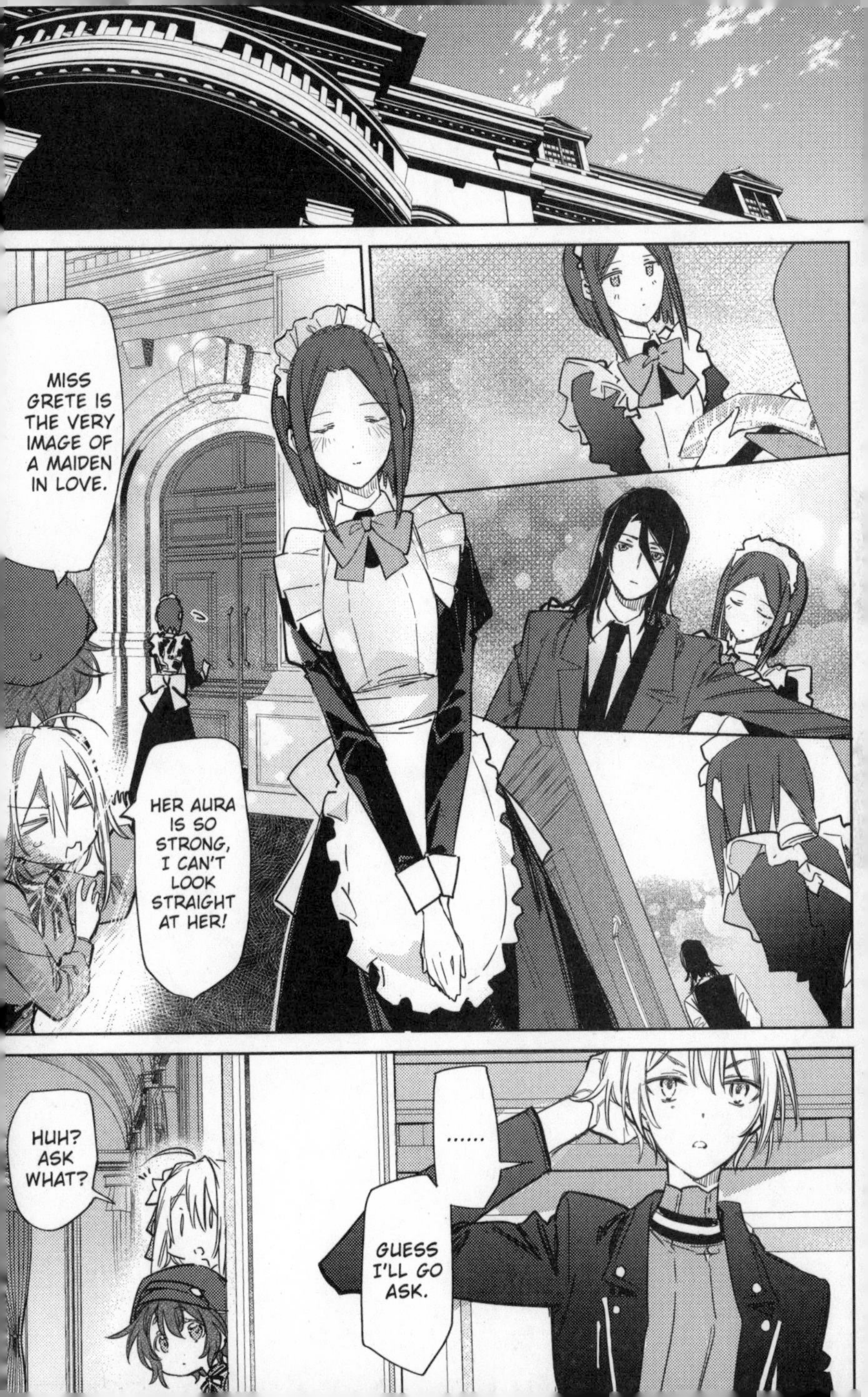
MISS GRETE IS THE VERY IMAGE OF A MAIDEN IN LOVE.
HER AURA IS SO STRONG, I CAN'T LOOK STRAIGHT AT HER!
......
GUESS I'LL GO ASK.
HUH? ASK WHAT?

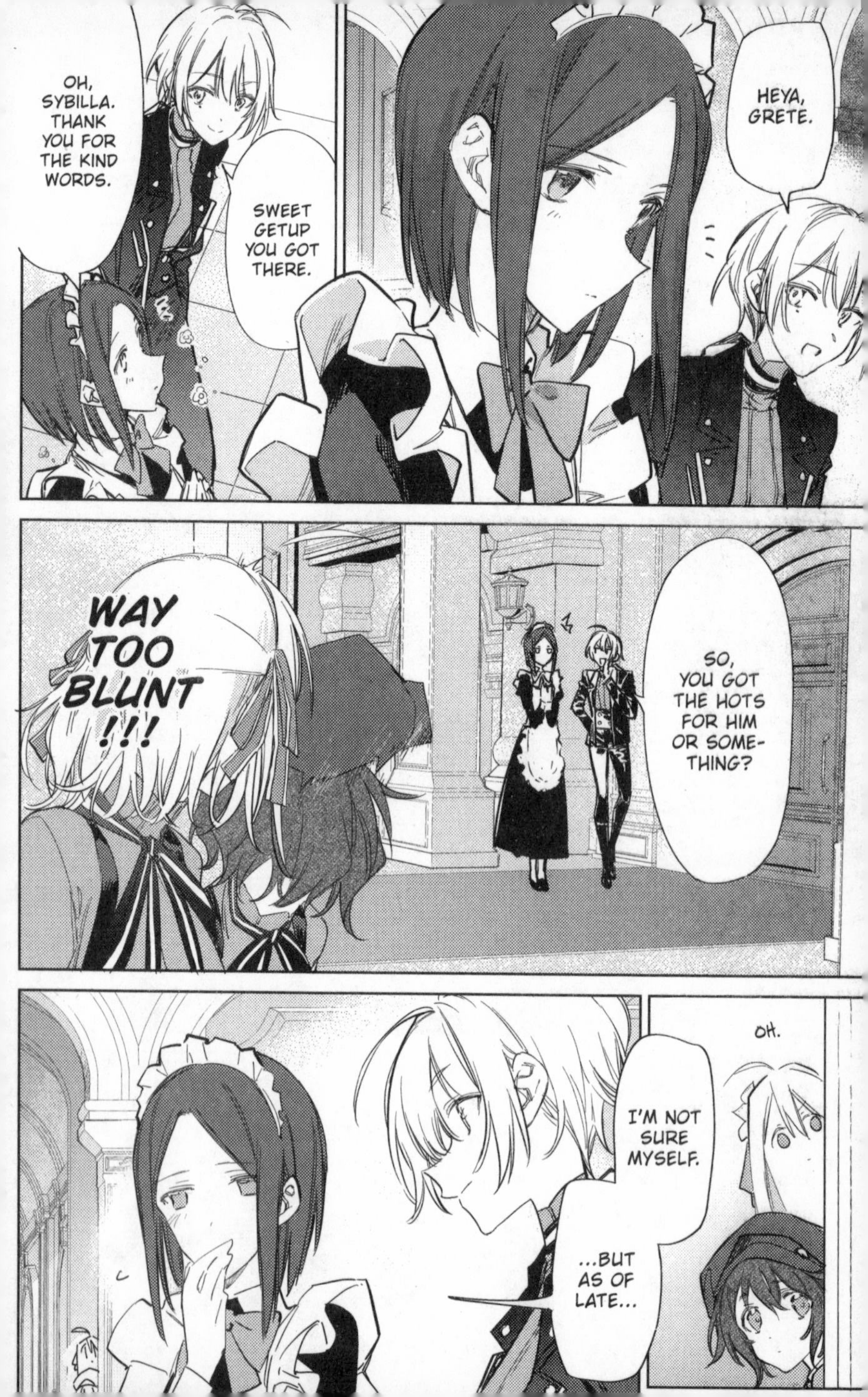
HEYA, GRETE.
SWEET GETUP YOU GOT THERE.
OH, SYBILLA. THANK YOU FOR THE KIND WORDS.
SO, YOU GOT THE HOTS FOR HIM OR SOME-THING?
WAY TOO BLUNT!!!
OH.
I'M NOT SURE MYSELF.
...BUT AS OF LATE...

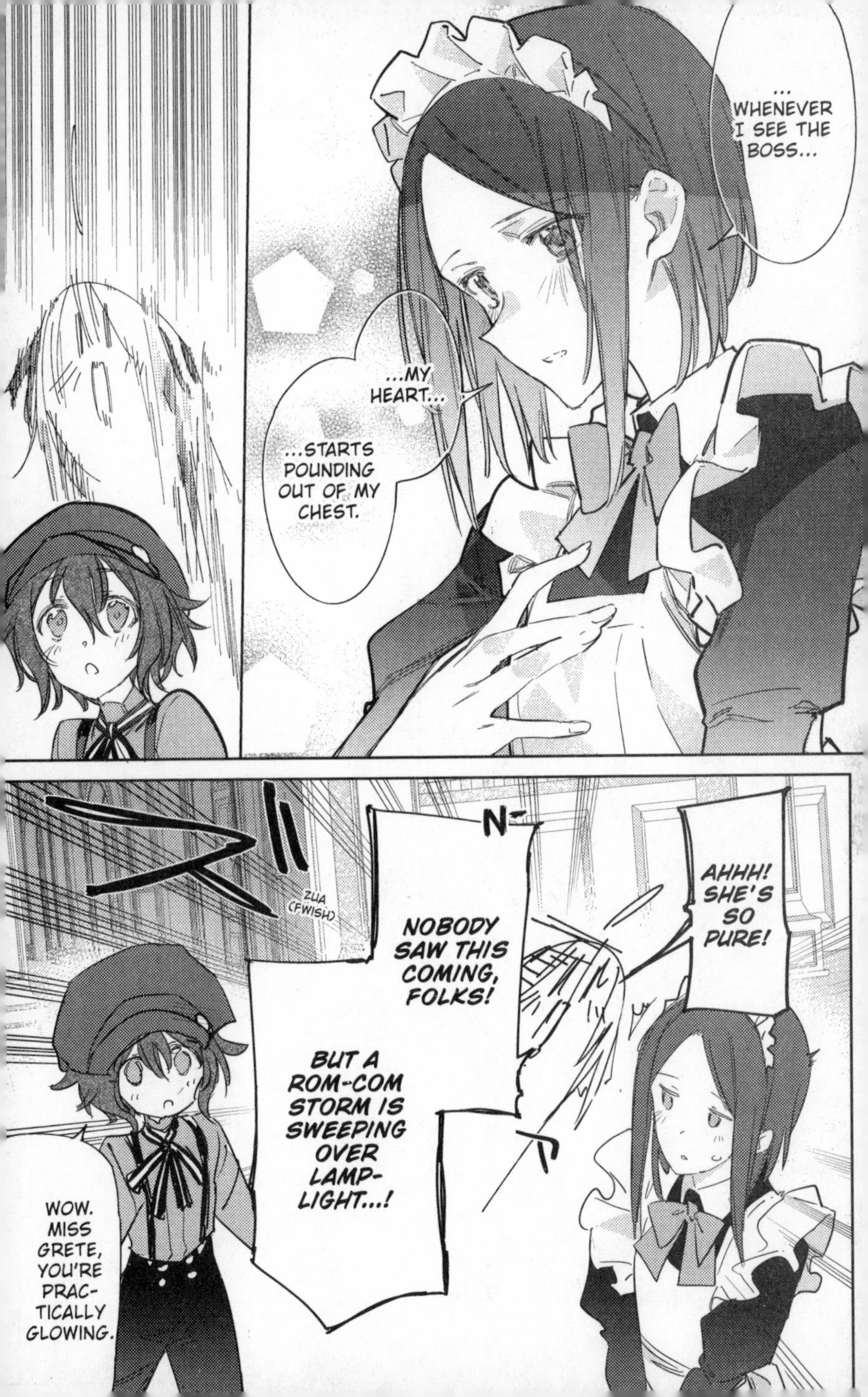

... WHENEVER I SEE THE BOSS...
...MY HEART...
...STARTS POUNDING OUT OF MY CHEST.
N-
AHHH! SHE'S SO PURE!
NOBODY SAW THIS COMING, FOLKS!
BUT A ROM-COM STORM IS SWEEPING OVER LAMP-LIGHT...!
ZUA (FWISH)
WOW. MISS GRETE, YOU'RE PRAC-TICALLY GLOWING.

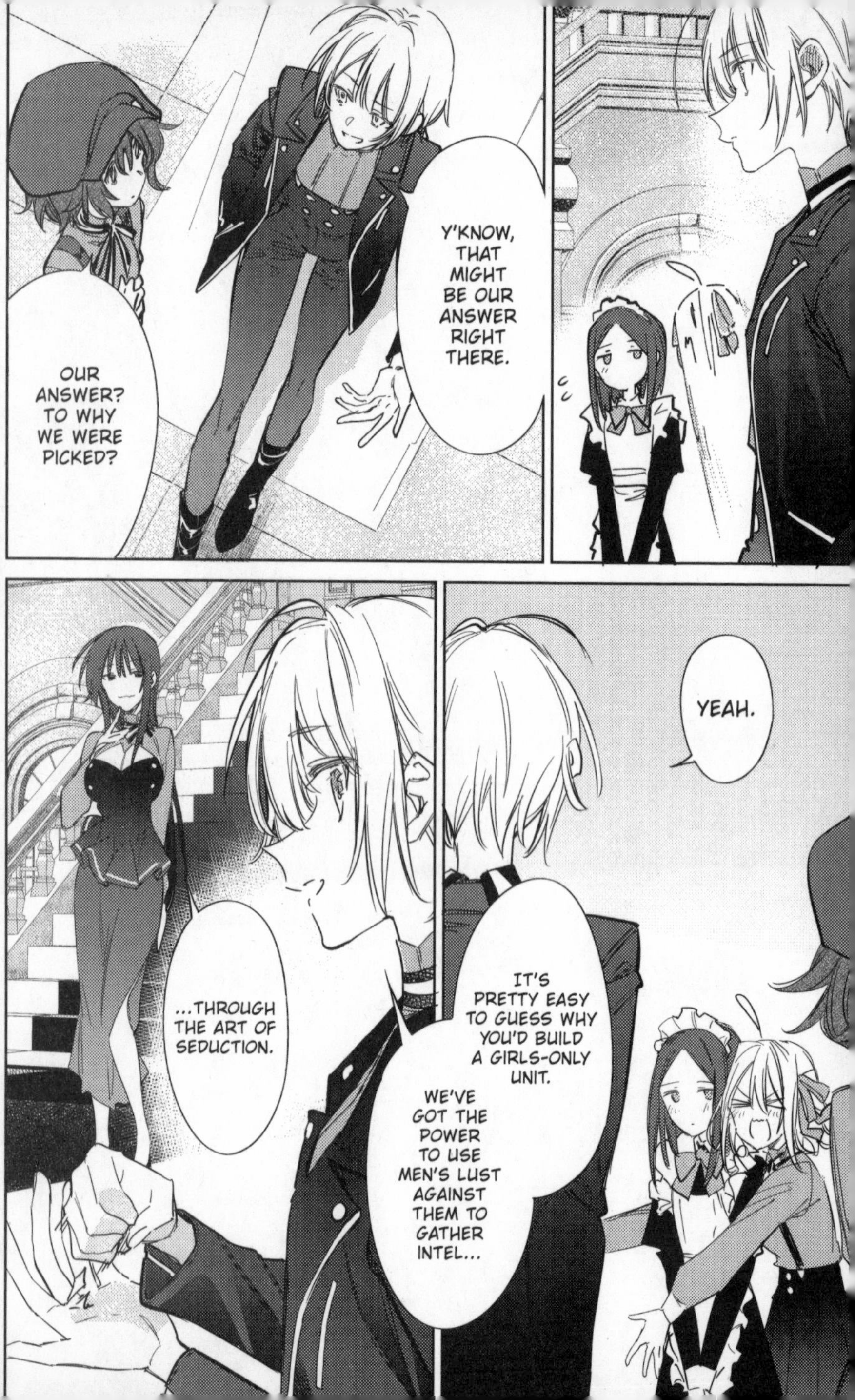
Y'KNOW, THAT MIGHT BE OUR ANSWER RIGHT THERE.
OUR ANSWER? TO WHY WE WERE PICKED?
YEAH.
IT'S PRETTY EASY TO GUESS WHY YOU'D BUILD A GIRLS-ONLY UNIT.
WE'VE GOT THE POWER TO USE MEN'S LUST AGAINST THEM TO GATHER INTEL...
...THROUGH THE ART OF SEDUCTION.

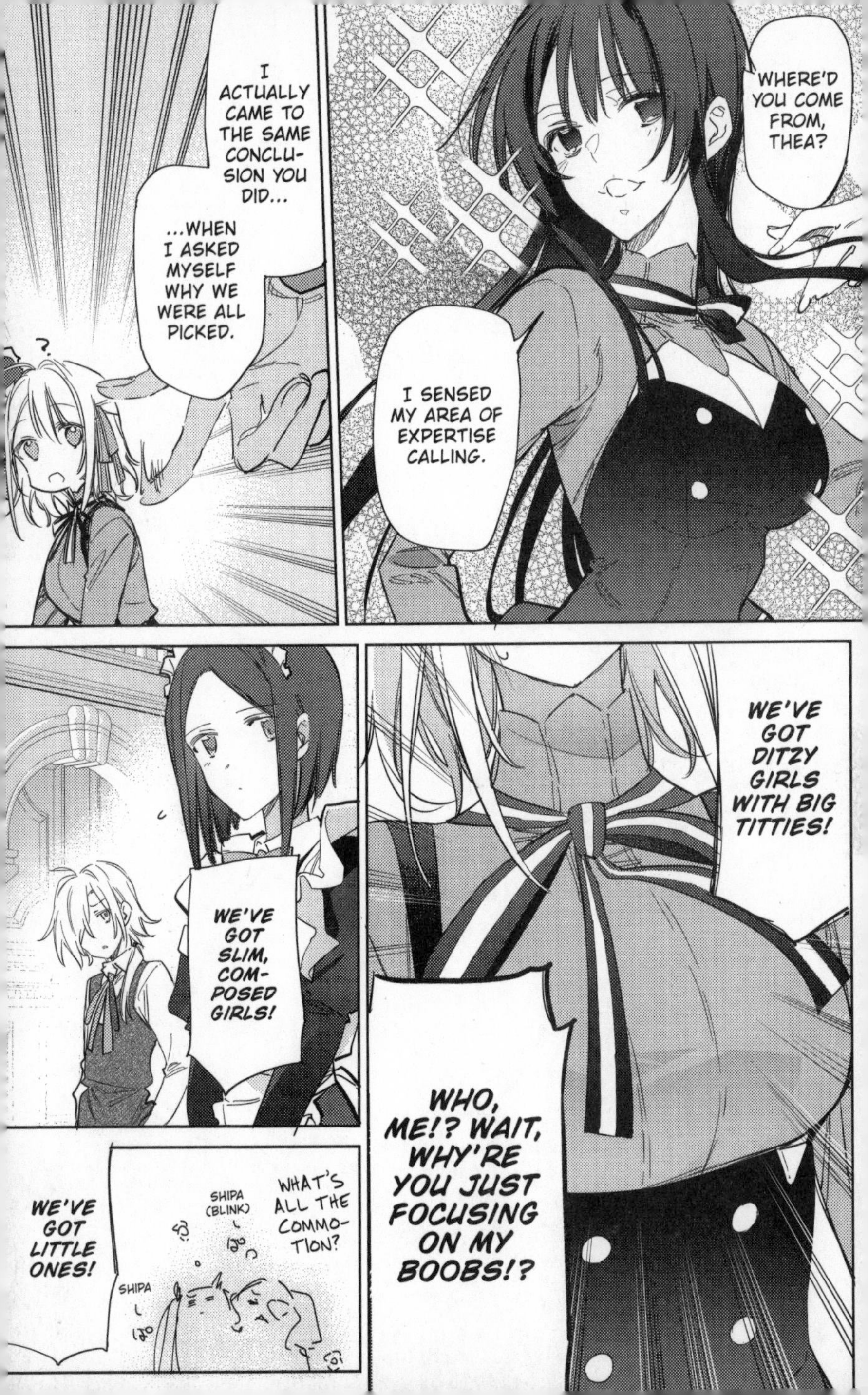
WHERE'D YOU COME FROM, THEA?
I SENSED MY AREA OF EXPERTISE CALLING.
I ACTUALLY CAME TO THE SAME CONCLUSION YOU DID...
...WHEN I ASKED MYSELF WHY WE WERE ALL PICKED.
?
WE'VE GOT DITZY GIRLS WITH BIG TITTIES!
WHO, ME!? WAIT, WHY'RE YOU JUST FOCUSING ON MY BOOBS!?
WE'VE GOT SLIM, COMPOSED GIRLS!
WHAT'S ALL THE COMMOTION?
SHIPA (BLINK)
SHIPA
WE'VE GOT LITTLE ONES!

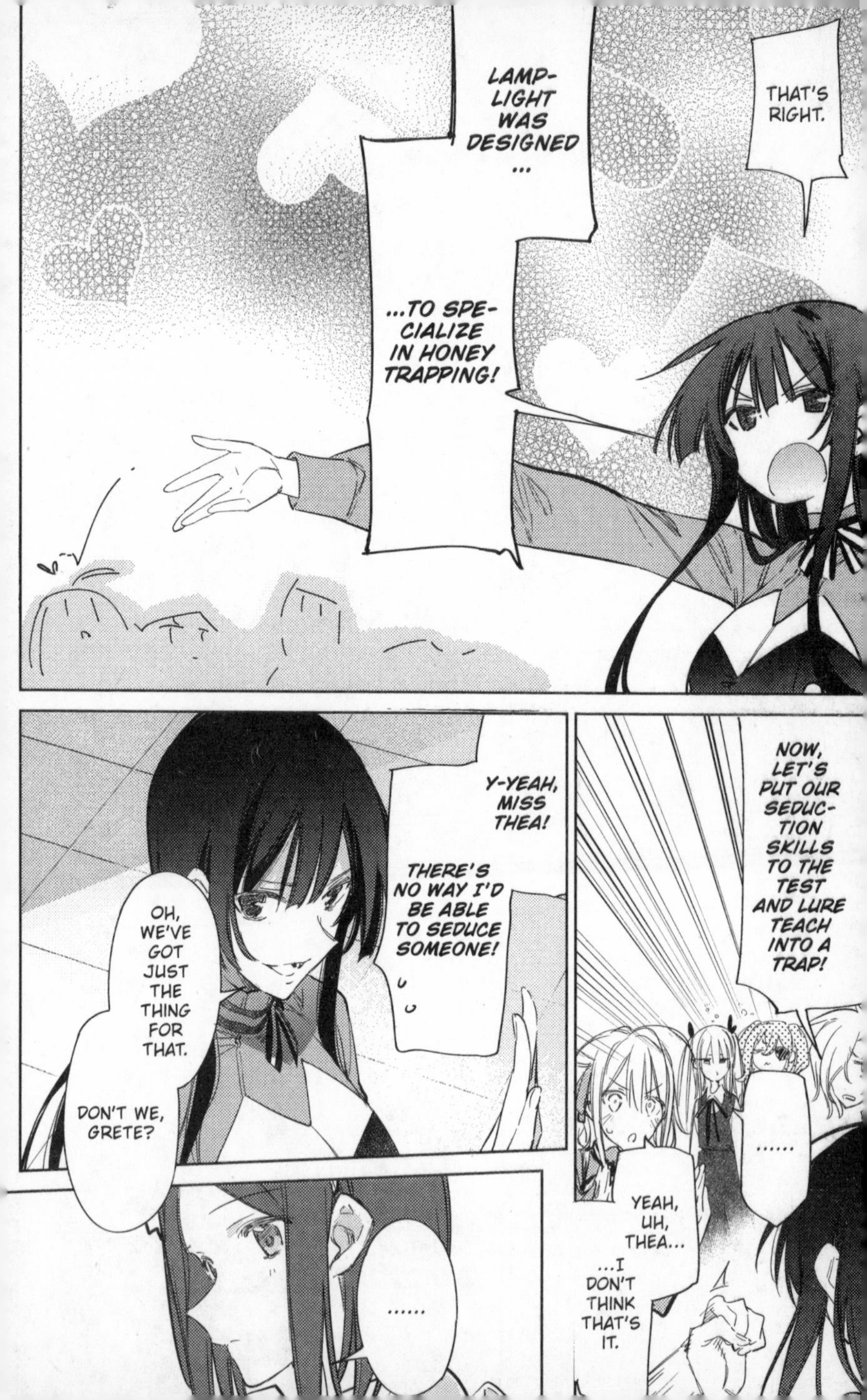
THAT'S RIGHT.
LAMP-LIGHT WAS DESIGNED...
...TO SPE-CIALIZE IN HONEY TRAPPING!
NOW, LET'S PUT OUR SEDUC-TION SKILLS TO THE TEST AND LURE TEACH INTO A TRAP!
......
YEAH, UH, THEA...
...I DON'T THINK THAT'S IT.
Y-YEAH, MISS THEA!
THERE'S NO WAY I'D BE ABLE TO SEDUCE SOMEONE!
OH, WE'VE GOT JUST THE THING FOR THAT.
DON'T WE, GRETE?
......

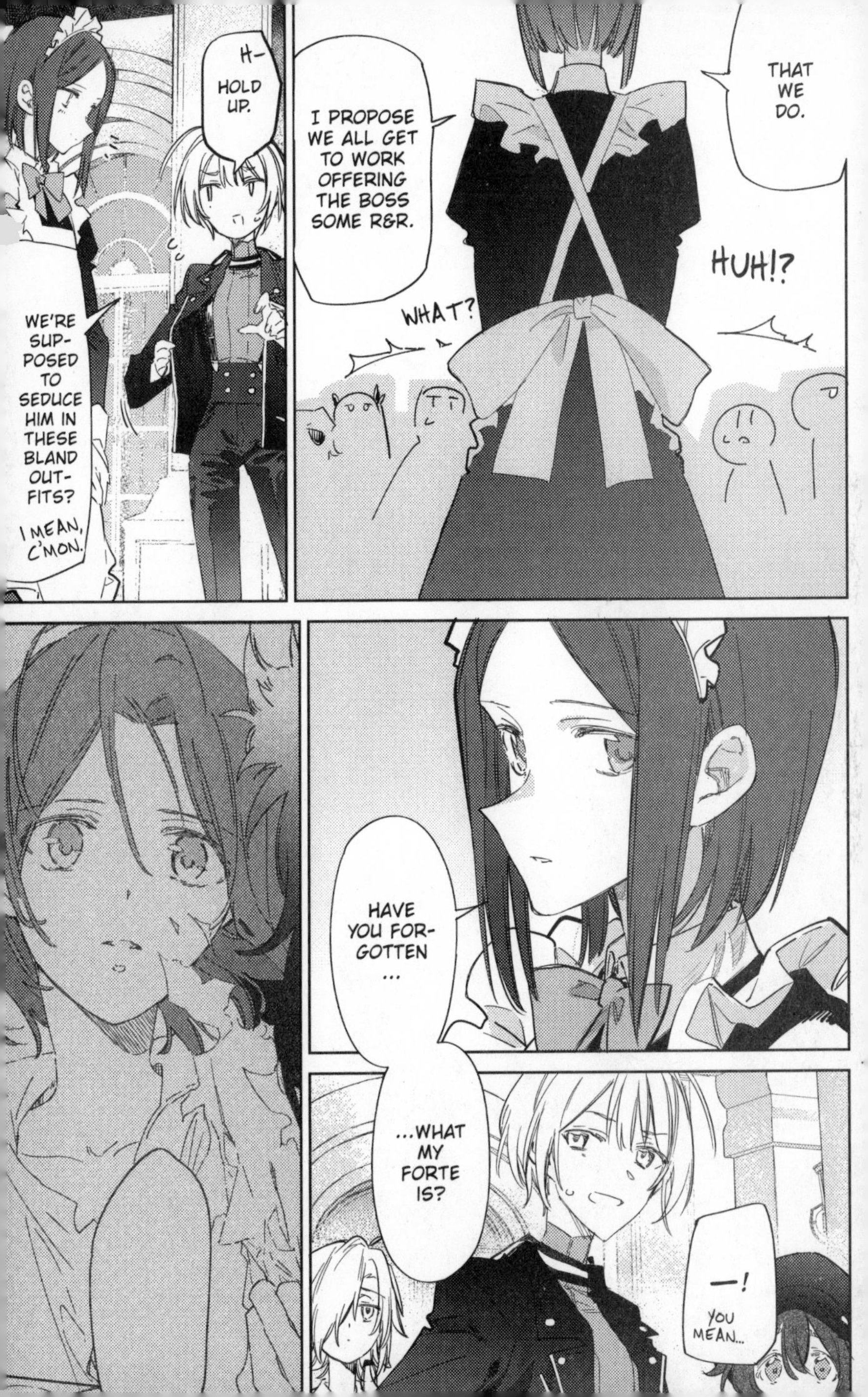
THAT WE DO.
I PROPOSE WE ALL GET TO WORK OFFERING THE BOSS SOME R&R.
HUH!?
WHAT?
H- HOLD UP.
WE'RE SUP-POSED TO SEDUCE HIM IN THESE BLAND OUT-FITS?
I MEAN, C'MON.
HAVE YOU FOR-GOTTEN...
...WHAT MY FORTE IS?
—!
YOU MEAN...

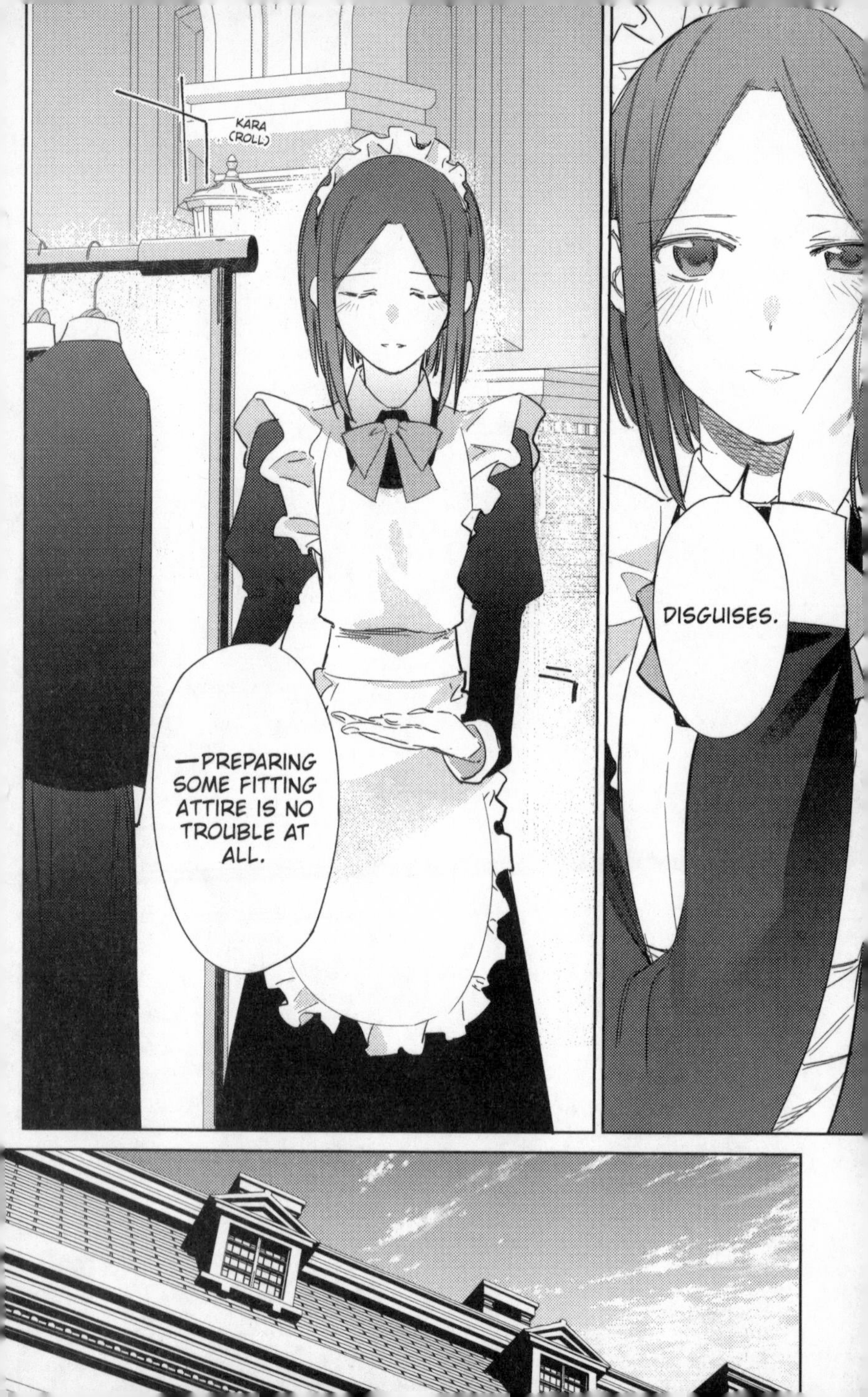
DISGUISES.
KARA (ROLL)
—PREPARING SOME FITTING ATTIRE IS NO TROUBLE AT ALL.

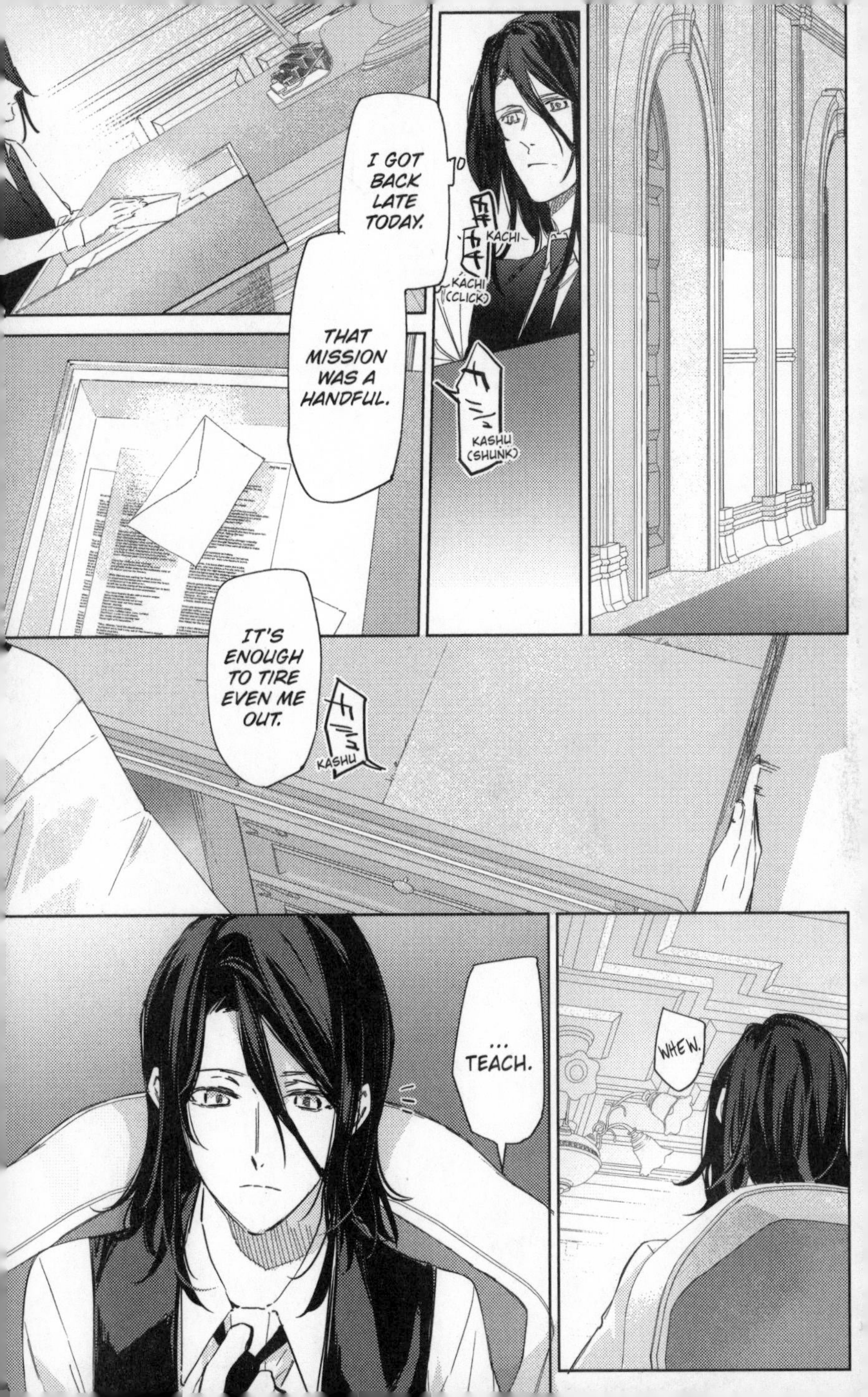
I GOT BACK LATE TODAY.
KACHI
KACHI (CLICK)
THAT MISSION WAS A HANDFUL.
KASHU (SHUNK)
IT'S ENOUGH TO TIRE EVEN ME OUT.
KASHU
WHEW.
...TEACH.

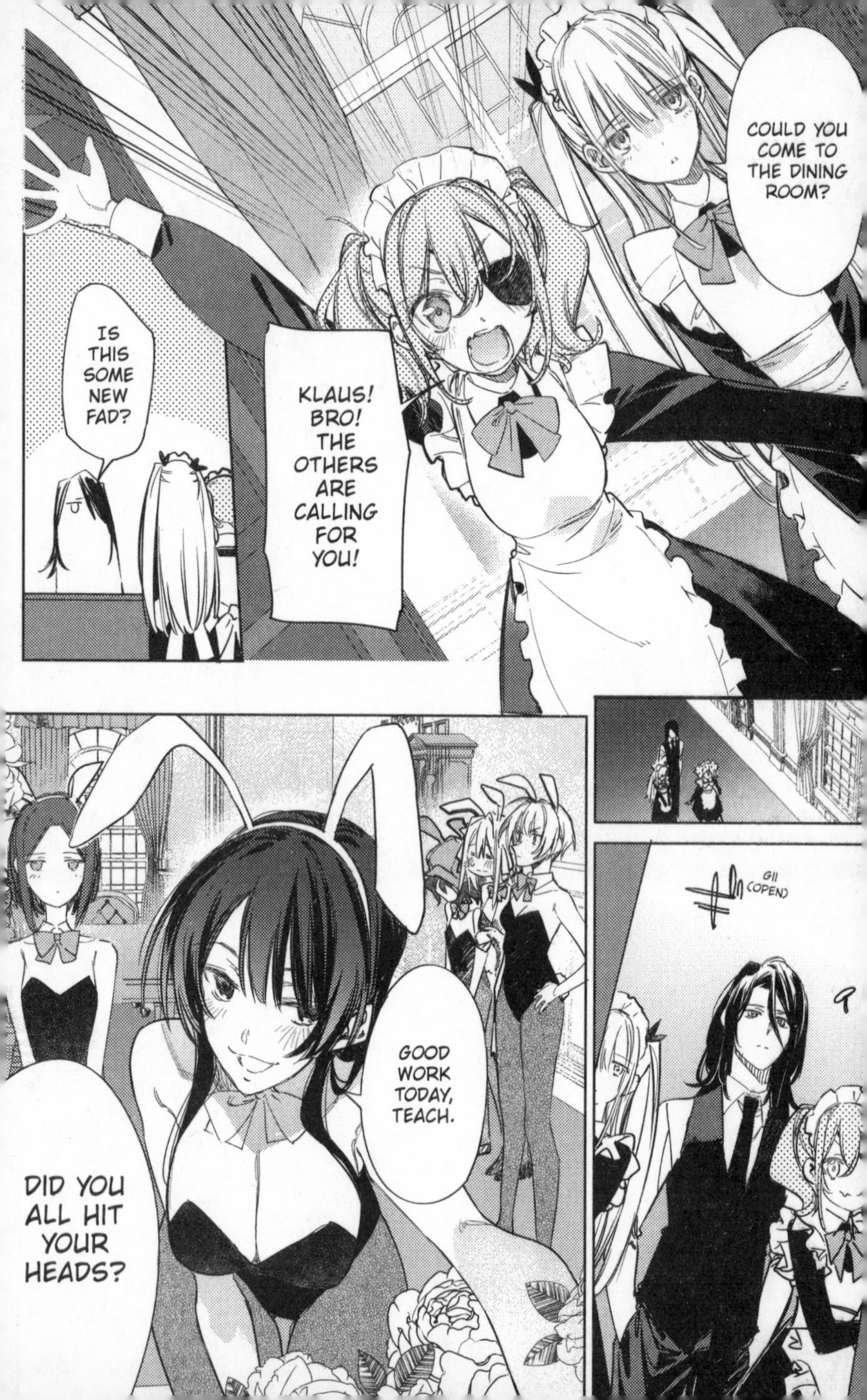
COULD YOU COME TO THE DINING ROOM?
KLAUS! BRO! THE OTHERS ARE CALLING FOR YOU!
IS THIS SOME NEW FAD?
GII (OPEN)
GOOD WORK TODAY, TEACH.
DID YOU ALL HIT YOUR HEADS?

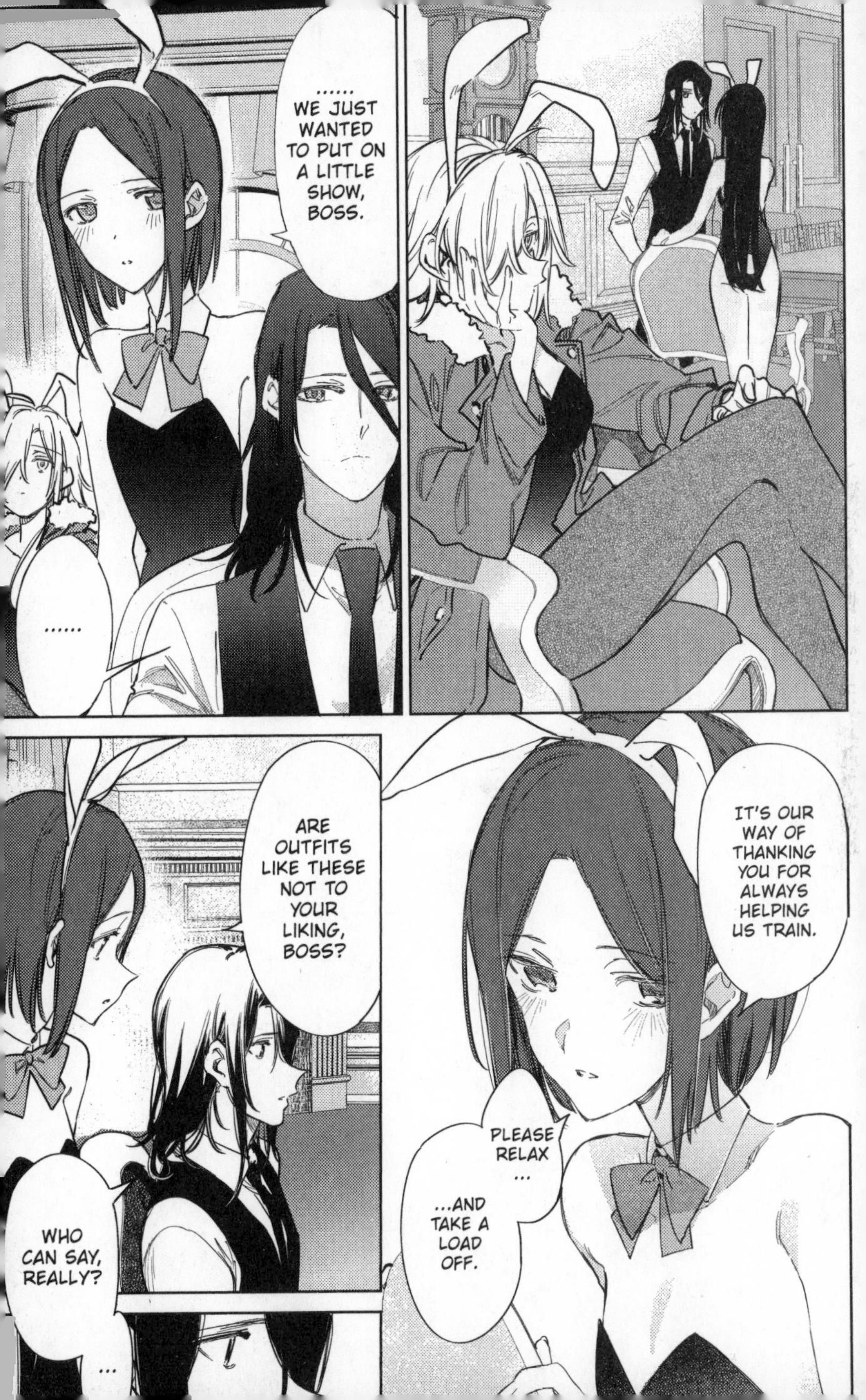
......
WE JUST WANTED TO PUT ON A LITTLE SHOW, BOSS.
......
IT'S OUR WAY OF THANKING YOU FOR ALWAYS HELPING US TRAIN.
PLEASE RELAX ...
...AND TAKE A LOAD OFF.
ARE OUTFITS LIKE THESE NOT TO YOUR LIKING, BOSS?
WHO CAN SAY, REALLY?
...

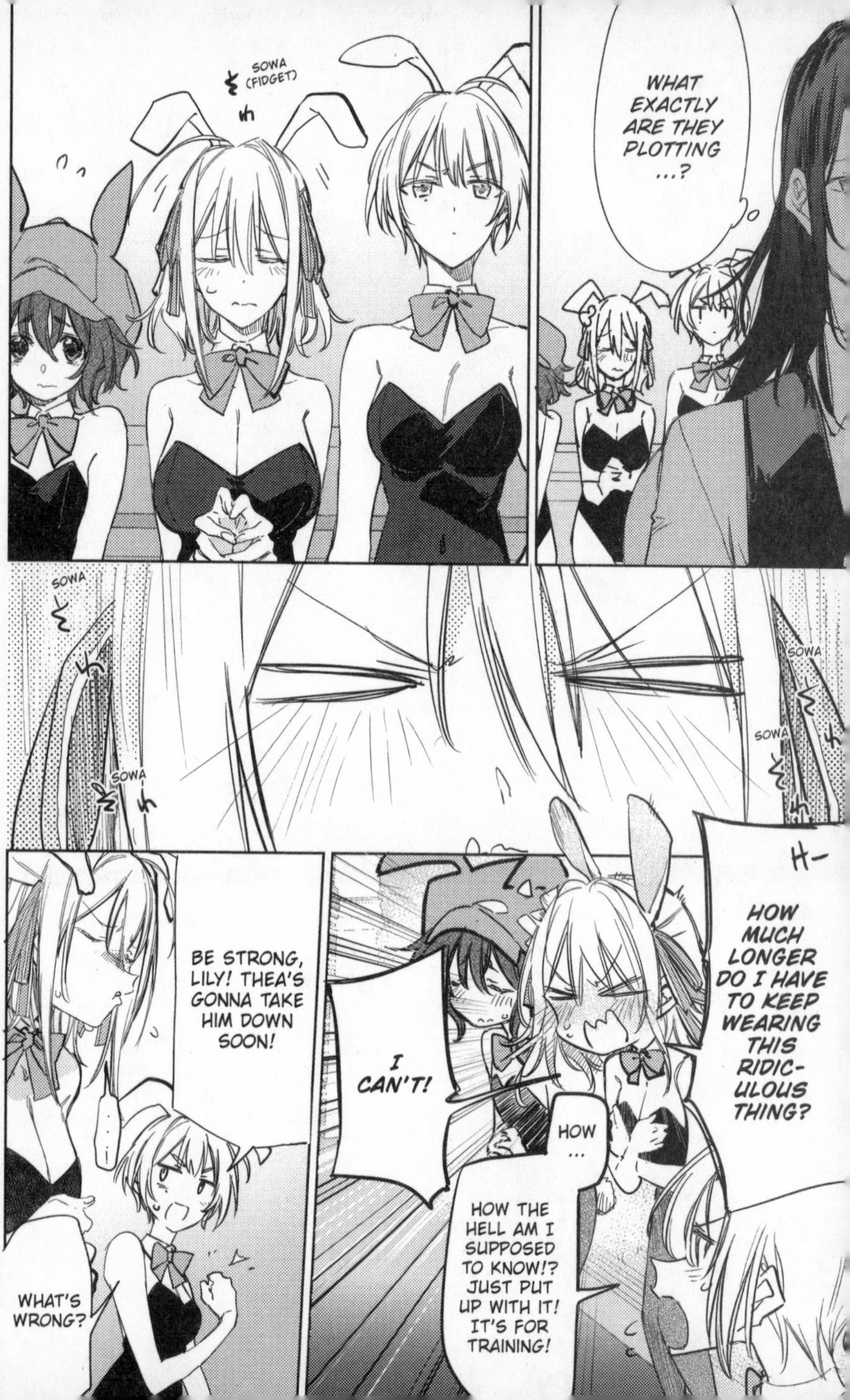
WHAT EXACTLY ARE THEY PLOTTING ...?
SOWA (FIDGET)
SOWA
SOWA
SOWA
SOWA
H—
HOW MUCH LONGER DO I HAVE TO KEEP WEARING THIS RIDIC-ULOUS THING?
I CAN'T!
HOW ...
HOW THE HELL AM I SUPPOSED TO KNOW!? JUST PUT UP WITH IT! IT'S FOR TRAINING!
BE STRONG, LILY! THEA'S GONNA TAKE HIM DOWN SOON!
...!
WHAT'S WRONG?

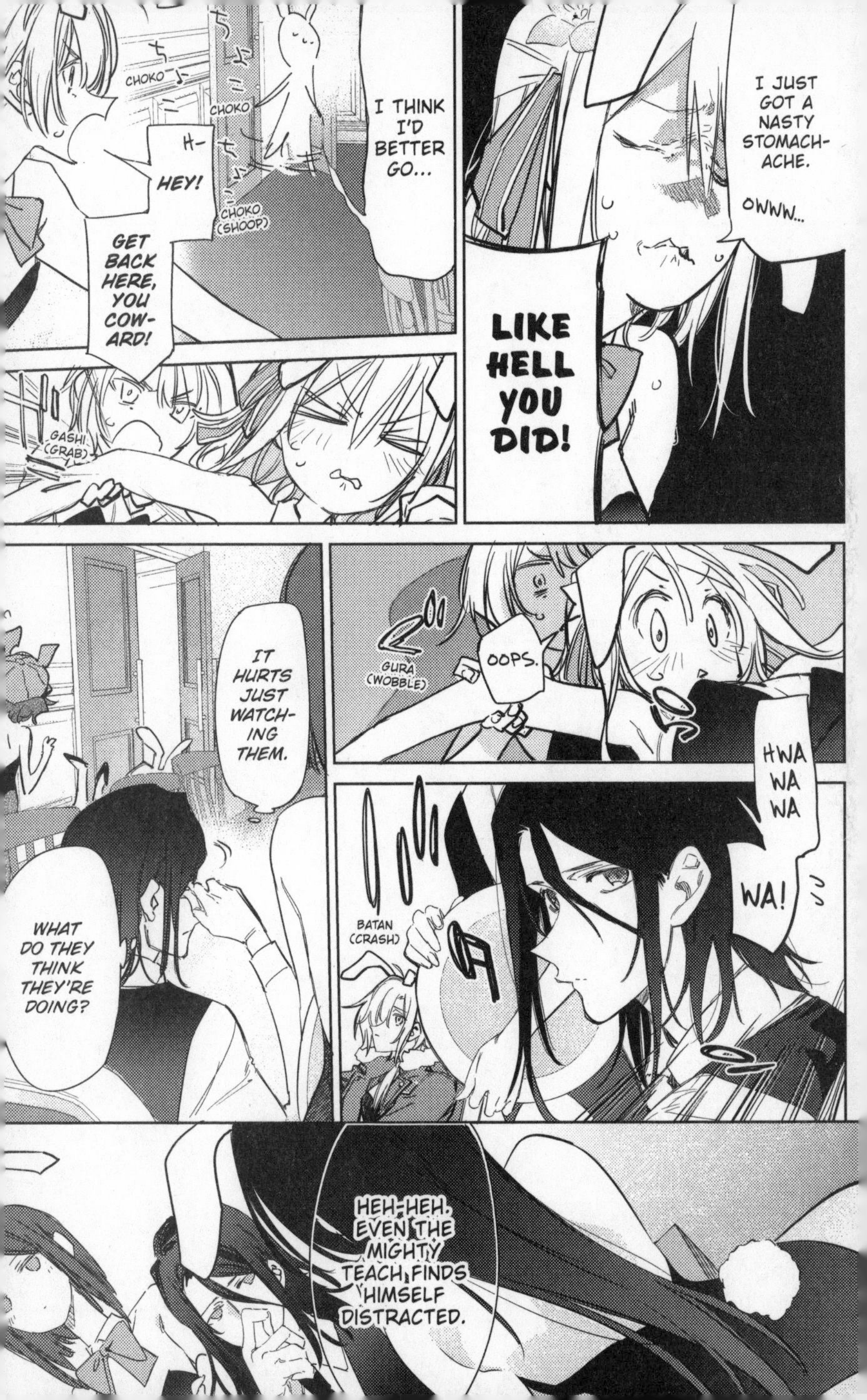
I JUST GOT A NASTY STOMACH-ACHE.
OWWW...
LIKE HELL YOU DID!
I THINK I'D BETTER GO...
CHOKO
CHOKO
CHOKO (SHOOP)
H-
HEY!
GET BACK HERE, YOU COWARD!
GASHI (GRAB)
OOPS.
GURA (WOBBLE)
HWA WA WA WA
WA!
BATAN (CRASH)
IT HURTS JUST WATCHING THEM.
WHAT DO THEY THINK THEY'RE DOING?
HEH-HEH. EVEN THE MIGHTY TEACH FINDS HIMSELF DISTRACTED.

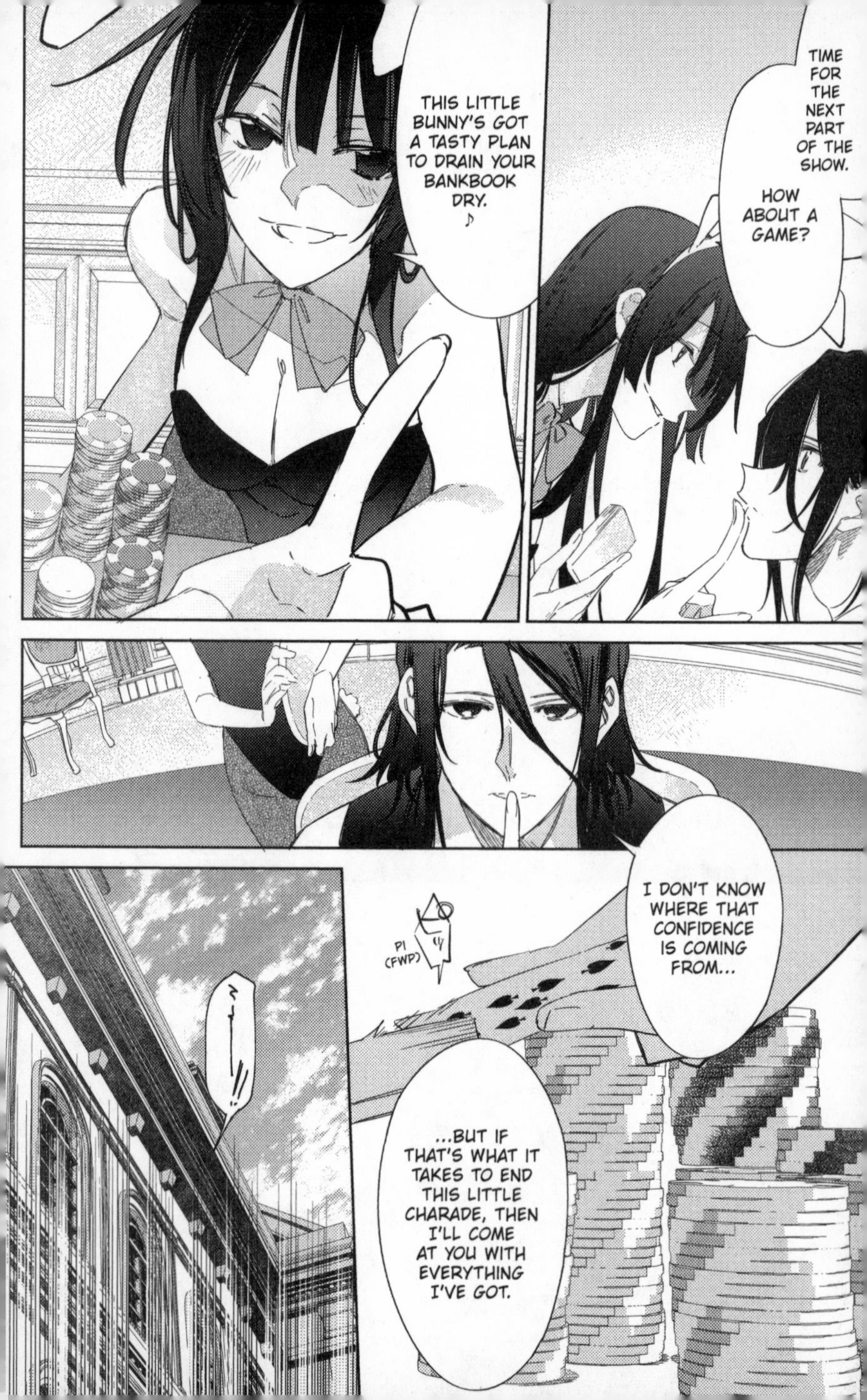
TIME FOR THE NEXT PART OF THE SHOW.
HOW ABOUT A GAME?
THIS LITTLE BUNNY'S GOT A TASTY PLAN TO DRAIN YOUR BANKBOOK DRY. ♪
I DON'T KNOW WHERE THAT CONFIDENCE IS COMING FROM...
PI (FWP)
...BUT IF THAT'S WHAT IT TAKES TO END THIS LITTLE CHARADE, THEN I'LL COME AT YOU WITH EVERYTHING I'VE GOT.

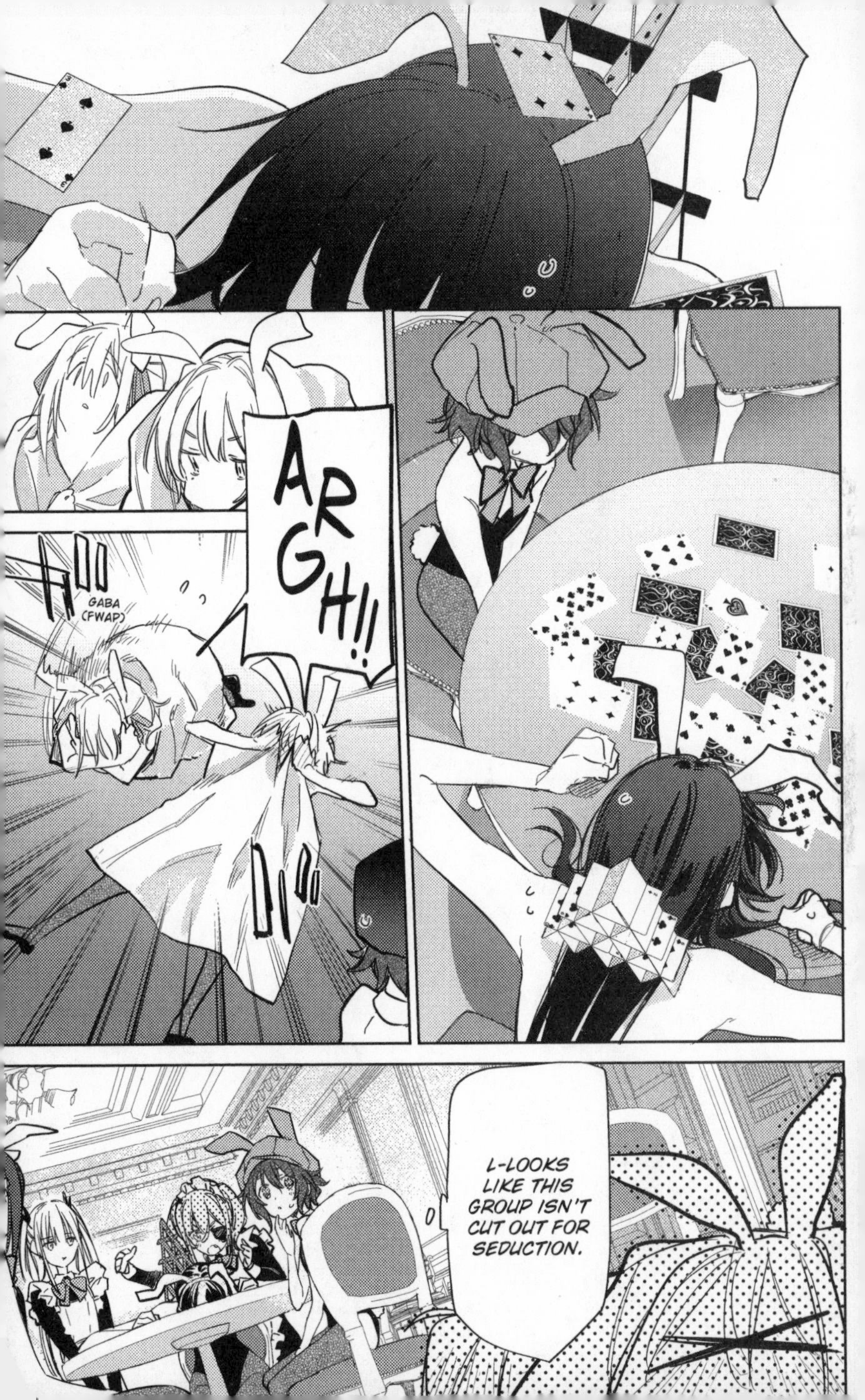
ARGH!!!
GABA (FWAP)
L-LOOKS LIKE THIS GROUP ISN'T CUT OUT FOR SEDUCTION.

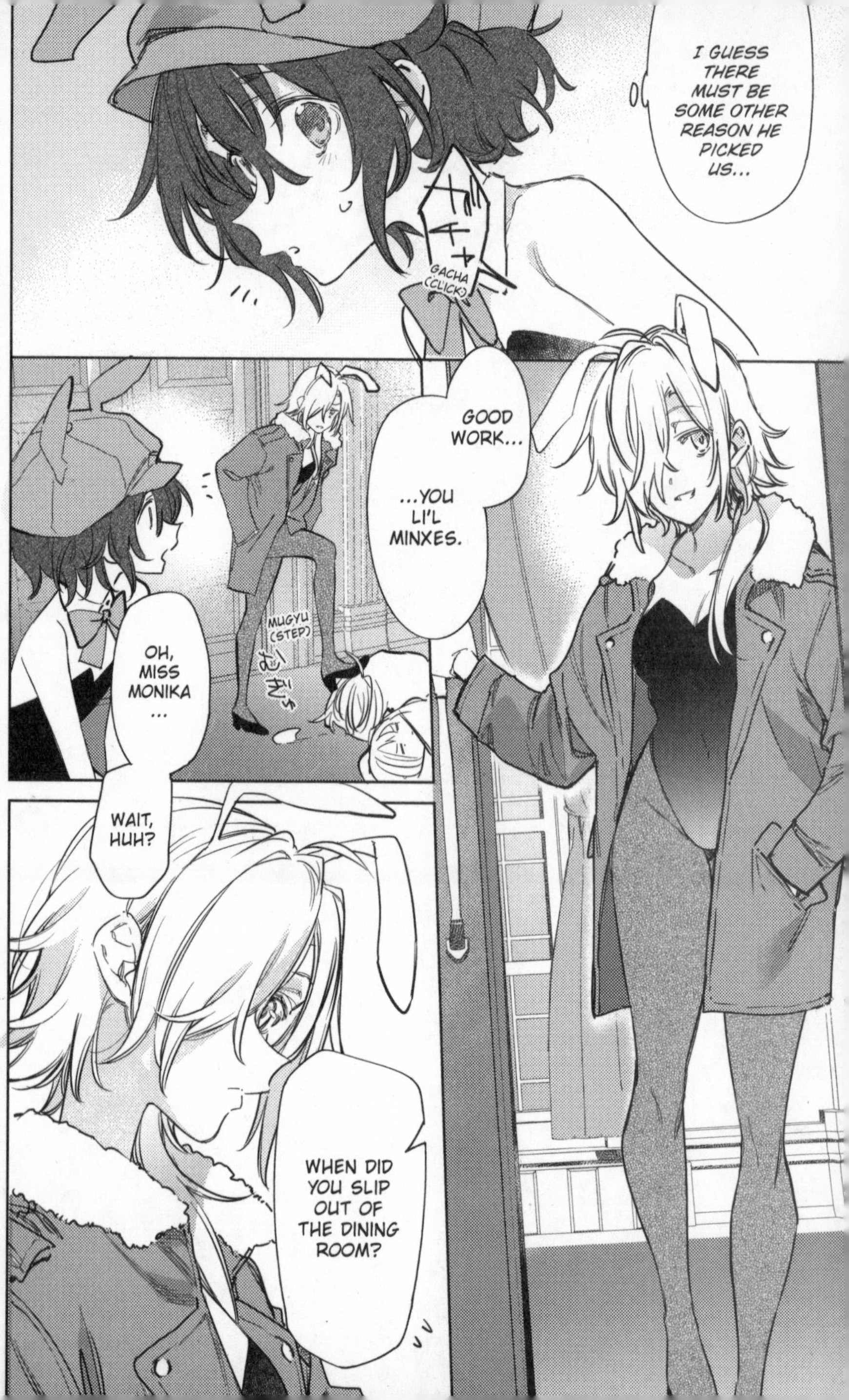
I GUESS THERE MUST BE SOME OTHER REASON HE PICKED US...
GACHA (CLICK)
GOOD WORK...
...YOU LI'L MINXES.
MUGYU (STEP)
OH, MISS MONIKA ...
WAIT, HUH?
WHEN DID YOU SLIP OUT OF THE DINING ROOM?

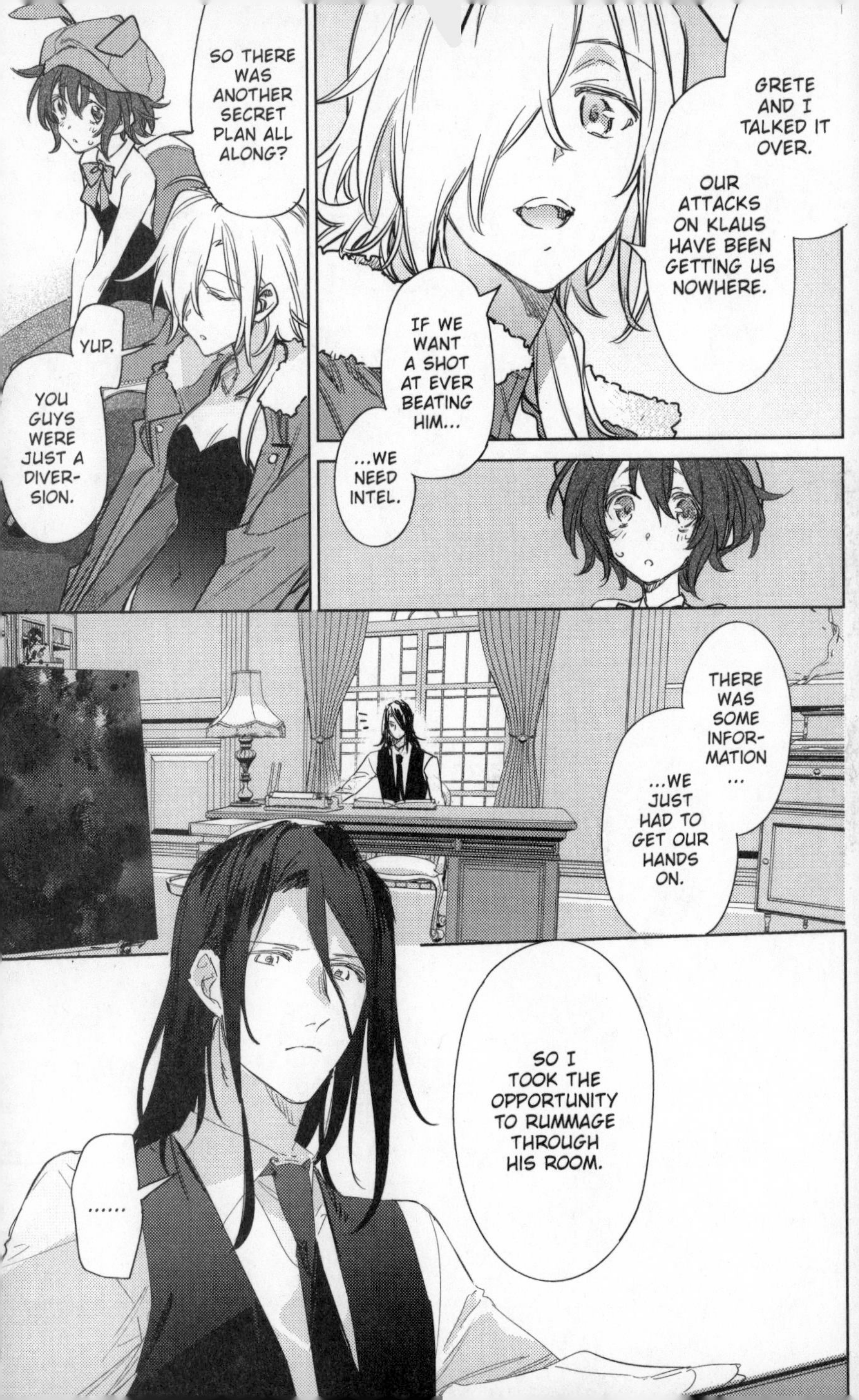
GRETE AND I TALKED IT OVER.
OUR ATTACKS ON KLAUS HAVE BEEN GETTING US NOWHERE.
IF WE WANT A SHOT AT EVER BEATING HIM...
...WE NEED INTEL.
SO THERE WAS ANOTHER SECRET PLAN ALL ALONG?
YUP.
YOU GUYS WERE JUST A DIVER-SION.
THERE WAS SOME INFOR-MATION...
...WE JUST HAD TO GET OUR HANDS ON.
SO I TOOK THE OPPORTUNITY TO RUMMAGE THROUGH HIS ROOM.
......

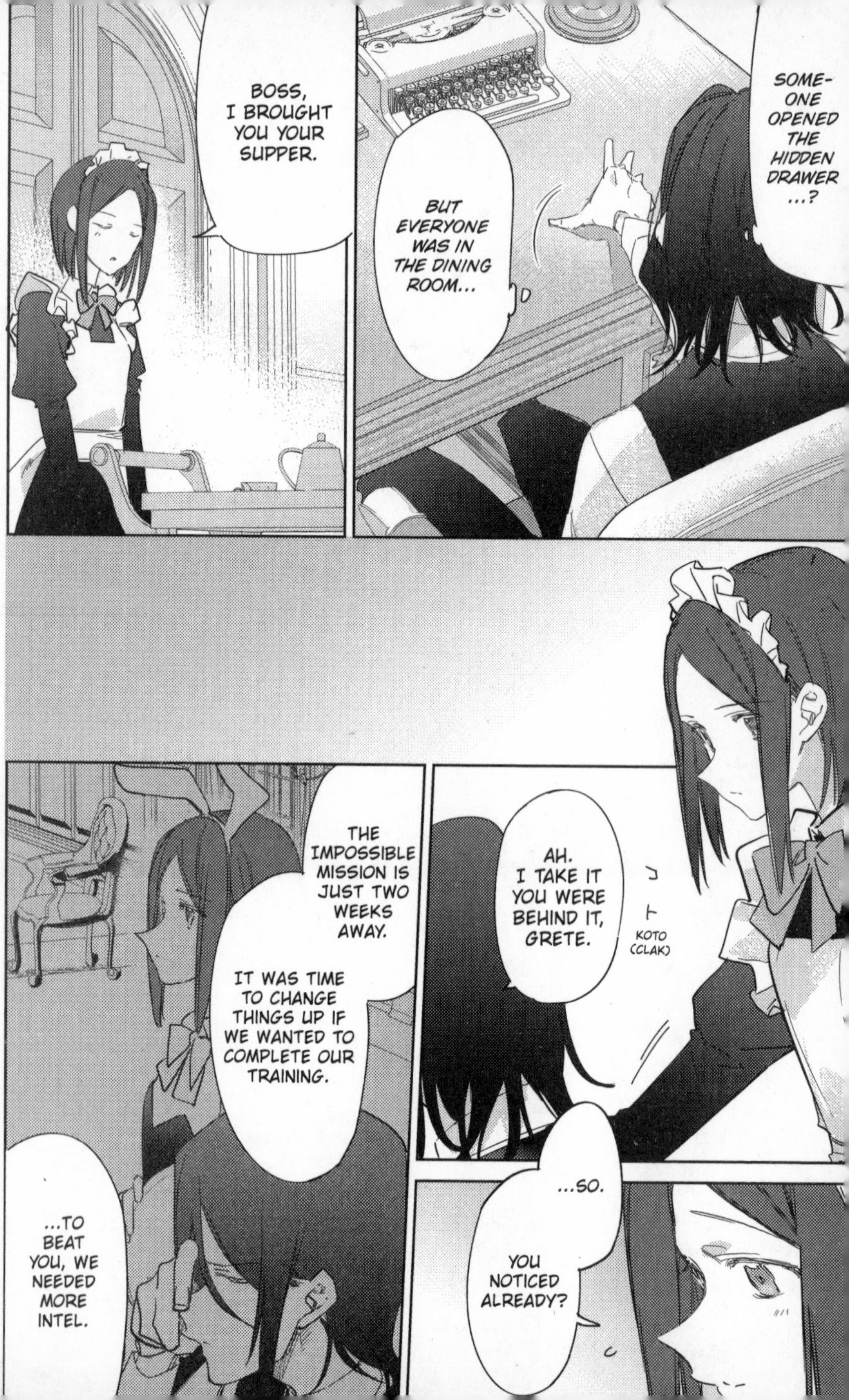
SOME-ONE OPENED THE HIDDEN DRAWER...?
BUT EVERYONE WAS IN THE DINING ROOM...
BOSS, I BROUGHT YOU YOUR SUPPER.
AH. I TAKE IT YOU WERE BEHIND IT, GRETE.
コト
KOTO (CLAK)
...SO.
YOU NOTICED ALREADY?
THE IMPOSSIBLE MISSION IS JUST TWO WEEKS AWAY.
IT WAS TIME TO CHANGE THINGS UP IF WE WANTED TO COMPLETE OUR TRAINING.
...TO BEAT YOU, WE NEEDED MORE INTEL.

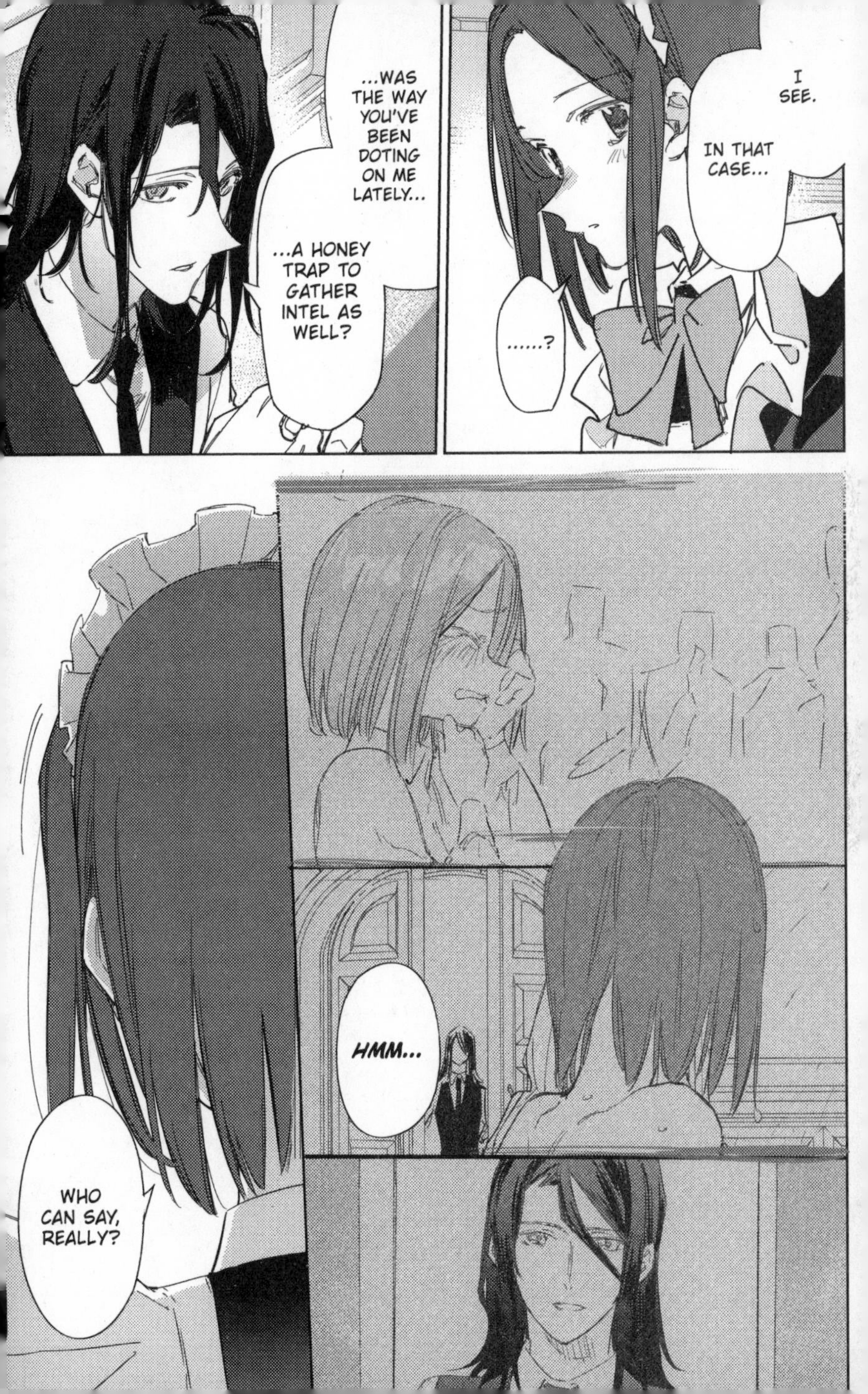
I SEE.
IN THAT CASE...
......?
...WAS THE WAY YOU'VE BEEN DOTING ON ME LATELY...
...A HONEY TRAP TO GATHER INTEL AS WELL?
HMM...
WHO CAN SAY, REALLY?

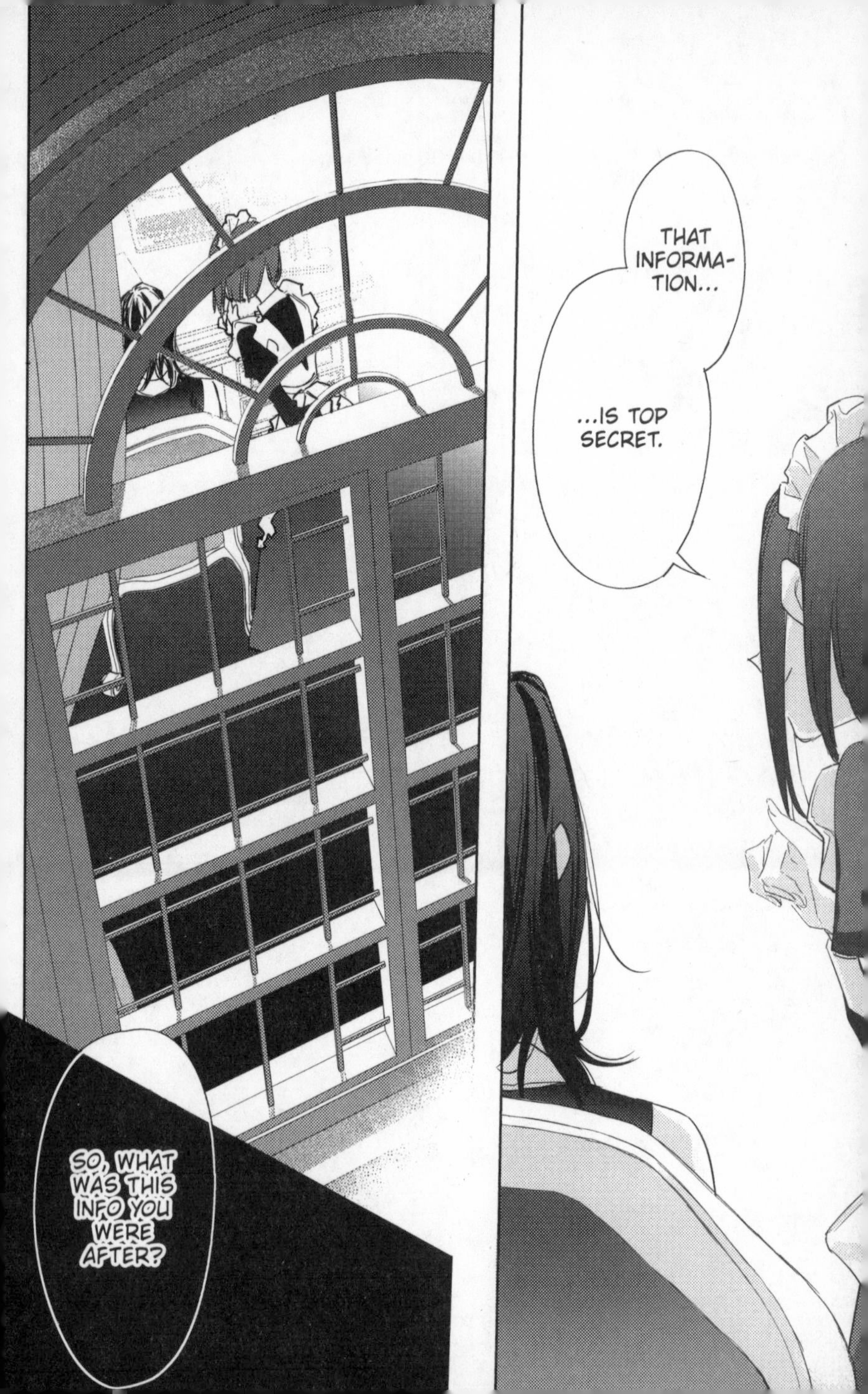
THAT INFORMATION...
...IS TOP SECRET.
SO, WHAT WAS THIS INFO YOU WERE AFTER?

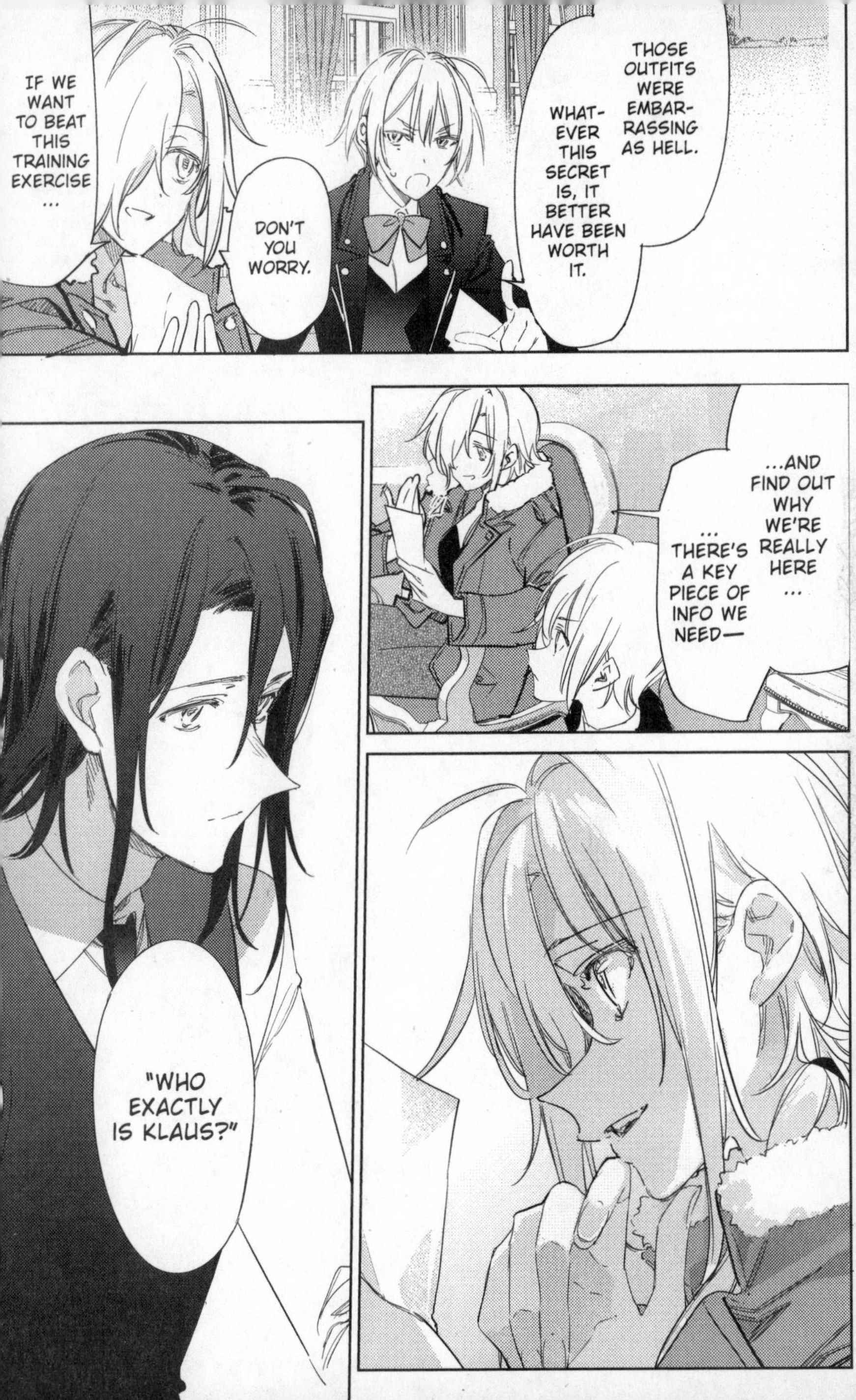
THOSE OUTFITS WERE EMBAR-RASSING AS HELL.
WHAT-EVER THIS SECRET IS, IT BETTER HAVE BEEN WORTH IT.
DON'T YOU WORRY.
IF WE WANT TO BEAT THIS TRAINING EXERCISE ...
...AND FIND OUT WHY WE'RE REALLY HERE ...
... THERE'S A KEY PIECE OF INFO WE NEED—
"WHO EXACTLY IS KLAUS?"

SPY
CLASSROOM

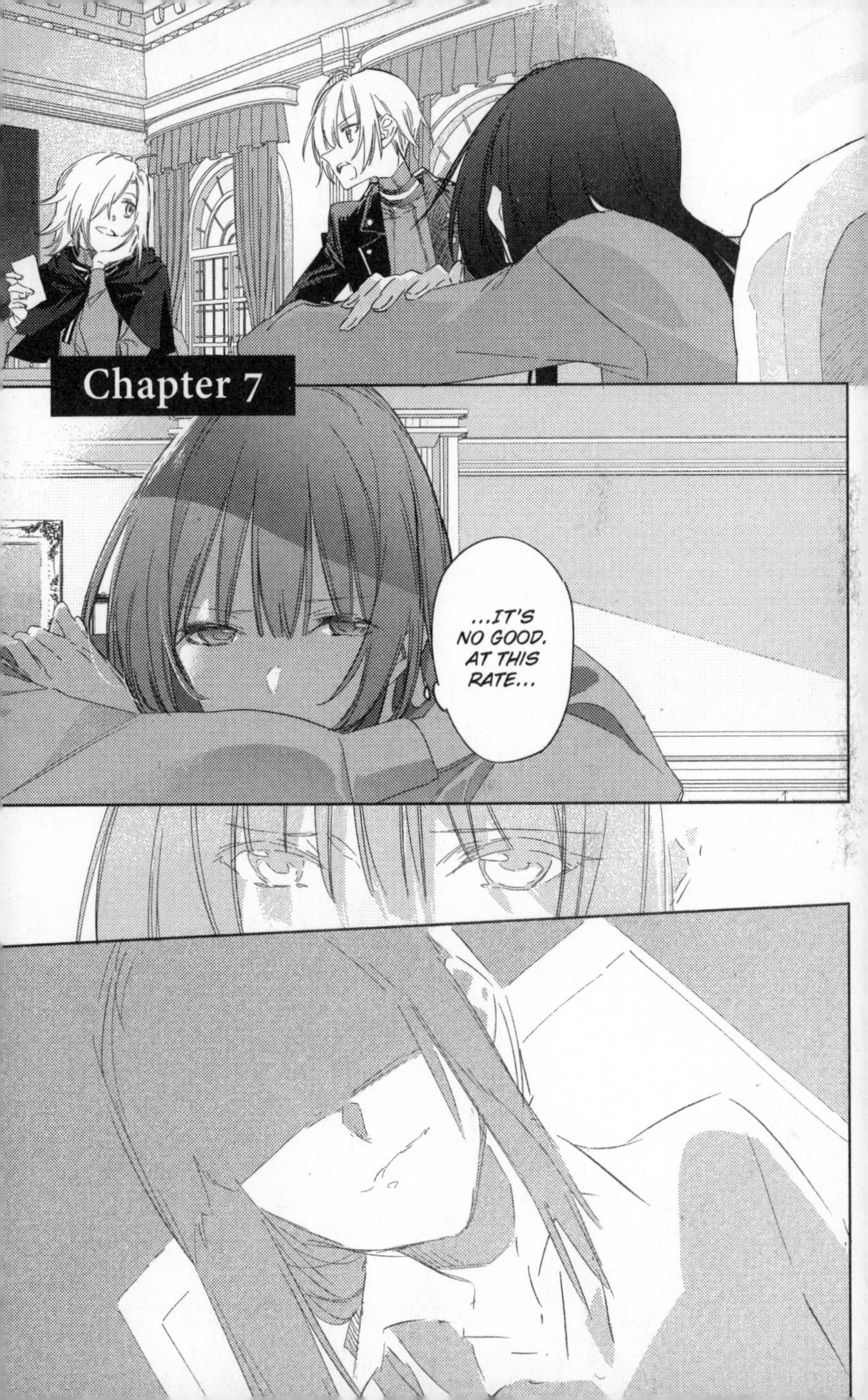
Chapter 7
...IT'S NO GOOD. AT THIS RATE...

Chapter 7 — Hostage Part 1

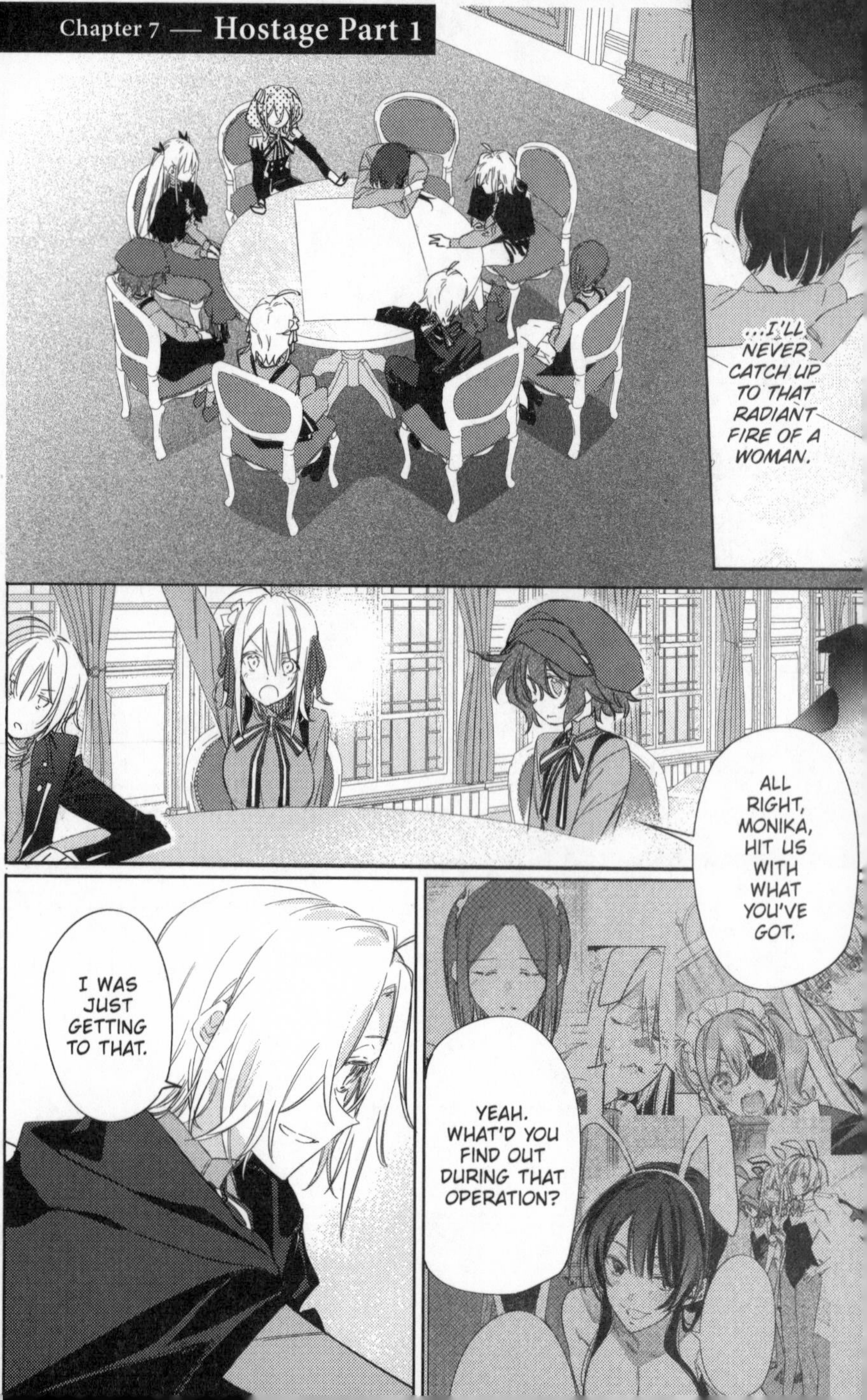

...I'LL NEVER CATCH UP TO THAT RADIANT FIRE OF A WOMAN.
ALL RIGHT, MONIKA, HIT US WITH WHAT YOU'VE GOT.
YEAH. WHAT'D YOU FIND OUT DURING THAT OPERATION?
I WAS JUST GETTING TO THAT.

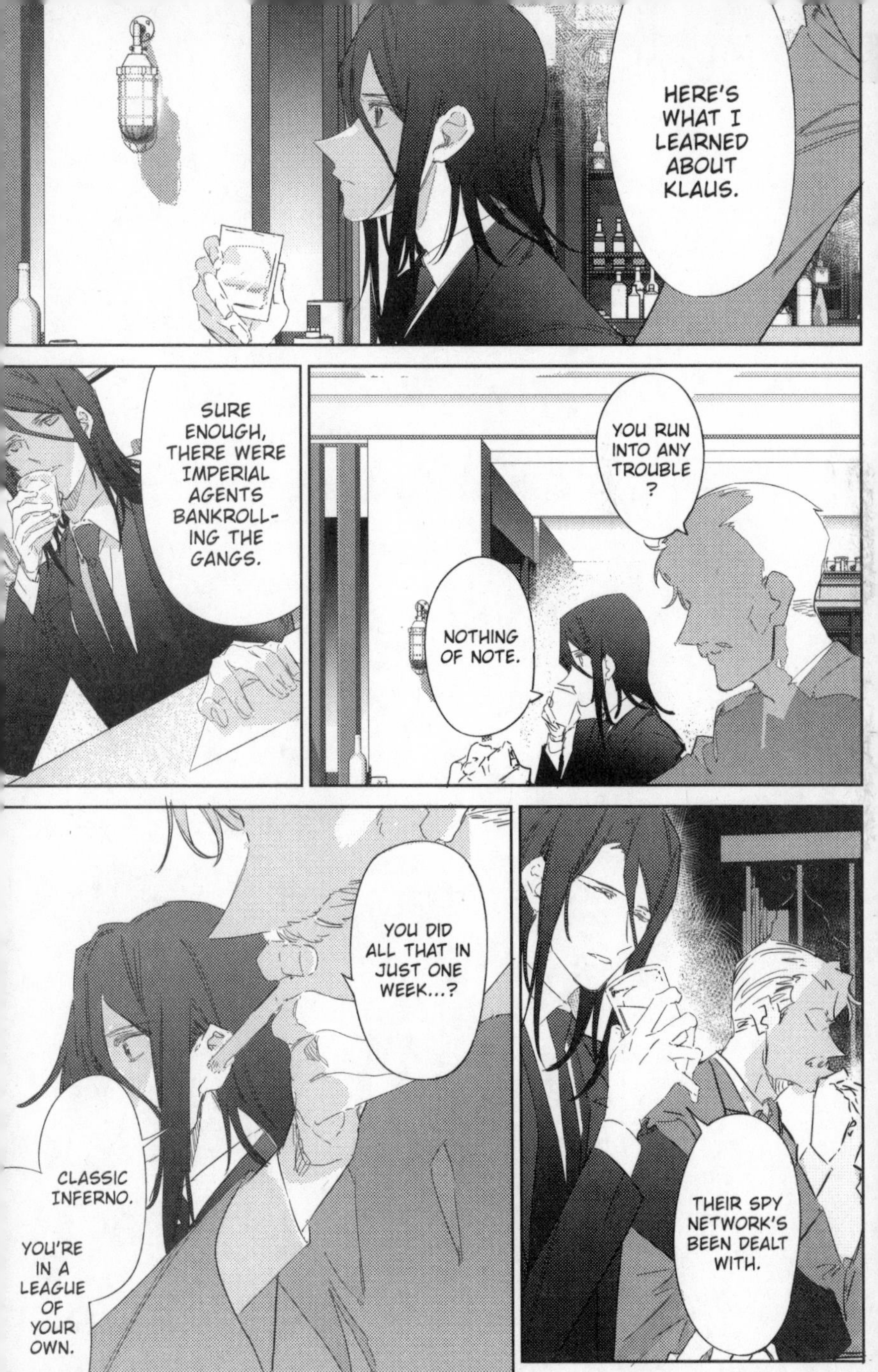
HERE'S WHAT I LEARNED ABOUT KLAUS.
YOU RUN INTO ANY TROUBLE?
NOTHING OF NOTE.
SURE ENOUGH, THERE WERE IMPERIAL AGENTS BANKROLLING THE GANGS.
THEIR SPY NETWORK'S BEEN DEALT WITH.
YOU DID ALL THAT IN JUST ONE WEEK...?
CLASSIC INFERNO.
YOU'RE IN A LEAGUE OF YOUR OWN.

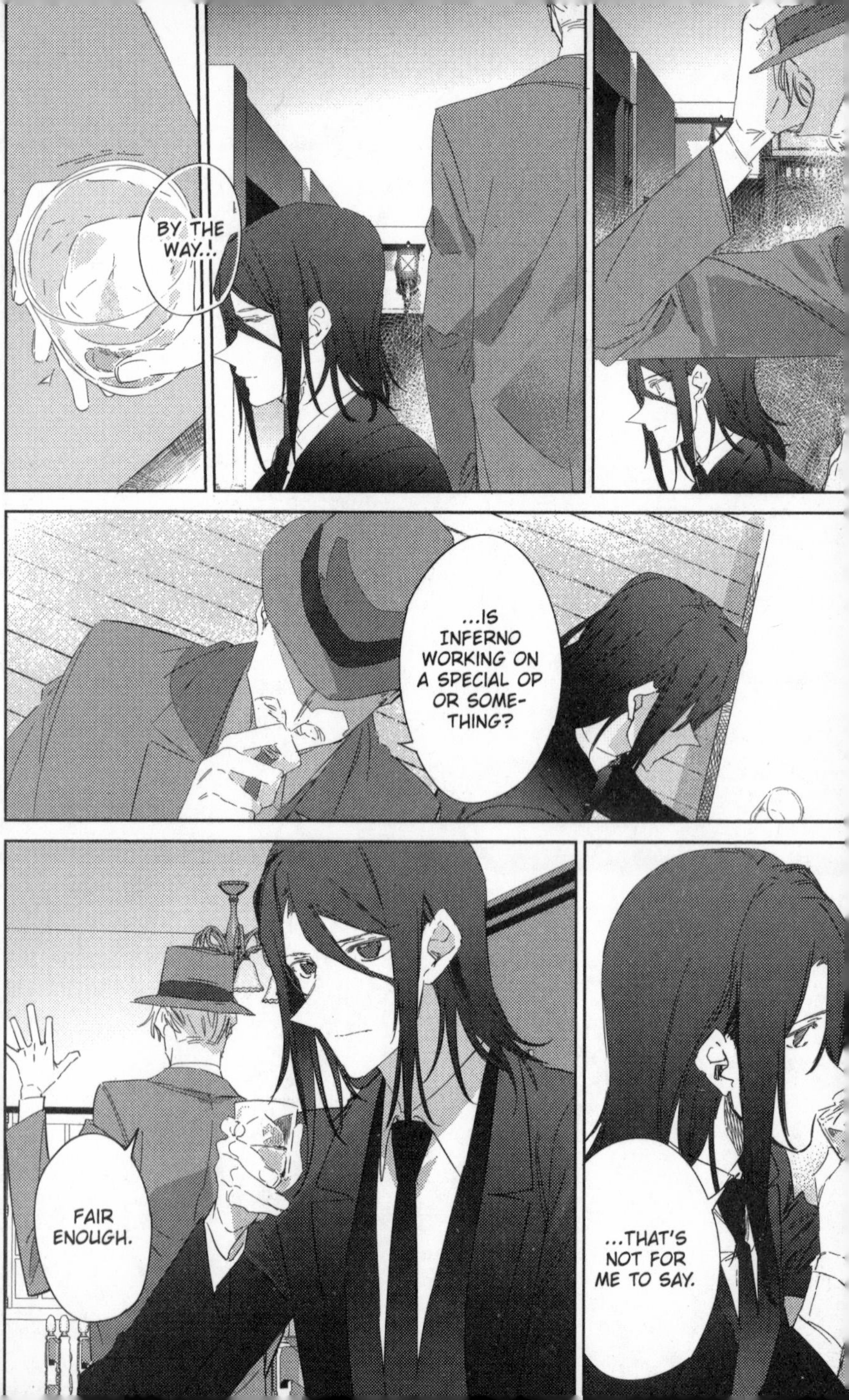
BY THE WAY...
...IS INFERNO WORKING ON A SPECIAL OP OR SOME-THING?
...THAT'S NOT FOR ME TO SAY.
FAIR ENOUGH.

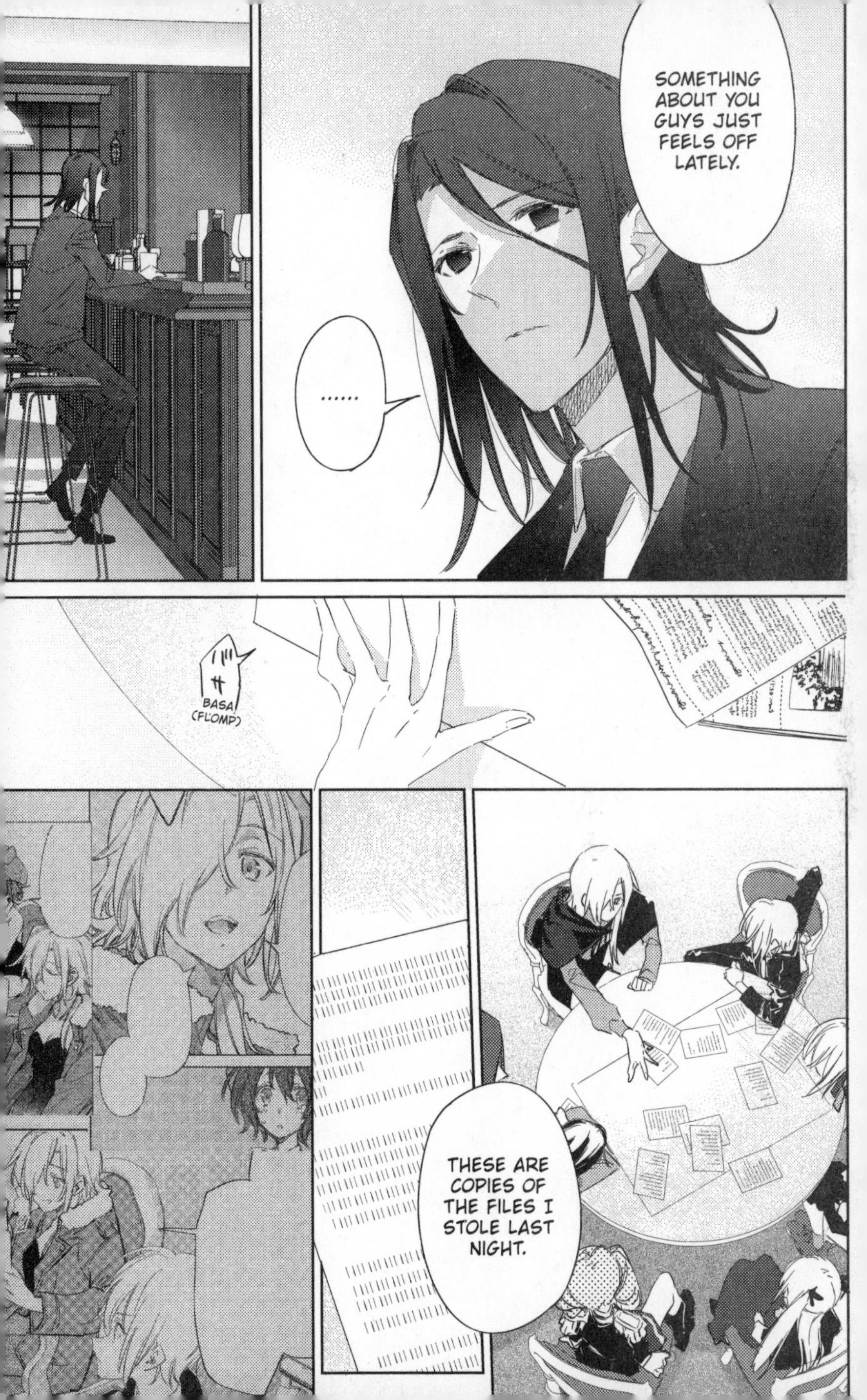
SOMETHING ABOUT YOU GUYS JUST FEELS OFF LATELY.
......
BASA (FLOMP)
THESE ARE COPIES OF THE FILES I STOLE LAST NIGHT.

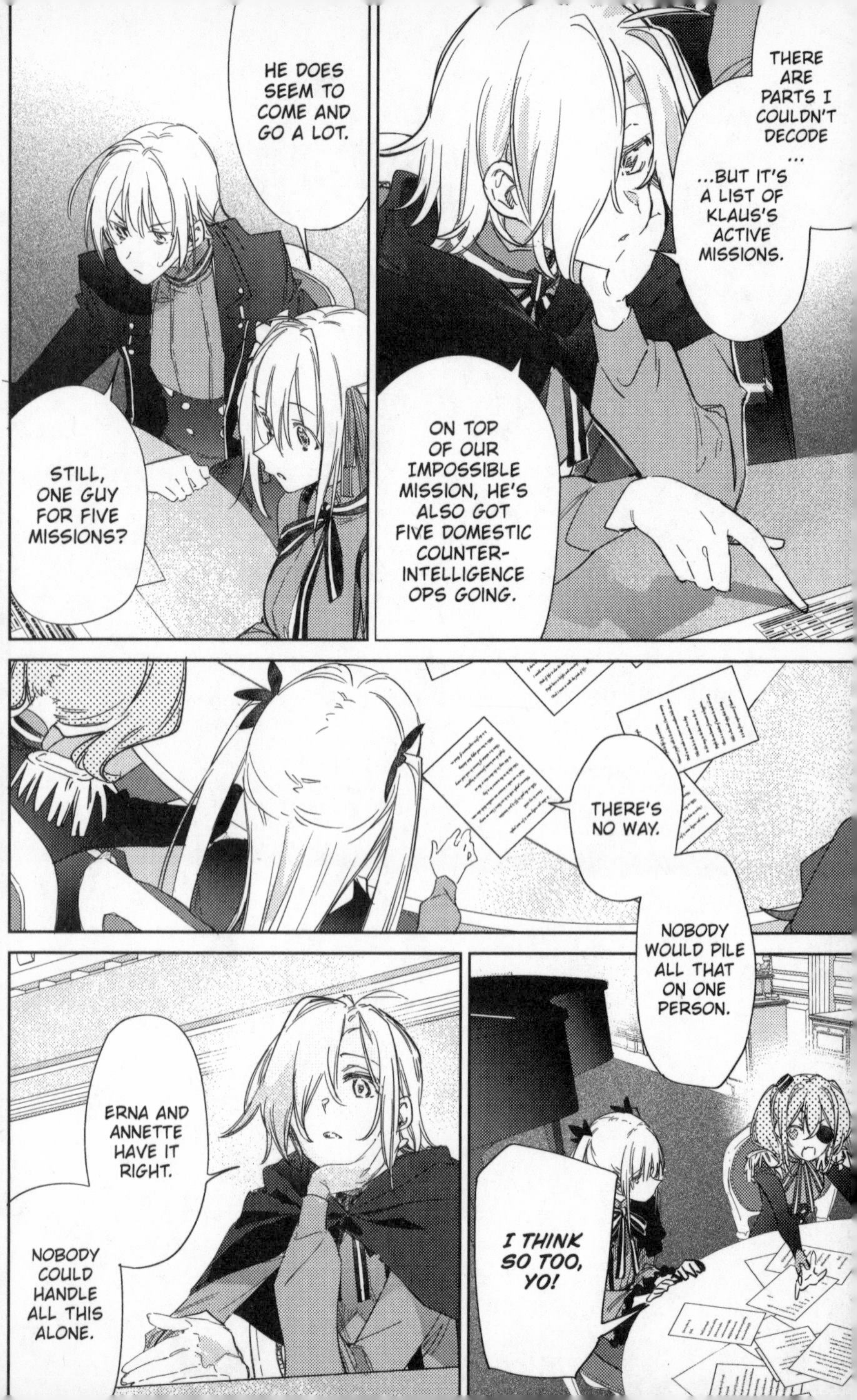
THERE ARE PARTS I COULDN'T DECODE...
...BUT IT'S A LIST OF KLAUS'S ACTIVE MISSIONS.
ON TOP OF OUR IMPOSSIBLE MISSION, HE'S ALSO GOT FIVE DOMESTIC COUNTER-INTELLIGENCE OPS GOING.
HE DOES SEEM TO COME AND GO A LOT.
STILL, ONE GUY FOR FIVE MISSIONS?
THERE'S NO WAY.
NOBODY WOULD PILE ALL THAT ON ONE PERSON.
I THINK SO TOO, YO!
ERNA AND ANNETTE HAVE IT RIGHT.
NOBODY COULD HANDLE ALL THIS ALONE.

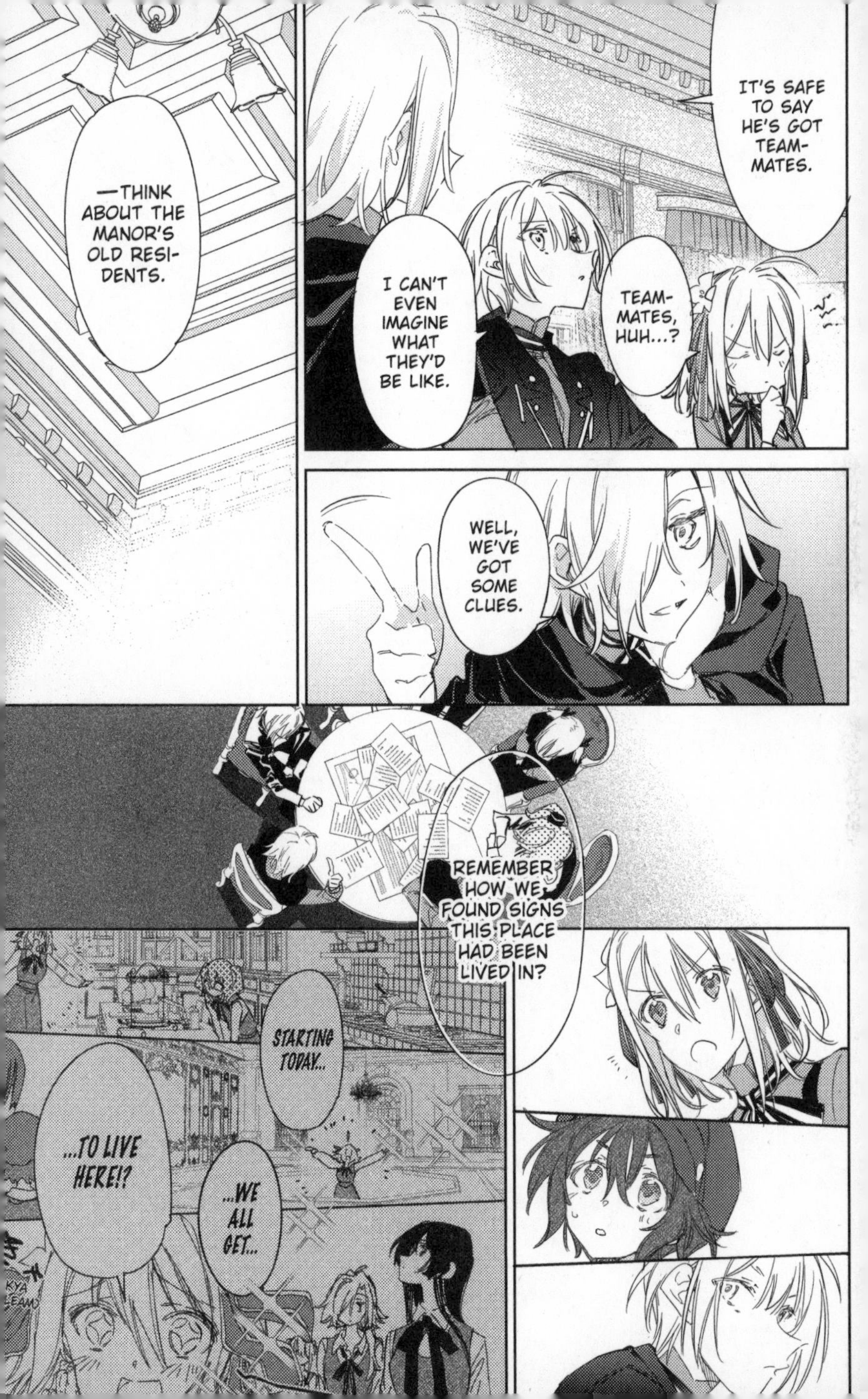
IT'S SAFE TO SAY HE'S GOT TEAM-MATES.
TEAM-MATES, HUH...?
I CAN'T EVEN IMAGINE WHAT THEY'D BE LIKE.
WELL, WE'VE GOT SOME CLUES.
—THINK ABOUT THE MANOR'S OLD RESI-DENTS.
REMEMBER HOW WE FOUND SIGNS THIS PLACE HAD BEEN LIVED IN?
STARTING TODAY...
...WE ALL GET...
...TO LIVE HERE!?

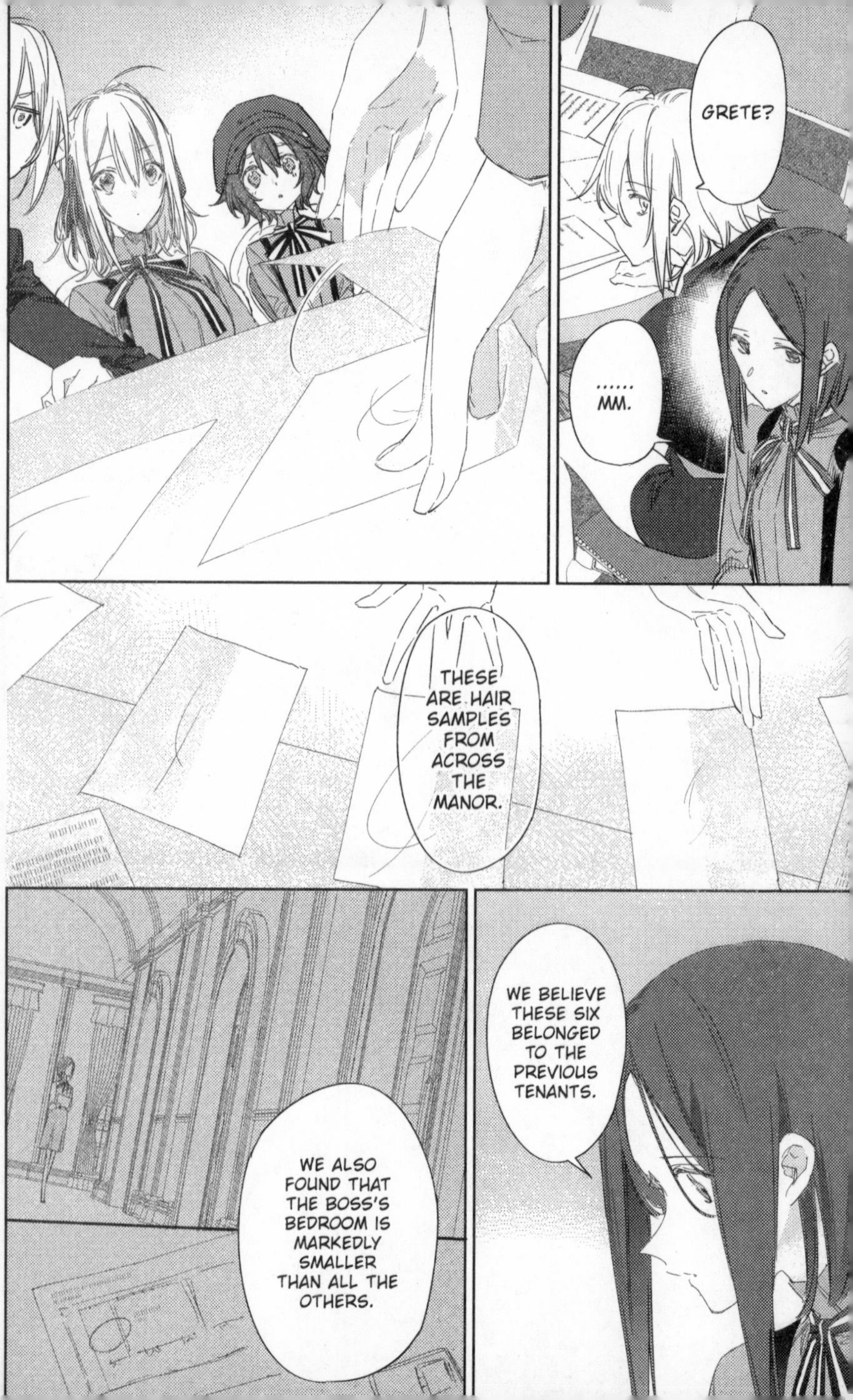
GRETE?
...... MM.
THESE ARE HAIR SAMPLES FROM ACROSS THE MANOR.
WE BELIEVE THESE SIX BELONGED TO THE PREVIOUS TENANTS.
WE ALSO FOUND THAT THE BOSS'S BEDROOM IS MARKEDLY SMALLER THAN ALL THE OTHERS.

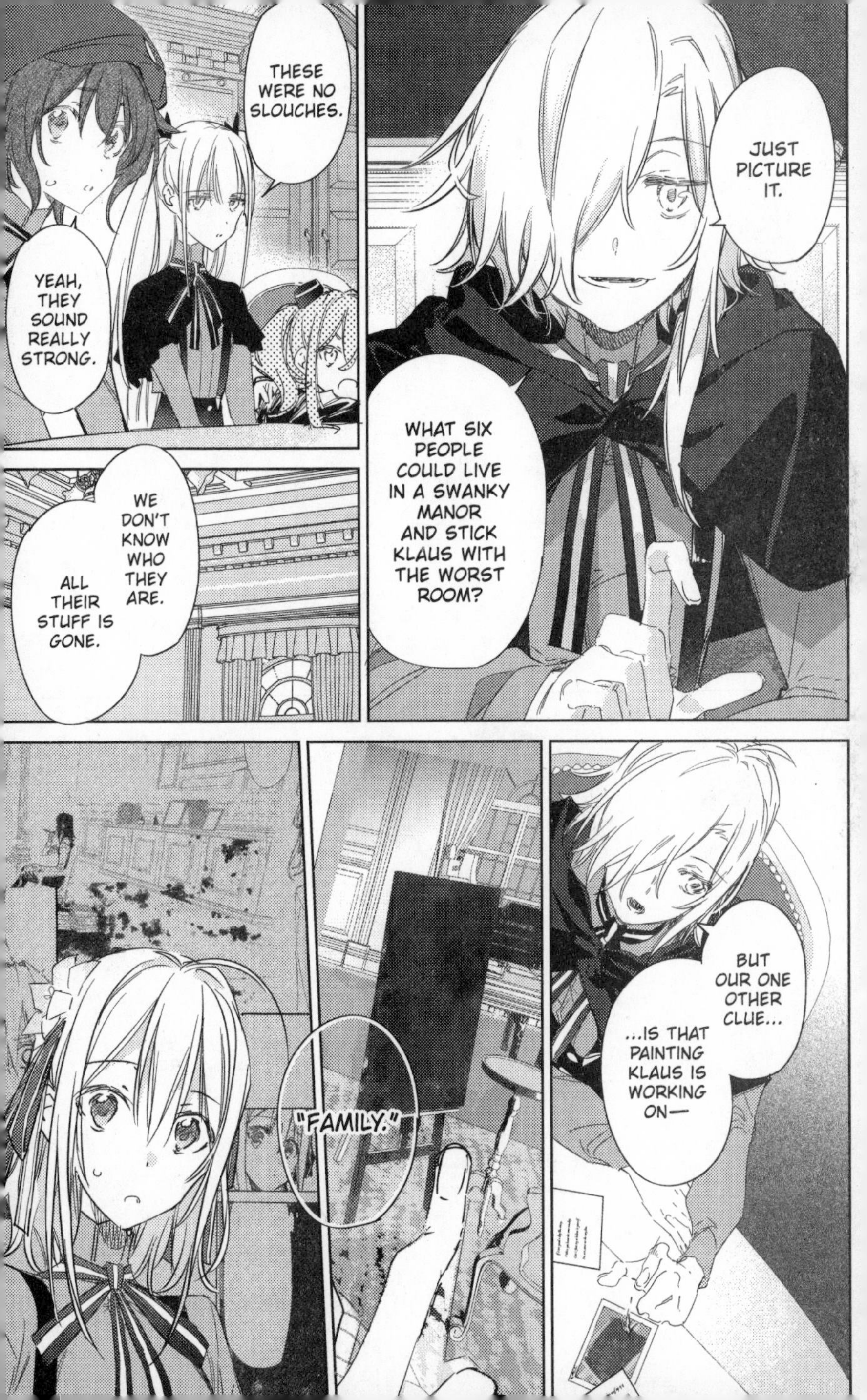
JUST PICTURE IT.
WHAT SIX PEOPLE COULD LIVE IN A SWANKY MANOR AND STICK KLAUS WITH THE WORST ROOM?
THESE WERE NO SLOUCHES.
YEAH, THEY SOUND REALLY STRONG.
WE DON'T KNOW WHO THEY ARE.
ALL THEIR STUFF IS GONE.
BUT OUR ONE OTHER CLUE...
...IS THAT PAINTING KLAUS IS WORKING ON—
"FAMILY."

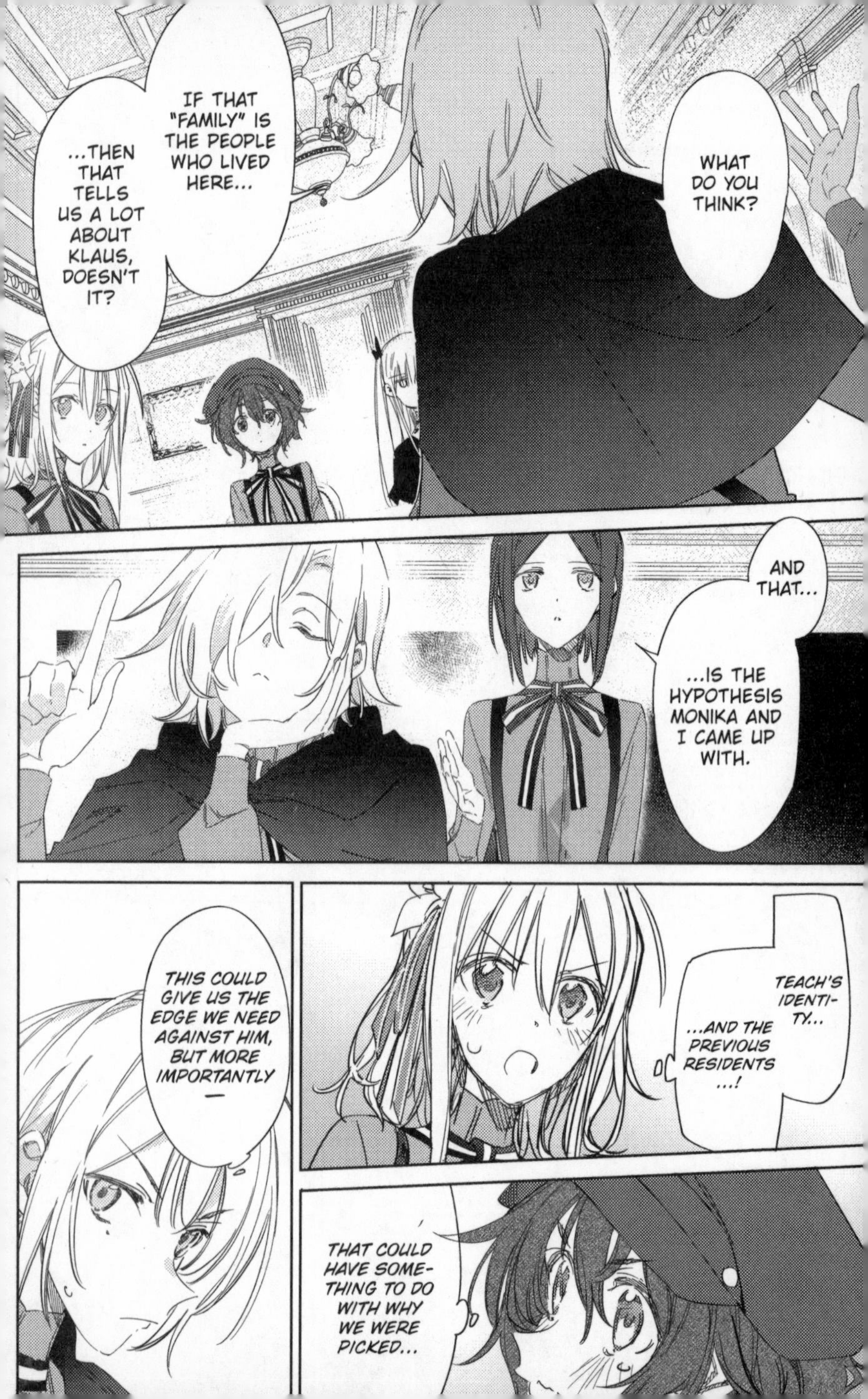
WHAT DO YOU THINK?
IF THAT "FAMILY" IS THE PEOPLE WHO LIVED HERE...
...THEN THAT TELLS US A LOT ABOUT KLAUS, DOESN'T IT?
AND THAT...
...IS THE HYPOTHESIS MONIKA AND I CAME UP WITH.
TEACH'S IDENTITY...
...AND THE PREVIOUS RESIDENTS ...!
THIS COULD GIVE US THE EDGE WE NEED AGAINST HIM, BUT MORE IMPORTANTLY —
THAT COULD HAVE SOMETHING TO DO WITH WHY WE WERE PICKED...

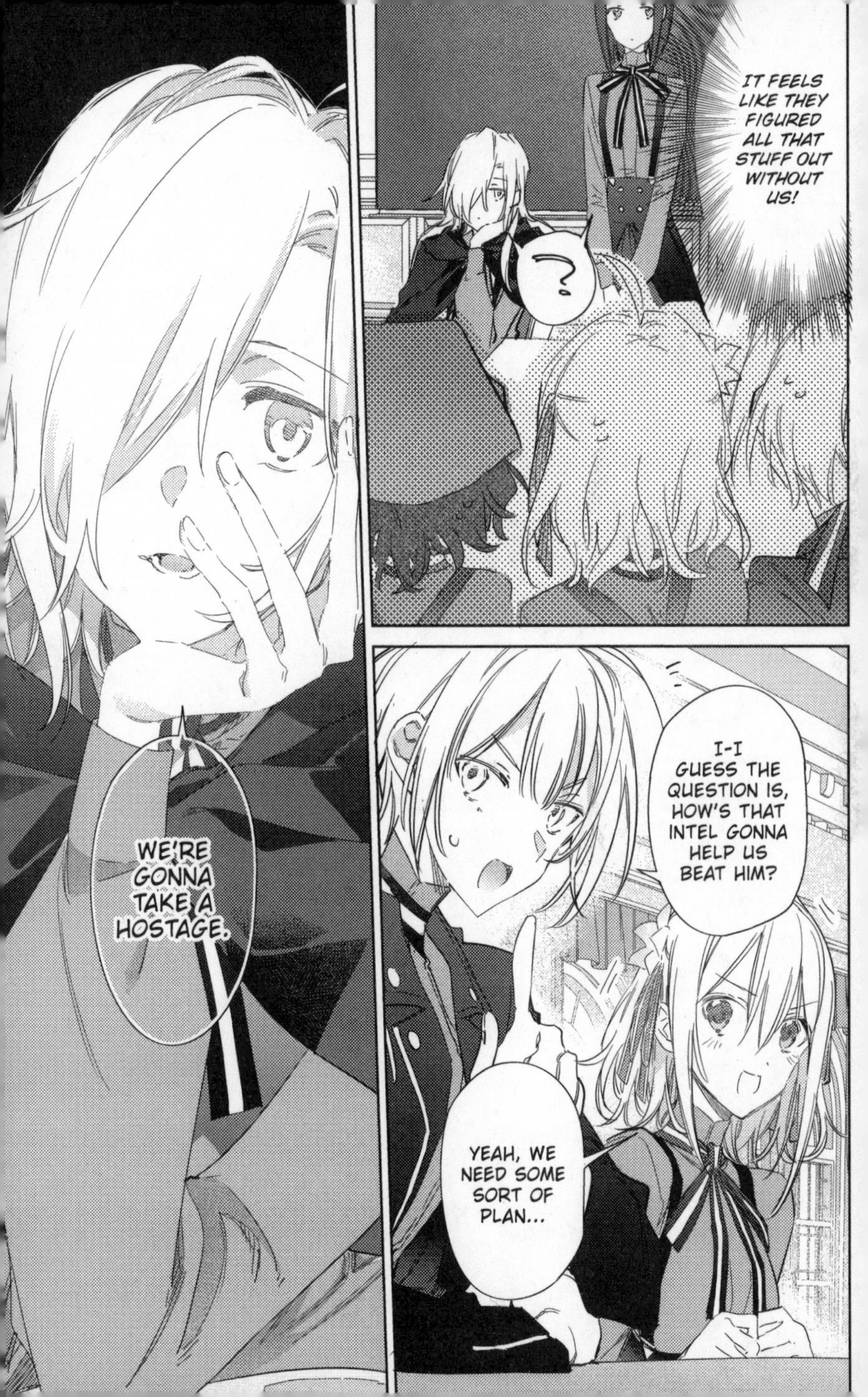
IT FEELS LIKE THEY FIGURED ALL THAT STUFF OUT WITHOUT US!
?
I-I GUESS THE QUESTION IS, HOW'S THAT INTEL GONNA HELP US BEAT HIM?
YEAH, WE NEED SOME SORT OF PLAN...
WE'RE GONNA TAKE A HOSTAGE.

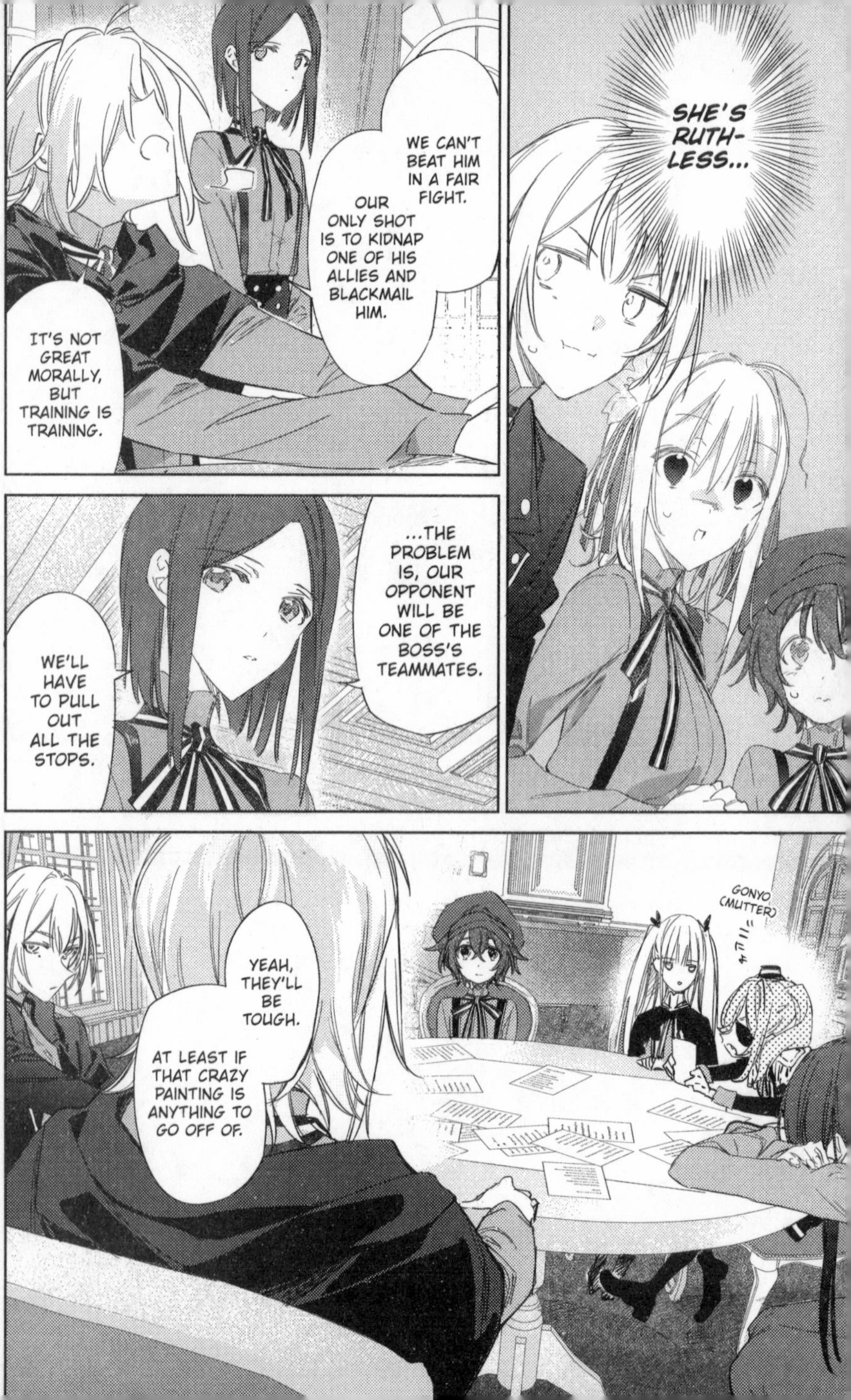
SHE'S RUTH-LESS...
WE CAN'T BEAT HIM IN A FAIR FIGHT.
OUR ONLY SHOT IS TO KIDNAP ONE OF HIS ALLIES AND BLACKMAIL HIM.
IT'S NOT GREAT MORALLY, BUT TRAINING IS TRAINING.
...THE PROBLEM IS, OUR OPPONENT WILL BE ONE OF THE BOSS'S TEAMMATES.
WE'LL HAVE TO PULL OUT ALL THE STOPS.
GONYO (MUTTER)
YEAH, THEY'LL BE TOUGH.
AT LEAST IF THAT CRAZY PAINTING IS ANYTHING TO GO OFF OF.

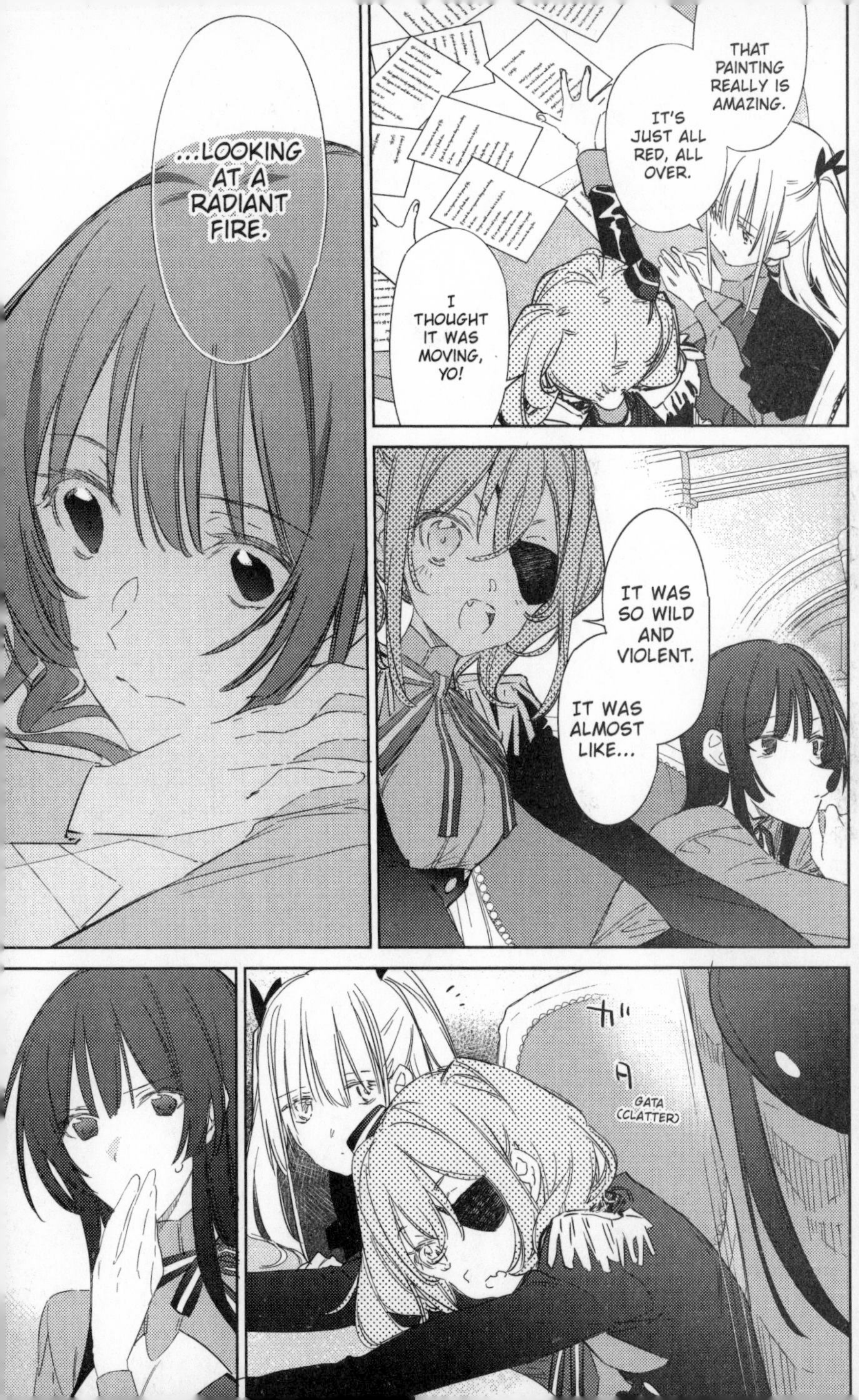
THAT PAINTING REALLY IS AMAZING.
IT'S JUST ALL RED, ALL OVER.
I THOUGHT IT WAS MOVING, YO!
IT WAS SO WILD AND VIOLENT.
IT WAS ALMOST LIKE...
...LOOKING AT A RADIANT FIRE.
ガタ
GATA (CLATTER)

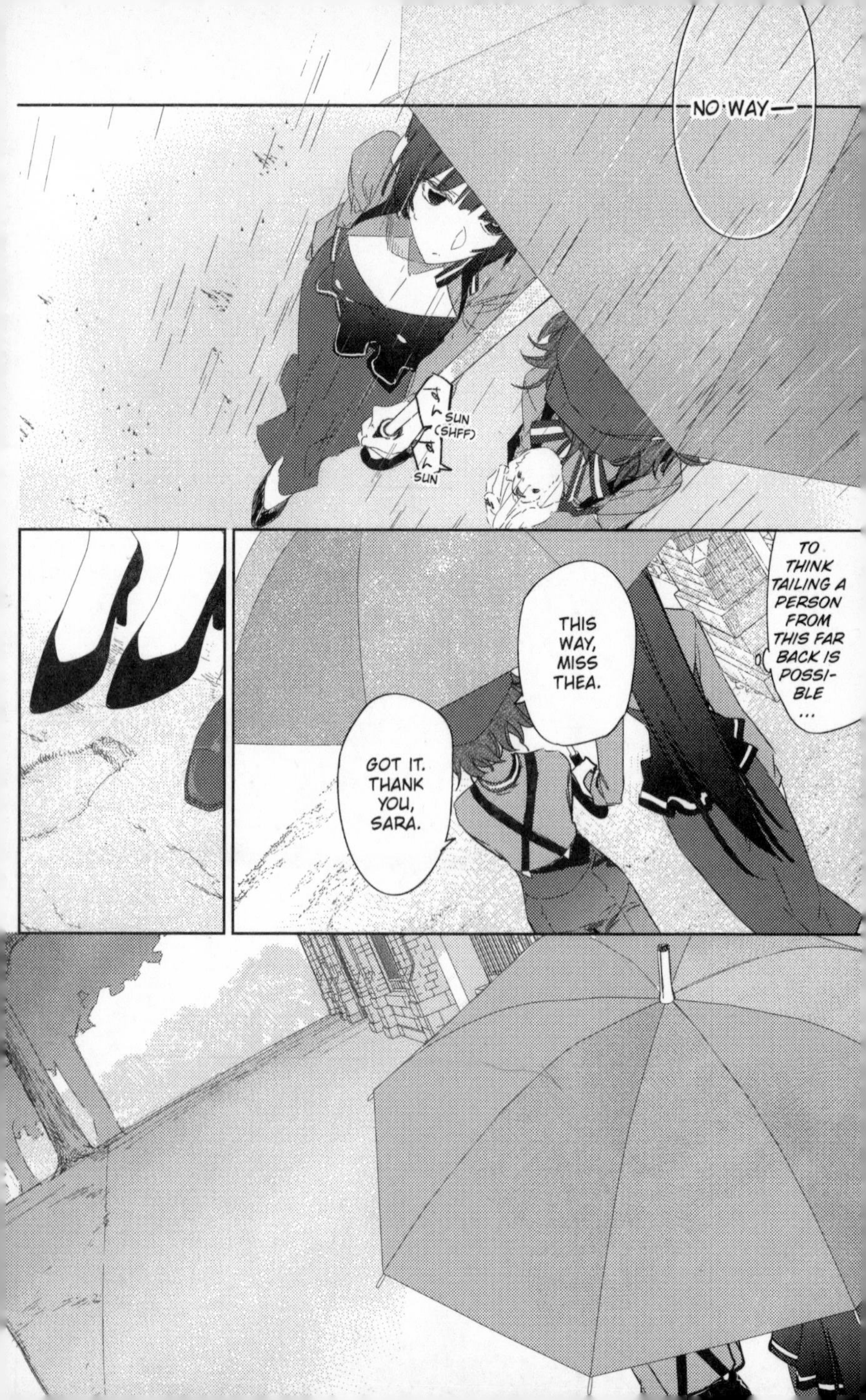
—NO WAY—
SUN (SHFF)
SUN
TO THINK TAILING A PERSON FROM THIS FAR BACK IS POSSIBLE...
THIS WAY, MISS THEA.
GOT IT. THANK YOU, SARA.

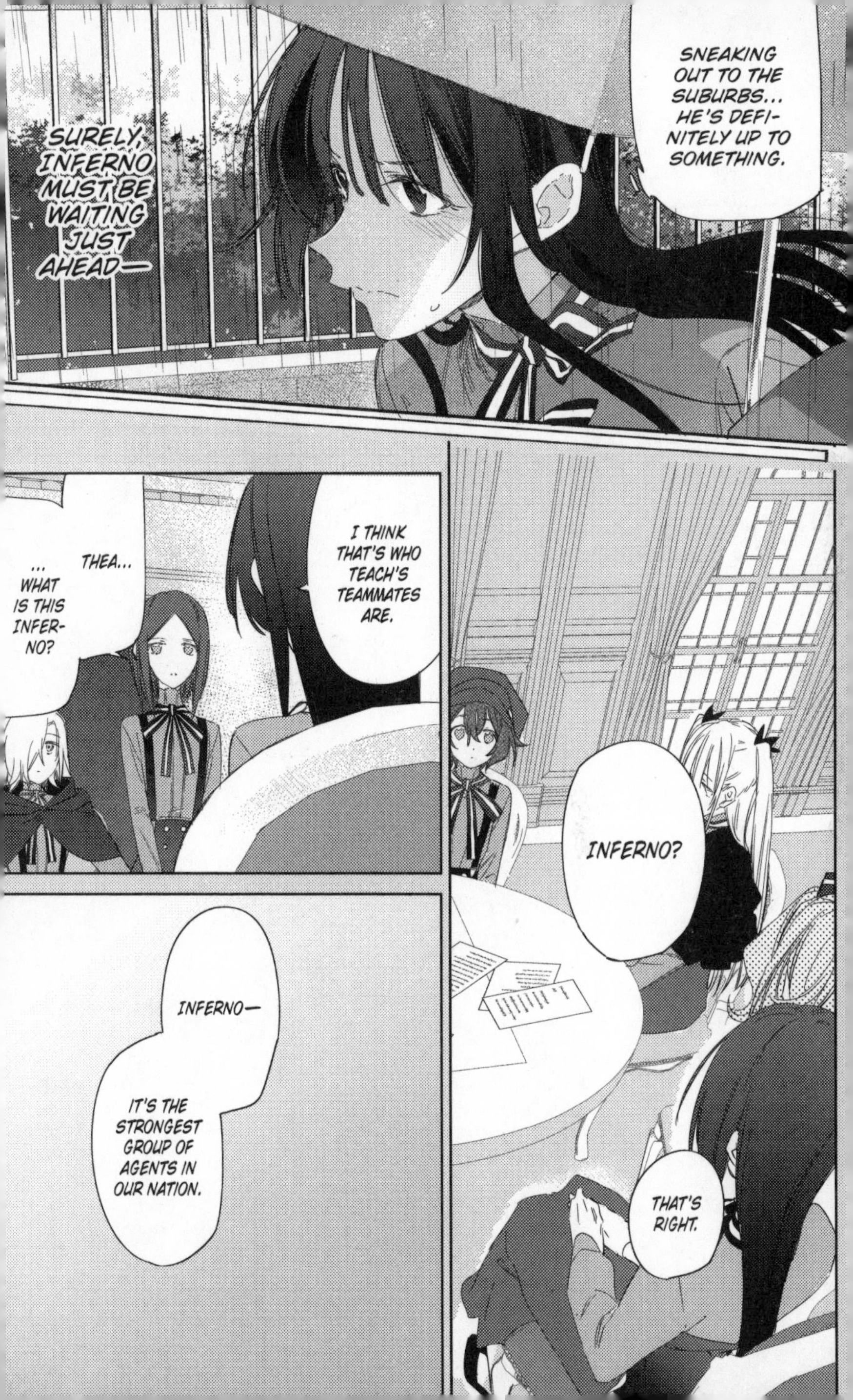
SNEAKING OUT TO THE SUBURBS... HE'S DEFINITELY UP TO SOMETHING.
SURELY, INFERNO MUST BE WAITING JUST AHEAD—
INFERNO?
THAT'S RIGHT.
I THINK THAT'S WHO TEACH'S TEAMMATES ARE.
THEA...
...WHAT IS THIS INFERNO?
INFERNO—
IT'S THE STRONGEST GROUP OF AGENTS IN OUR NATION.

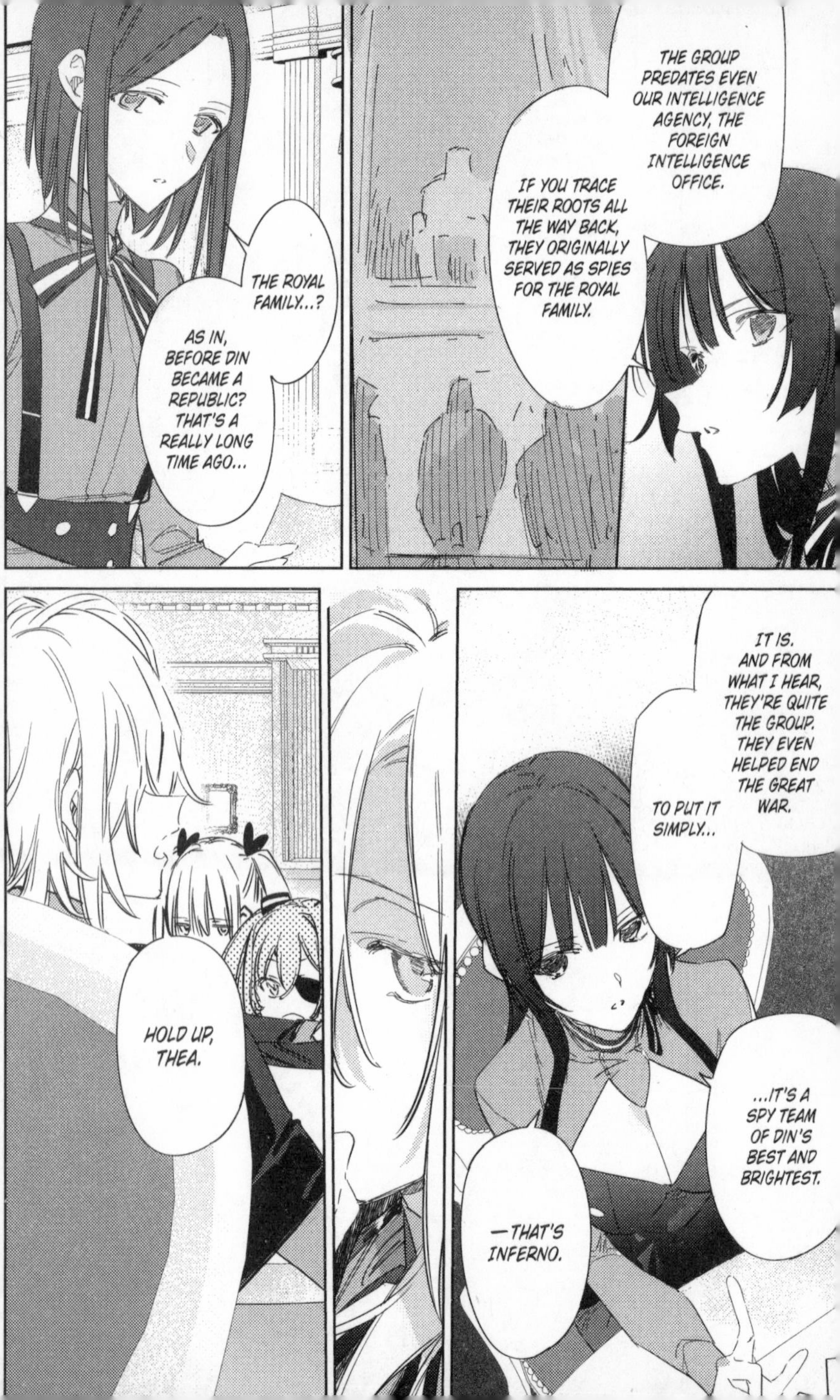
THE GROUP PREDATES EVEN OUR INTELLIGENCE AGENCY, THE FOREIGN INTELLIGENCE OFFICE.
IF YOU TRACE THEIR ROOTS ALL THE WAY BACK, THEY ORIGINALLY SERVED AS SPIES FOR THE ROYAL FAMILY.
THE ROYAL FAMILY...?
AS IN, BEFORE DIN BECAME A REPUBLIC? THAT'S A REALLY LONG TIME AGO...
IT IS. AND FROM WHAT I HEAR, THEY'RE QUITE THE GROUP. THEY EVEN HELPED END THE GREAT WAR.
TO PUT IT SIMPLY...
...IT'S A SPY TEAM OF DIN'S BEST AND BRIGHTEST.
—THAT'S INFERNO.
HOLD UP, THEA.

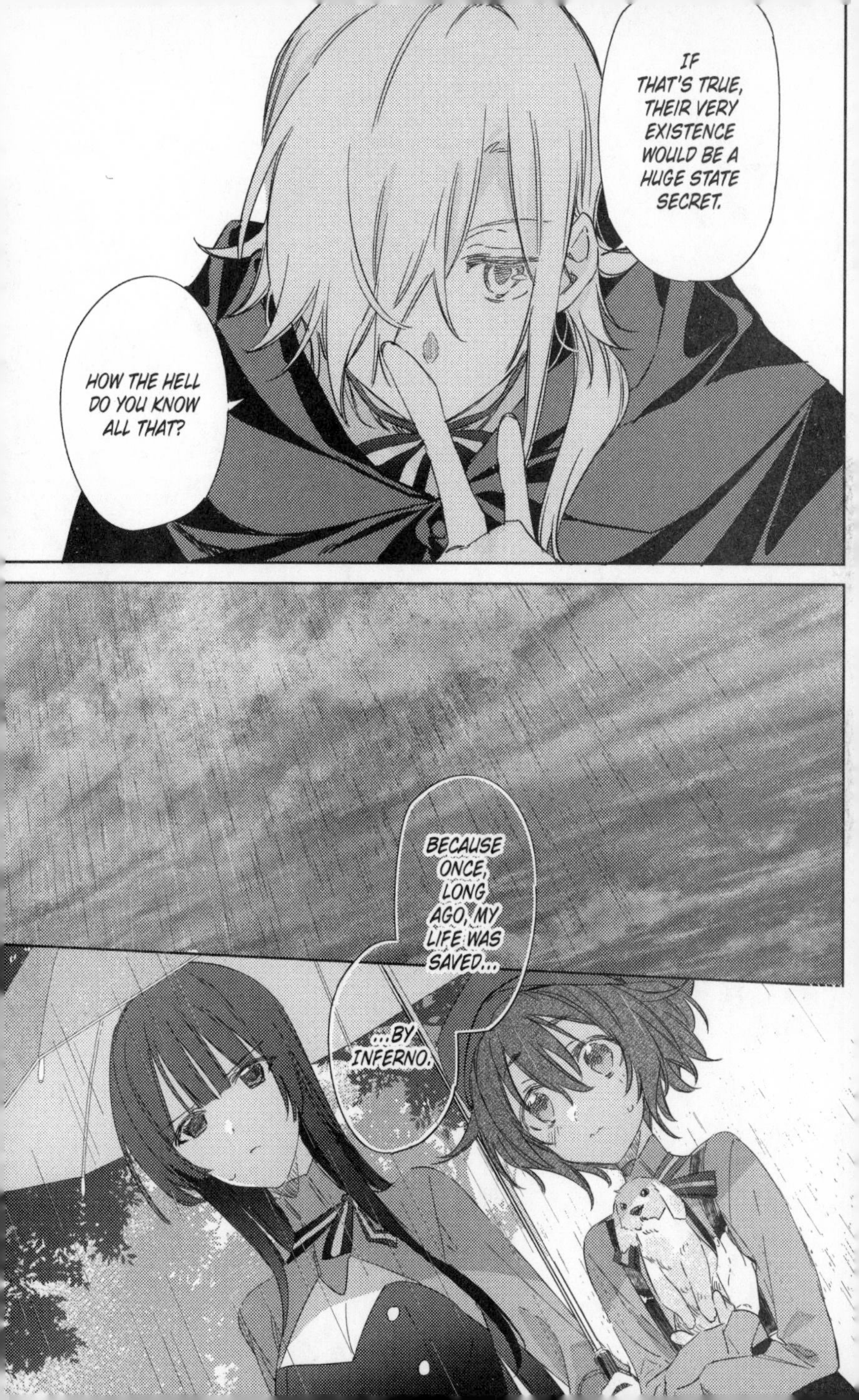
IF THAT'S TRUE, THEIR VERY EXISTENCE WOULD BE A HUGE STATE SECRET.
HOW THE HELL DO YOU KNOW ALL THAT?
BECAUSE ONCE, LONG AGO, MY LIFE WAS SAVED...
...BY INFERNO.

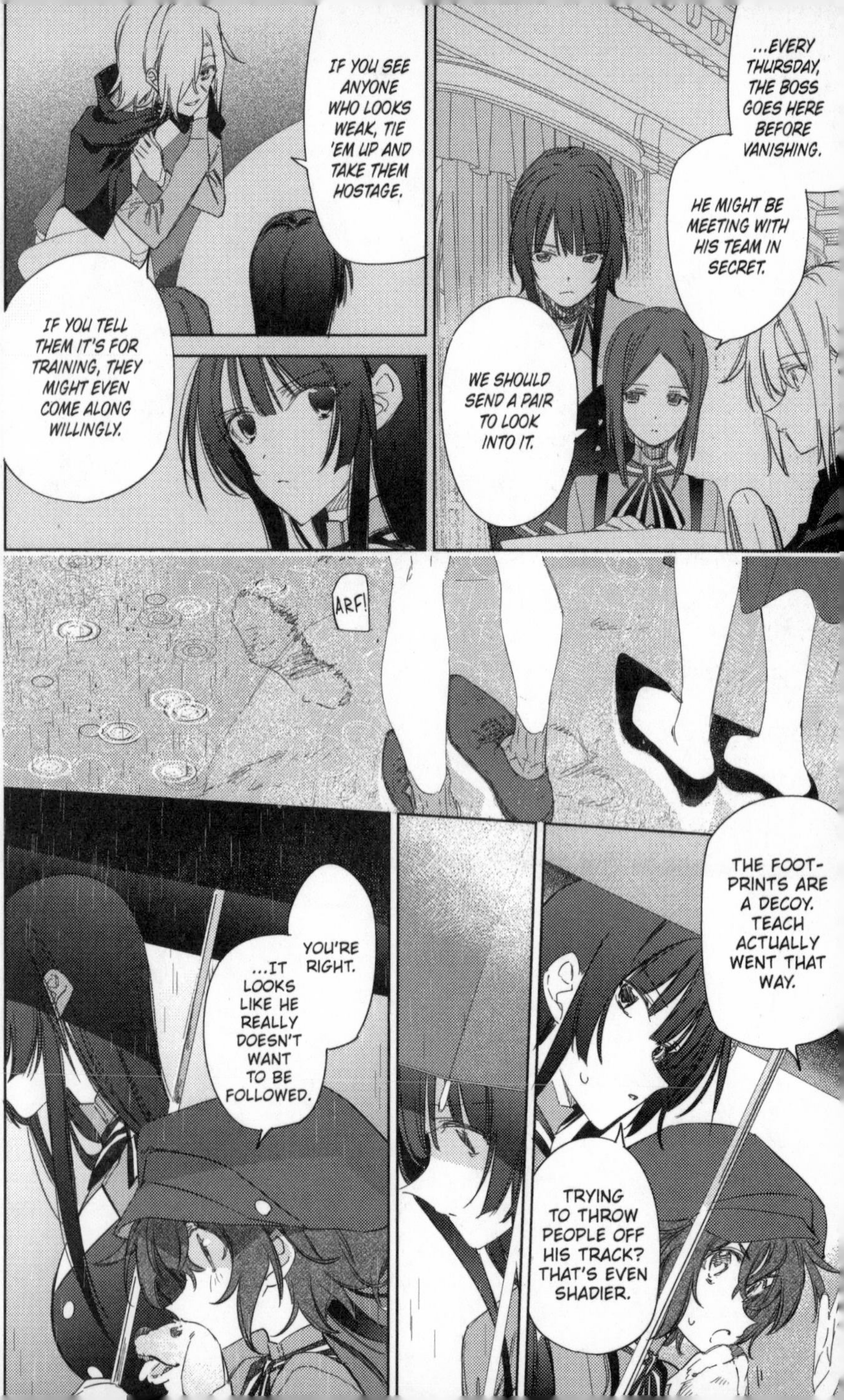
...EVERY THURSDAY, THE BOSS GOES HERE BEFORE VANISHING.
HE MIGHT BE MEETING WITH HIS TEAM IN SECRET.
WE SHOULD SEND A PAIR TO LOOK INTO IT.
IF YOU SEE ANYONE WHO LOOKS WEAK, TIE 'EM UP AND TAKE THEM HOSTAGE.
IF YOU TELL THEM IT'S FOR TRAINING, THEY MIGHT EVEN COME ALONG WILLINGLY.
ARF!
THE FOOT-PRINTS ARE A DECOY. TEACH ACTUALLY WENT THAT WAY.
TRYING TO THROW PEOPLE OFF HIS TRACK? THAT'S EVEN SHADIER.
YOU'RE RIGHT.
...IT LOOKS LIKE HE REALLY DOESN'T WANT TO BE FOLLOWED.

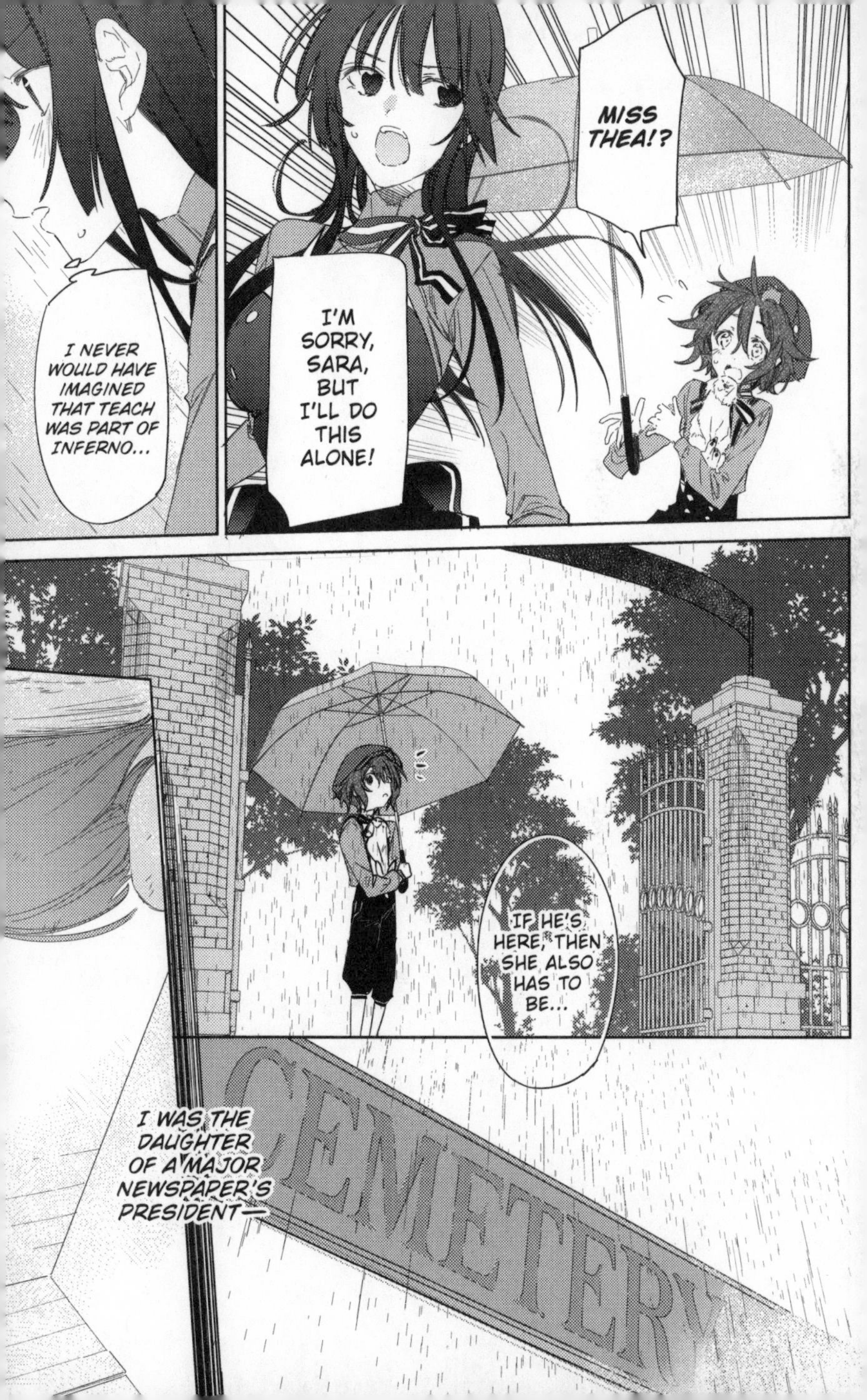
MISS THEA!?
I'M SORRY, SARA, BUT I'LL DO THIS ALONE!
I NEVER WOULD HAVE IMAGINED THAT TEACH WAS PART OF INFERNO...
IF HE'S HERE, THEN SHE ALSO HAS TO BE...
CEMETERY
I WAS THE DAUGHTER OF A MAJOR NEWSPAPER'S PRESIDENT—

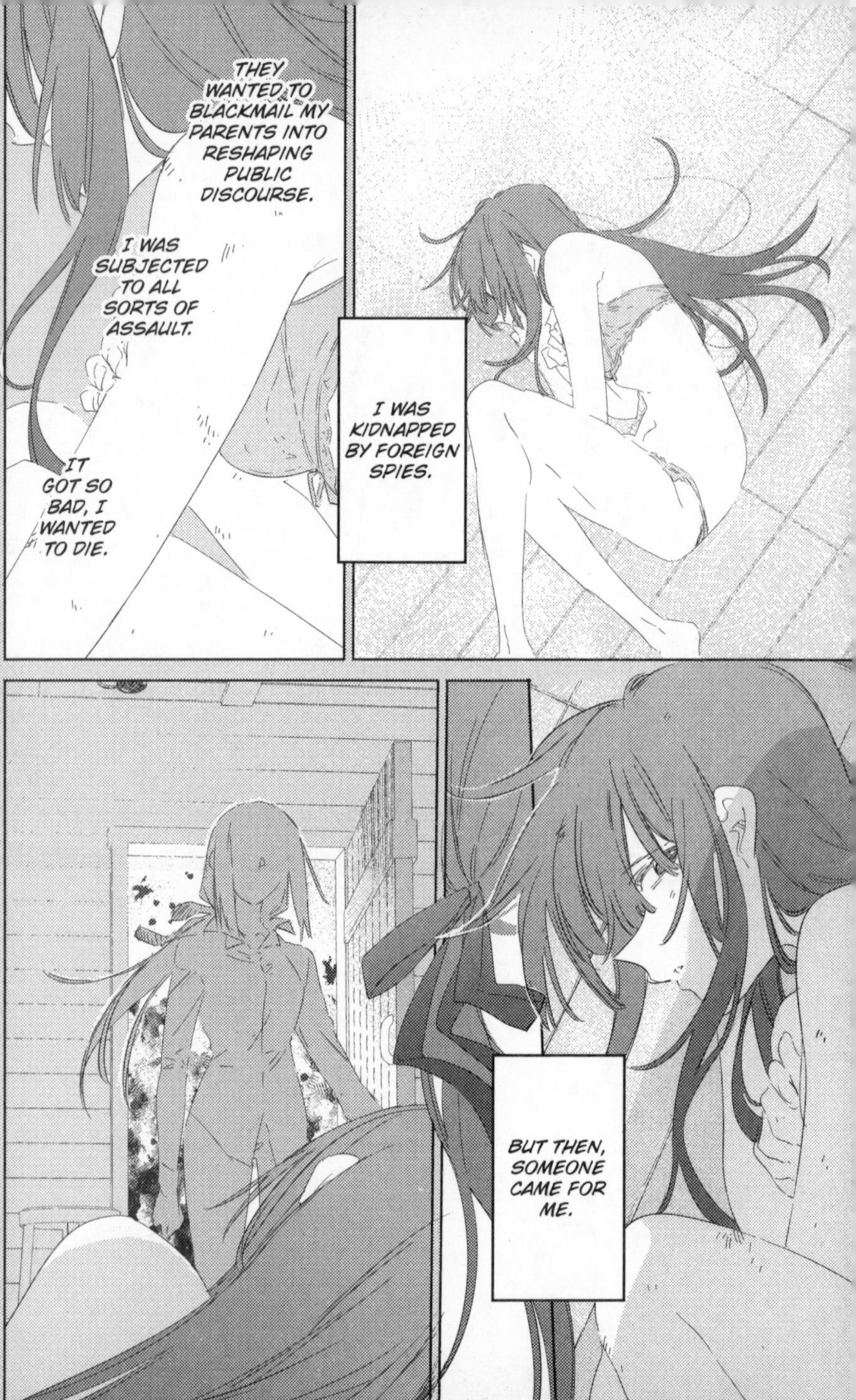
I WAS KIDNAPPED BY FOREIGN SPIES.
THEY WANTED TO BLACKMAIL MY PARENTS INTO RESHAPING PUBLIC DISCOURSE.
I WAS SUBJECTED TO ALL SORTS OF ASSAULT.
IT GOT SO BAD, I WANTED TO DIE.
BUT THEN, SOMEONE CAME FOR ME.

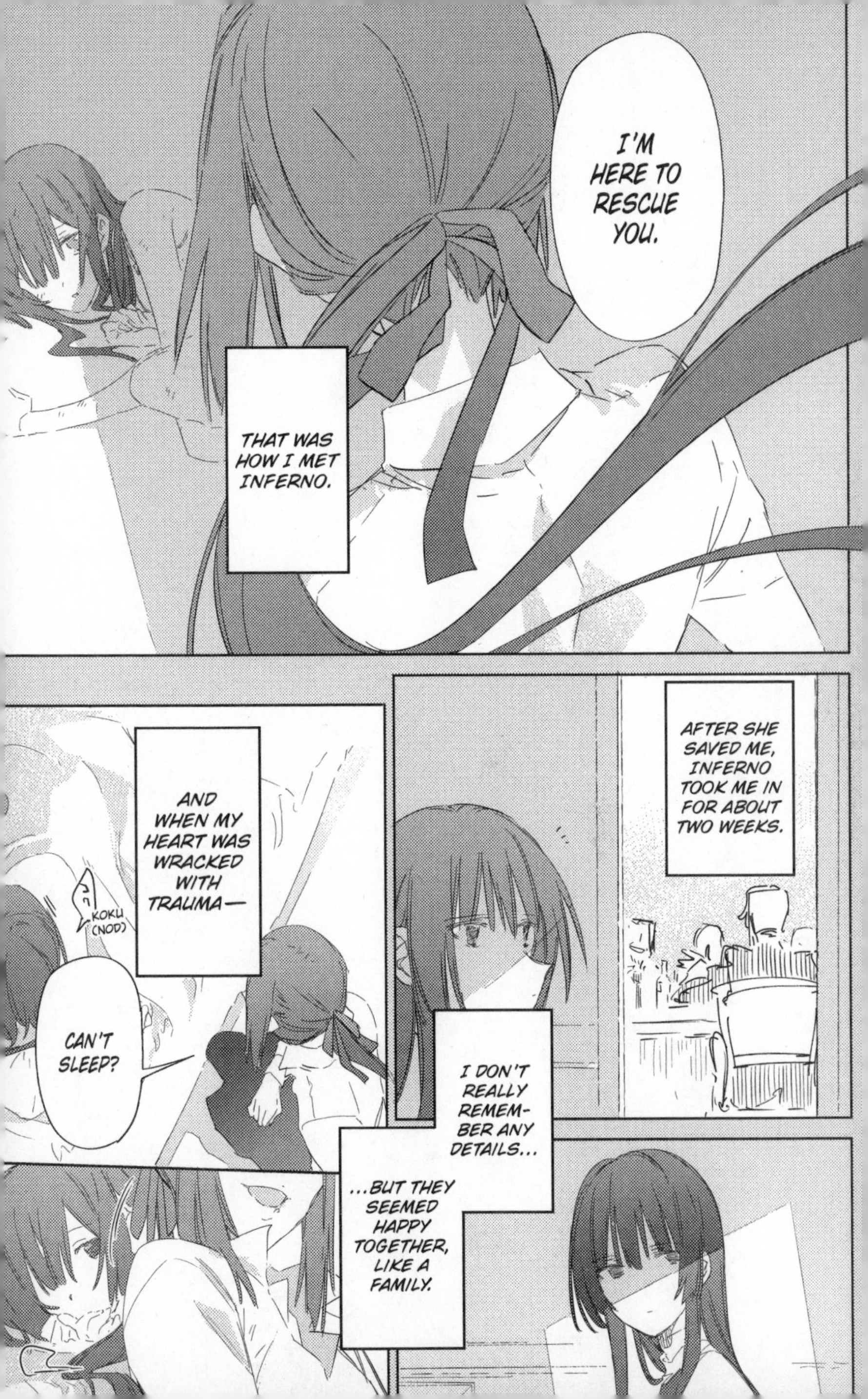
I'M HERE TO RESCUE YOU.
THAT WAS HOW I MET INFERNO.
AFTER SHE SAVED ME, INFERNO TOOK ME IN FOR ABOUT TWO WEEKS.
I DON'T REALLY REMEMBER ANY DETAILS...
...BUT THEY SEEMED HAPPY TOGETHER, LIKE A FAMILY.
AND WHEN MY HEART WAS WRACKED WITH TRAUMA—
CAN'T SLEEP?
KOKU (NOD)

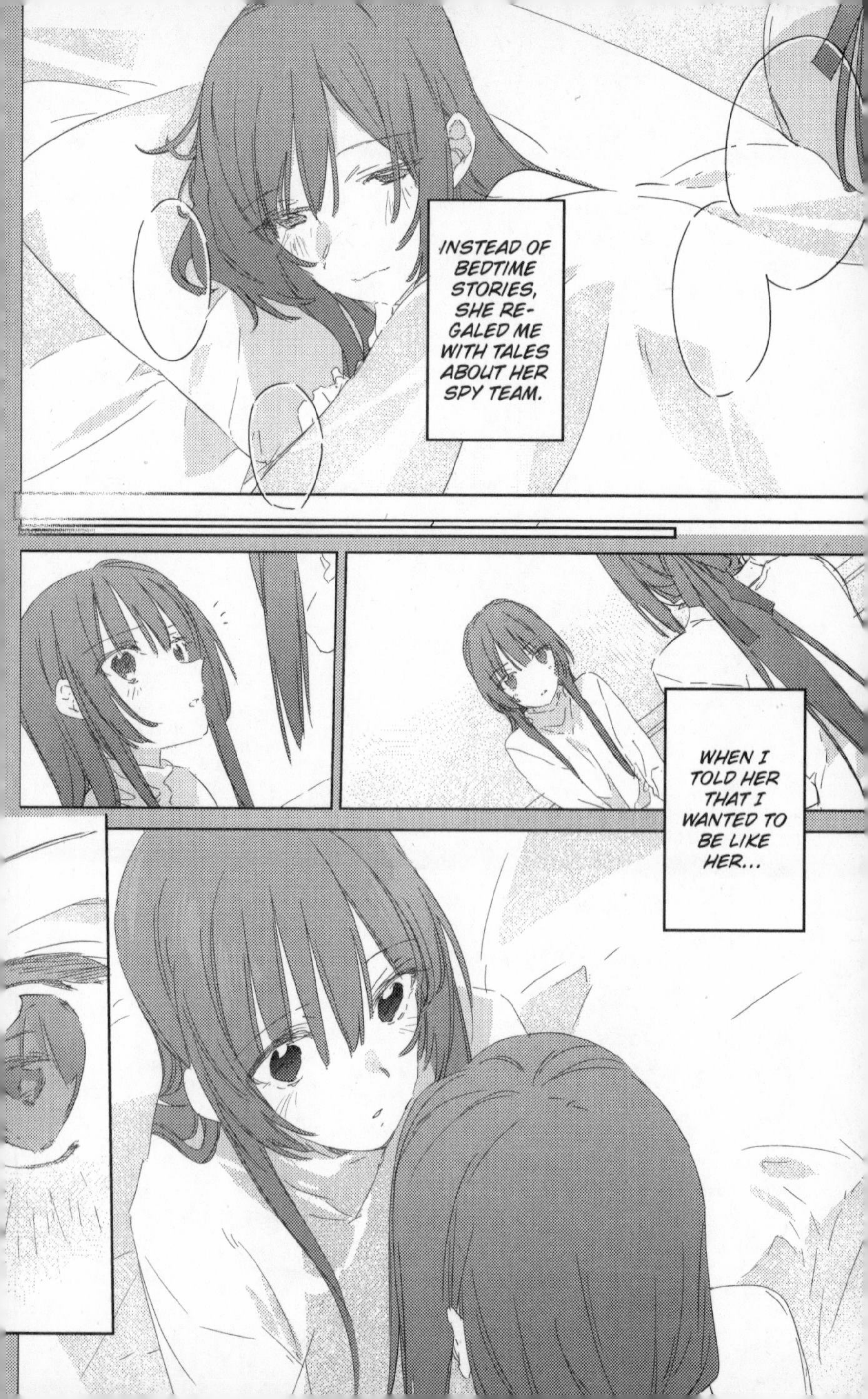
INSTEAD OF BEDTIME STORIES, SHE RE-GALED ME WITH TALES ABOUT HER SPY TEAM.
WHEN I TOLD HER THAT I WANTED TO BE LIKE HER...

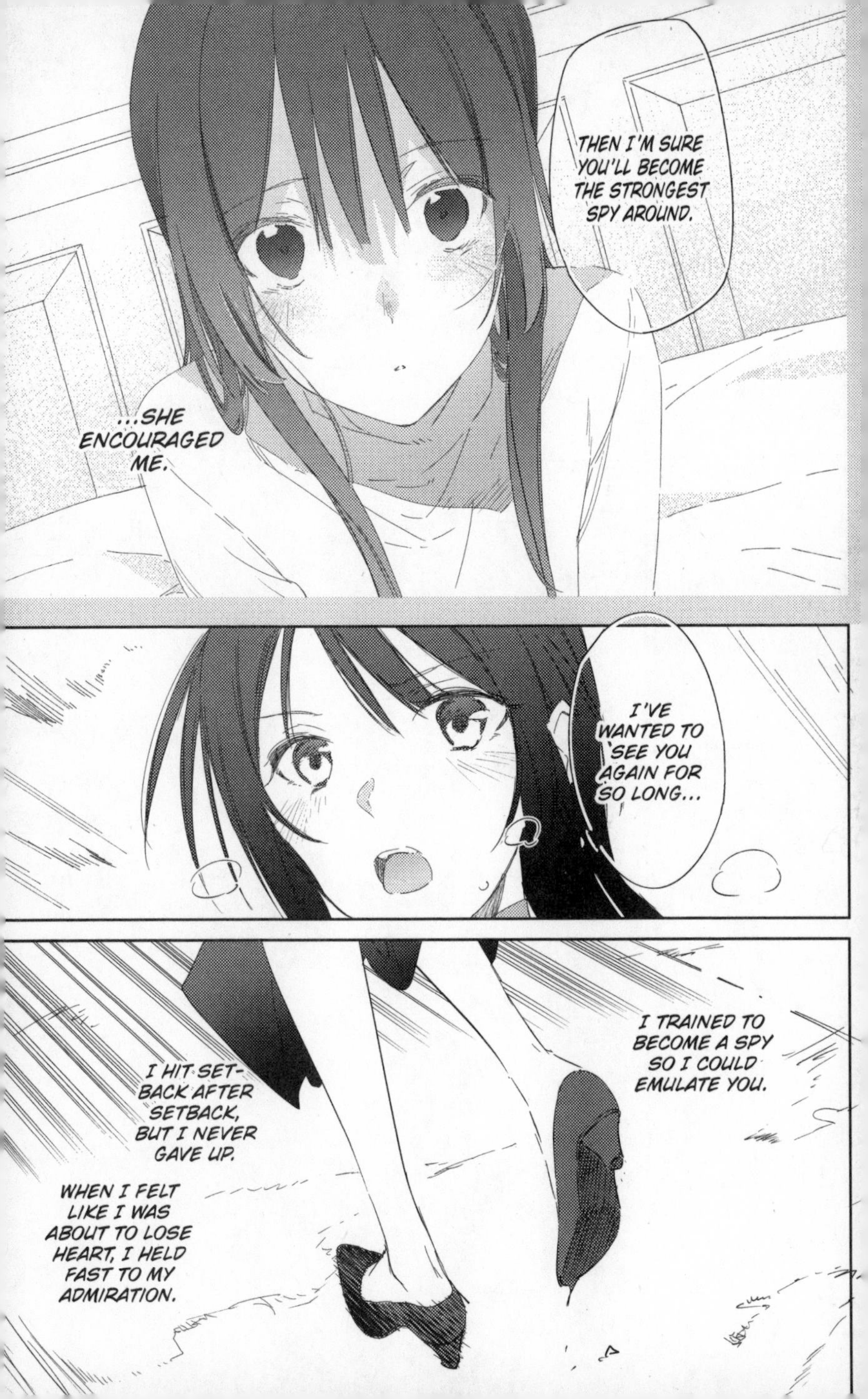
THEN I'M SURE YOU'LL BECOME THE STRONGEST SPY AROUND.
...SHE ENCOURAGED ME.
I'VE WANTED TO SEE YOU AGAIN FOR SO LONG...
I TRAINED TO BECOME A SPY SO I COULD EMULATE YOU.
I HIT SET-BACK AFTER SETBACK, BUT I NEVER GAVE UP.
WHEN I FELT LIKE I WAS ABOUT TO LOSE HEART, I HELD FAST TO MY ADMIRATION.

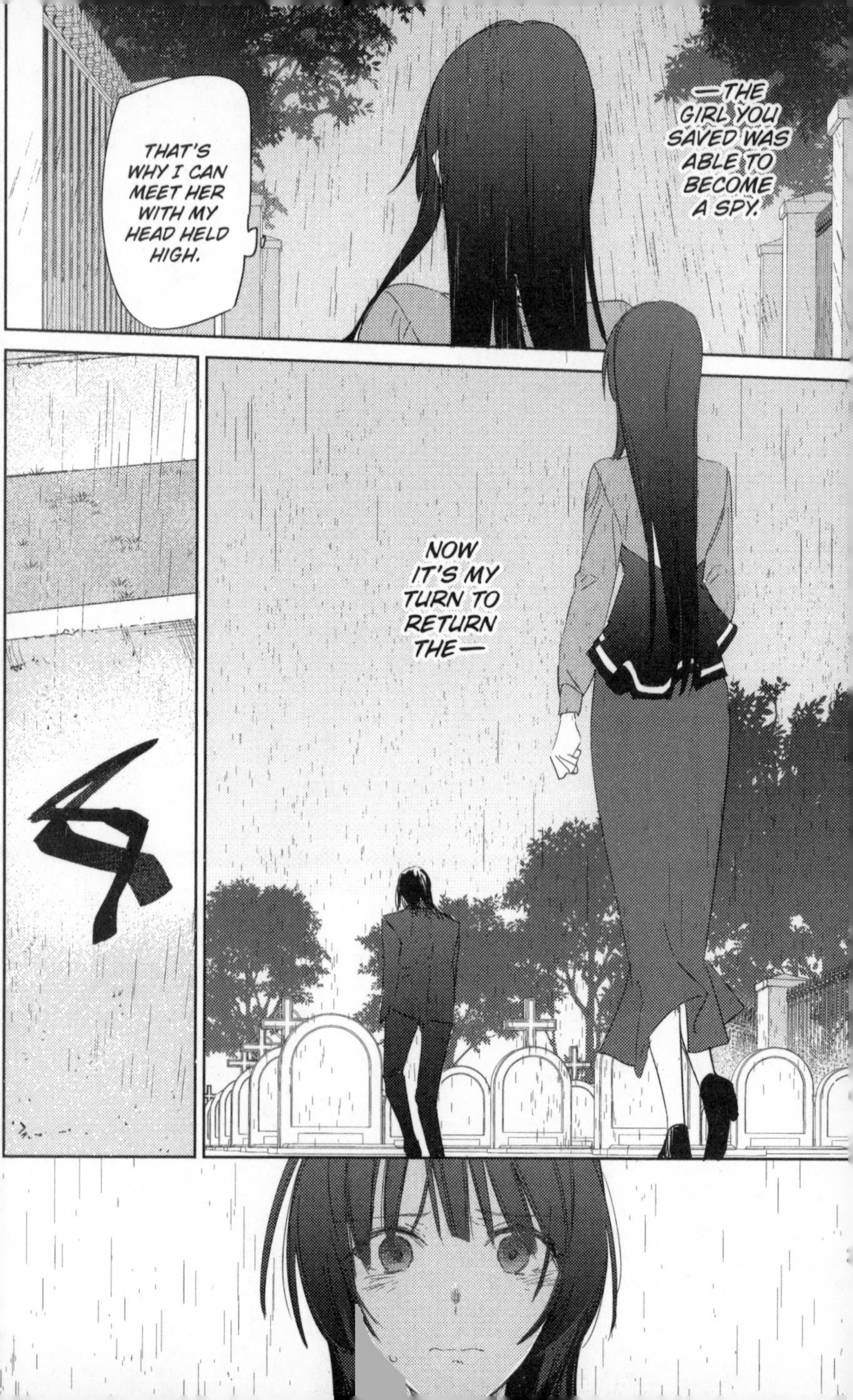
—THE GIRL YOU SAVED WAS ABLE TO BECOME A SPY.
THAT'S WHY I CAN MEET HER WITH MY HEAD HELD HIGH.
NOW IT'S MY TURN TO RETURN THE—

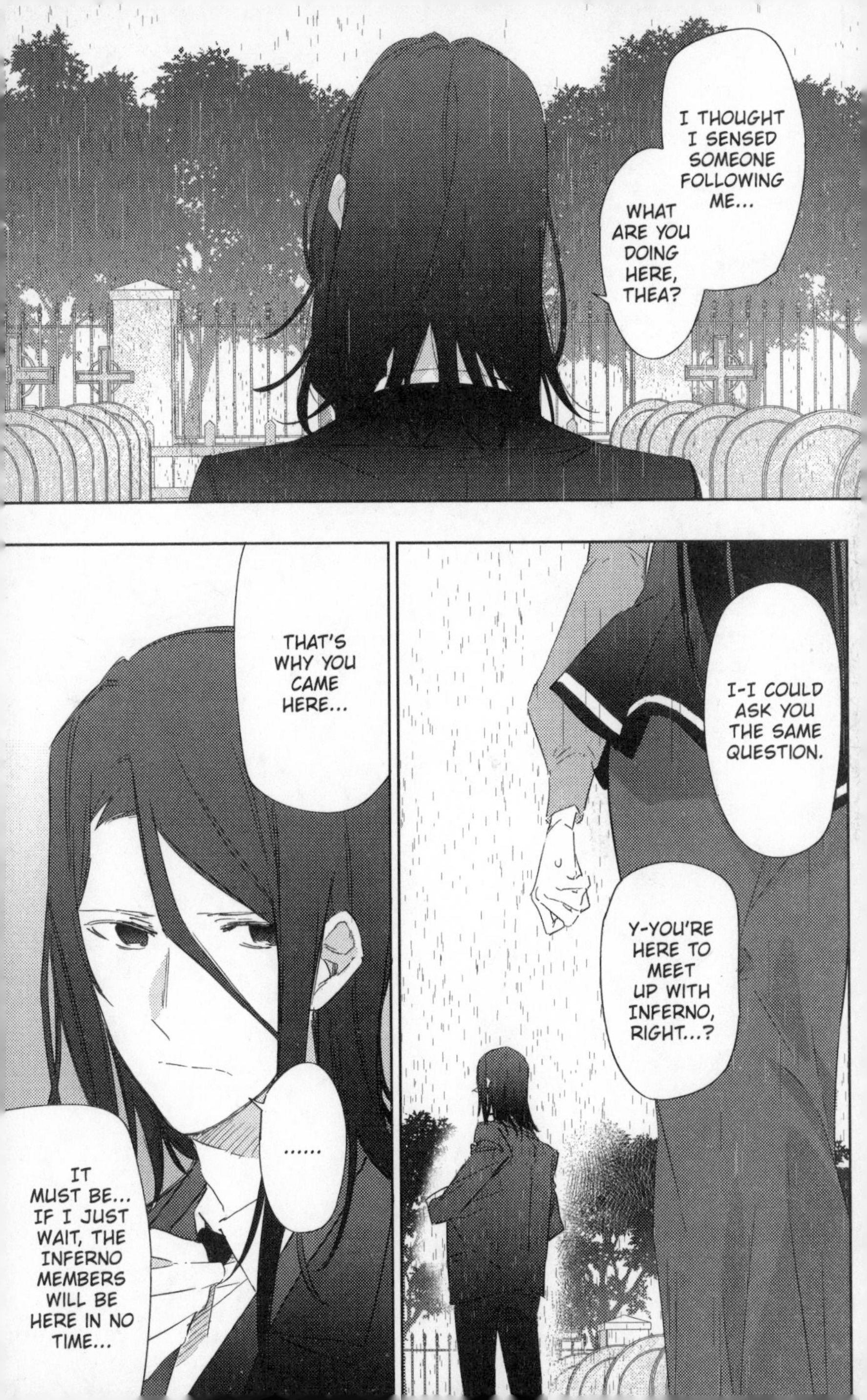
I THOUGHT I SENSED SOMEONE FOLLOWING ME...
WHAT ARE YOU DOING HERE, THEA?
I-I COULD ASK YOU THE SAME QUESTION.
Y-YOU'RE HERE TO MEET UP WITH INFERNO, RIGHT...?
THAT'S WHY YOU CAME HERE...
......
IT MUST BE... IF I JUST WAIT, THE INFERNO MEMBERS WILL BE HERE IN NO TIME...

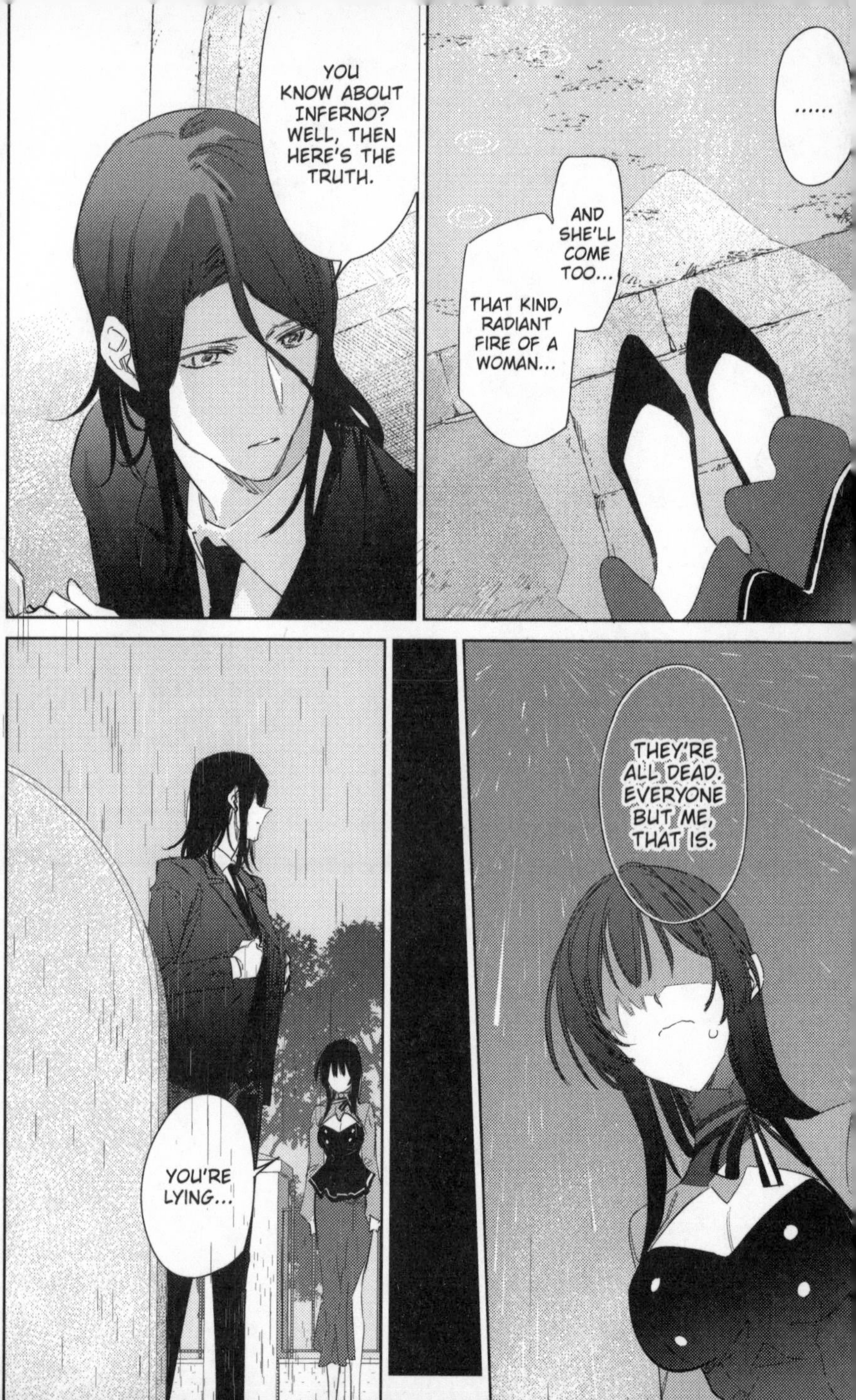
......
AND SHE'LL COME TOO...
THAT KIND, RADIANT FIRE OF A WOMAN...
YOU KNOW ABOUT INFERNO? WELL, THEN HERE'S THE TRUTH.
THEY'RE ALL DEAD. EVERYONE BUT ME, THAT IS.
YOU'RE LYING...

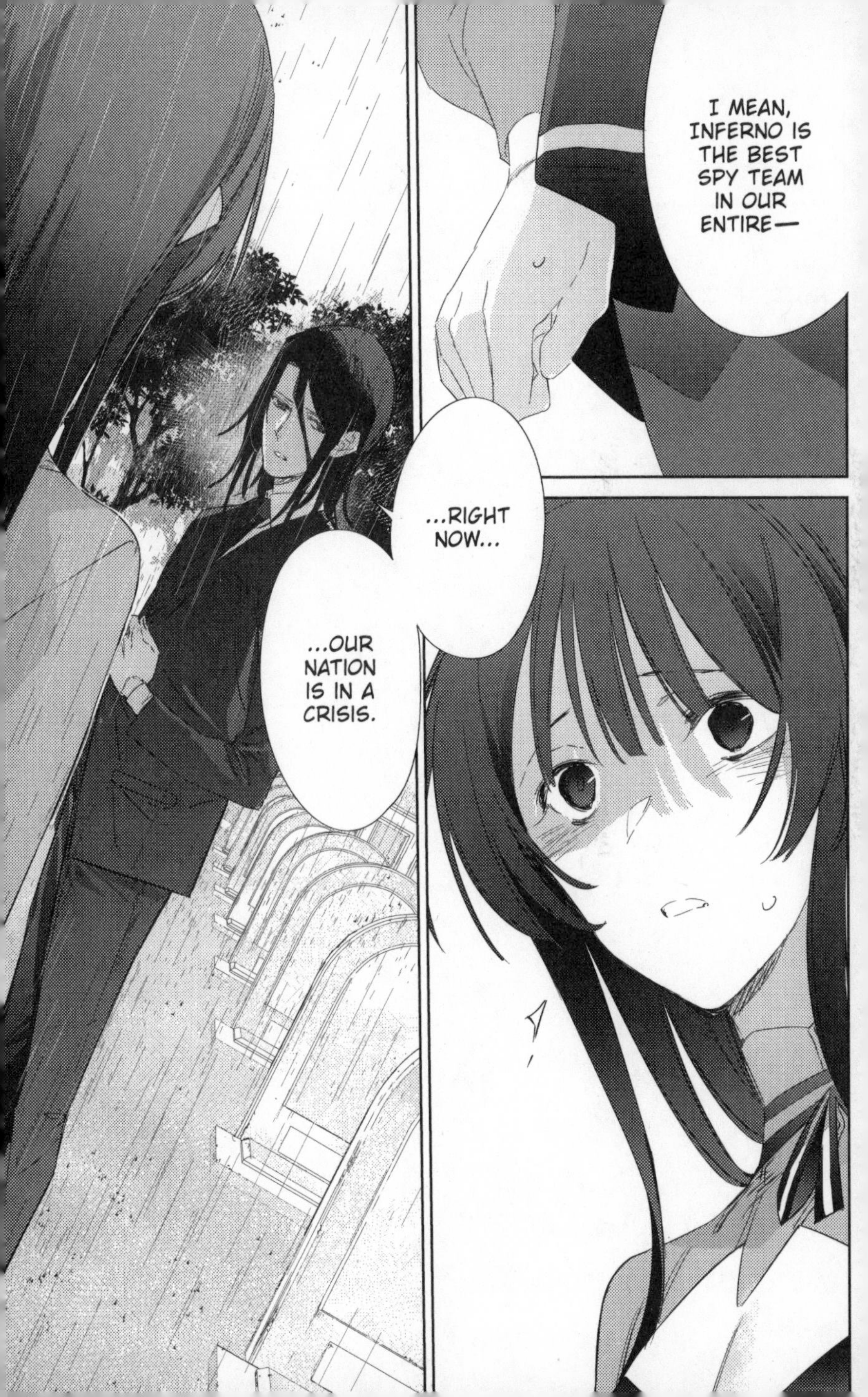
I MEAN, INFERNO IS THE BEST SPY TEAM IN OUR ENTIRE—
...RIGHT NOW...
...OUR NATION IS IN A CRISIS.

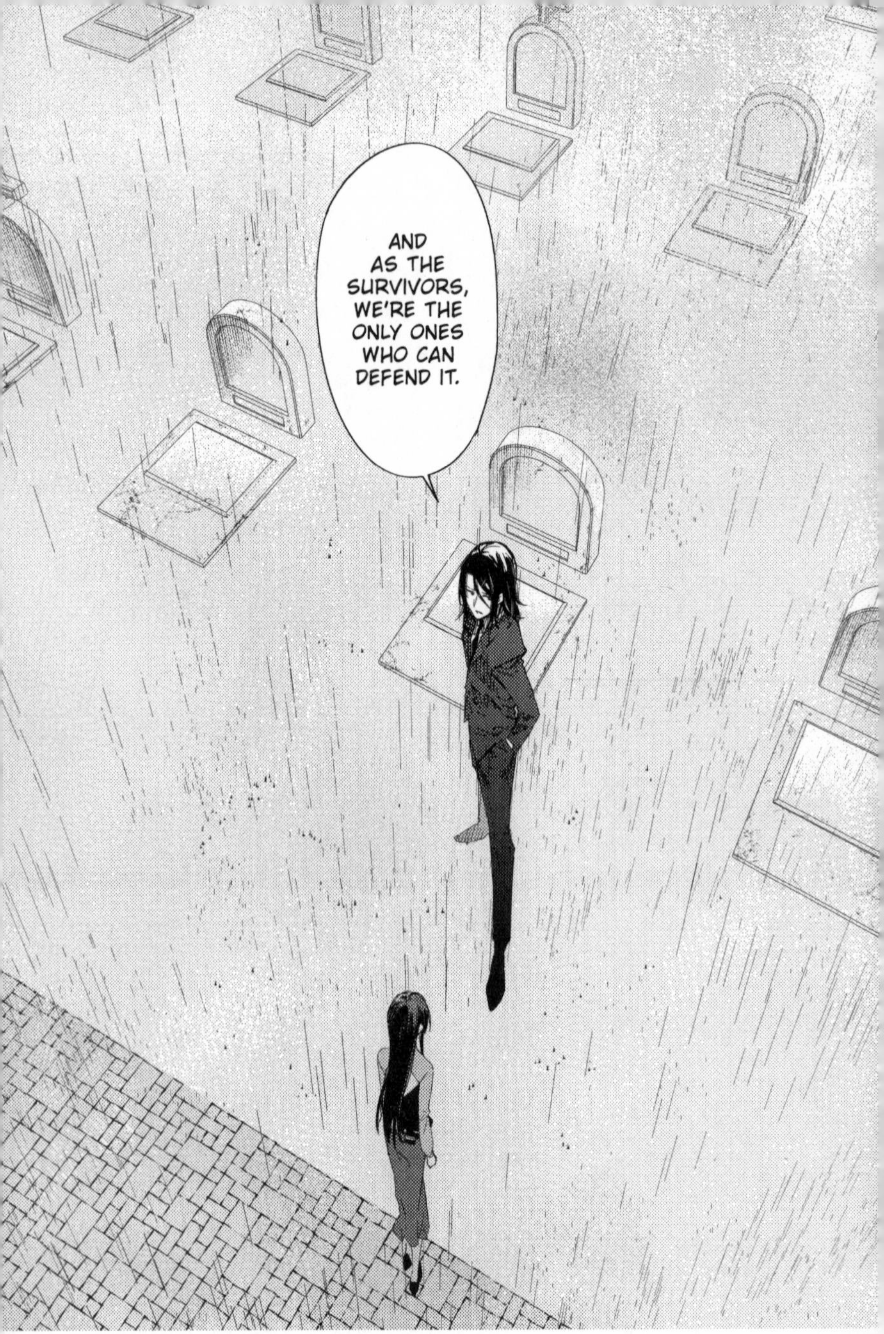
AND AS THE SURVIVORS, WE'RE THE ONLY ONES WHO CAN DEFEND IT.

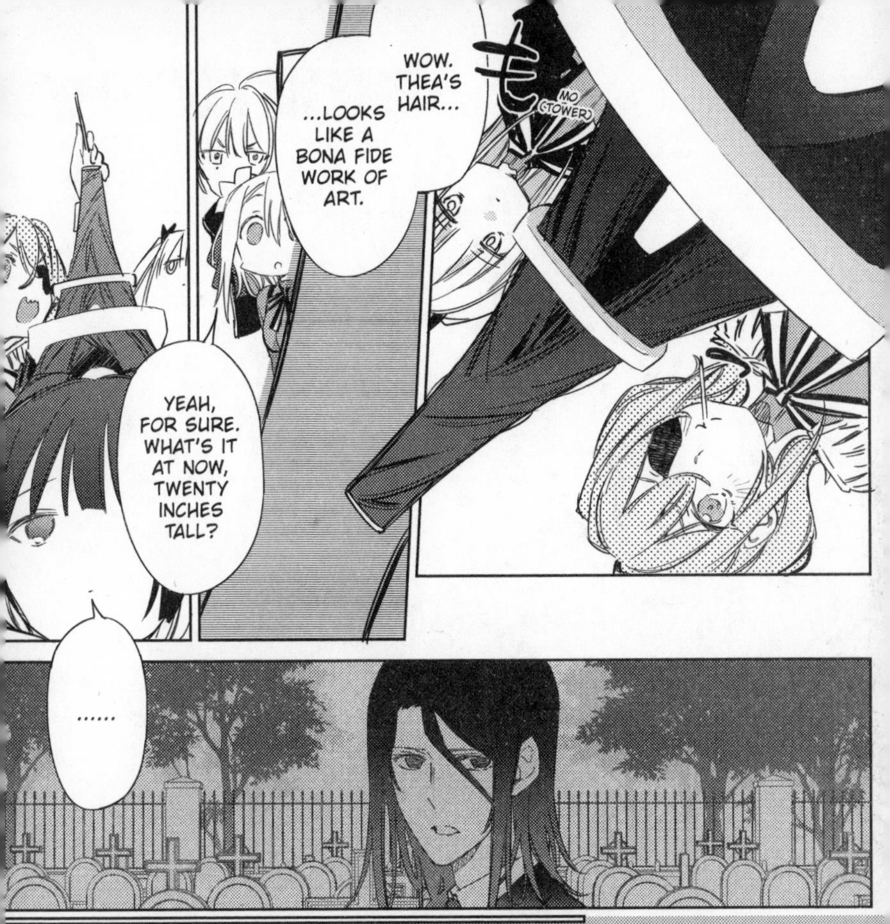
MO (TOWER)
WOW. THEA'S HAIR...
...LOOKS LIKE A BONA FIDE WORK OF ART.
YEAH, FOR SURE. WHAT'S IT AT NOW, TWENTY INCHES TALL?
......

Chapter 8

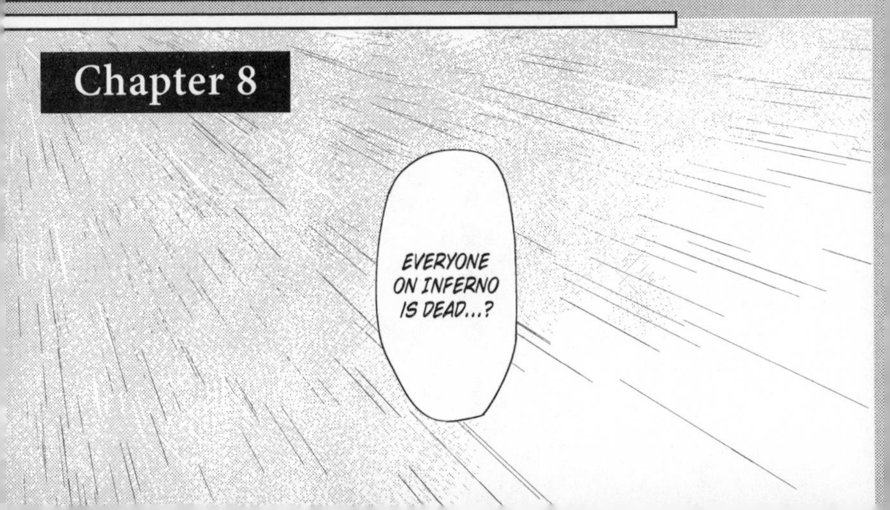
EVERYONE ON INFERNO IS DEAD...?

Chapter 8 — Hostage Part 2

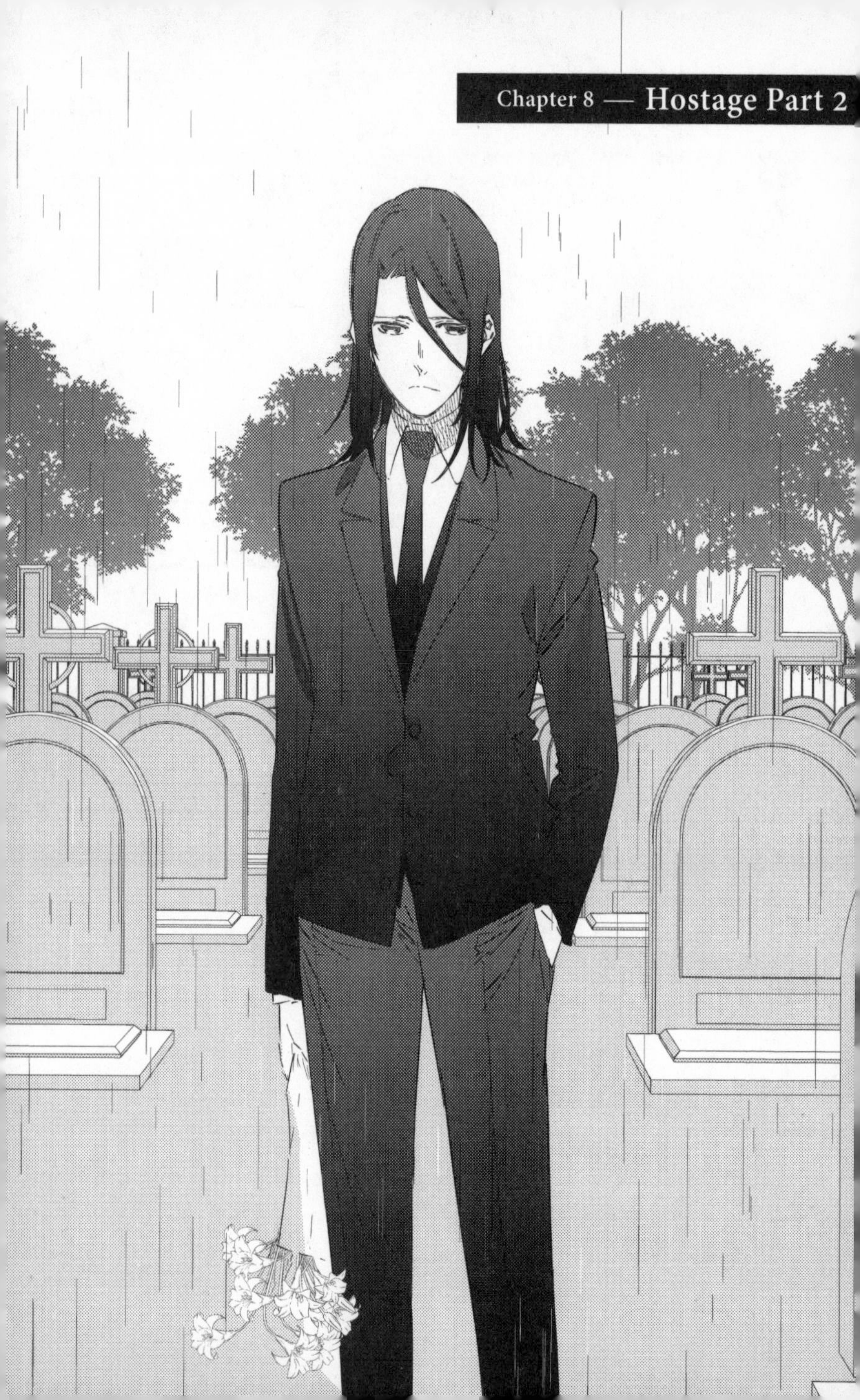

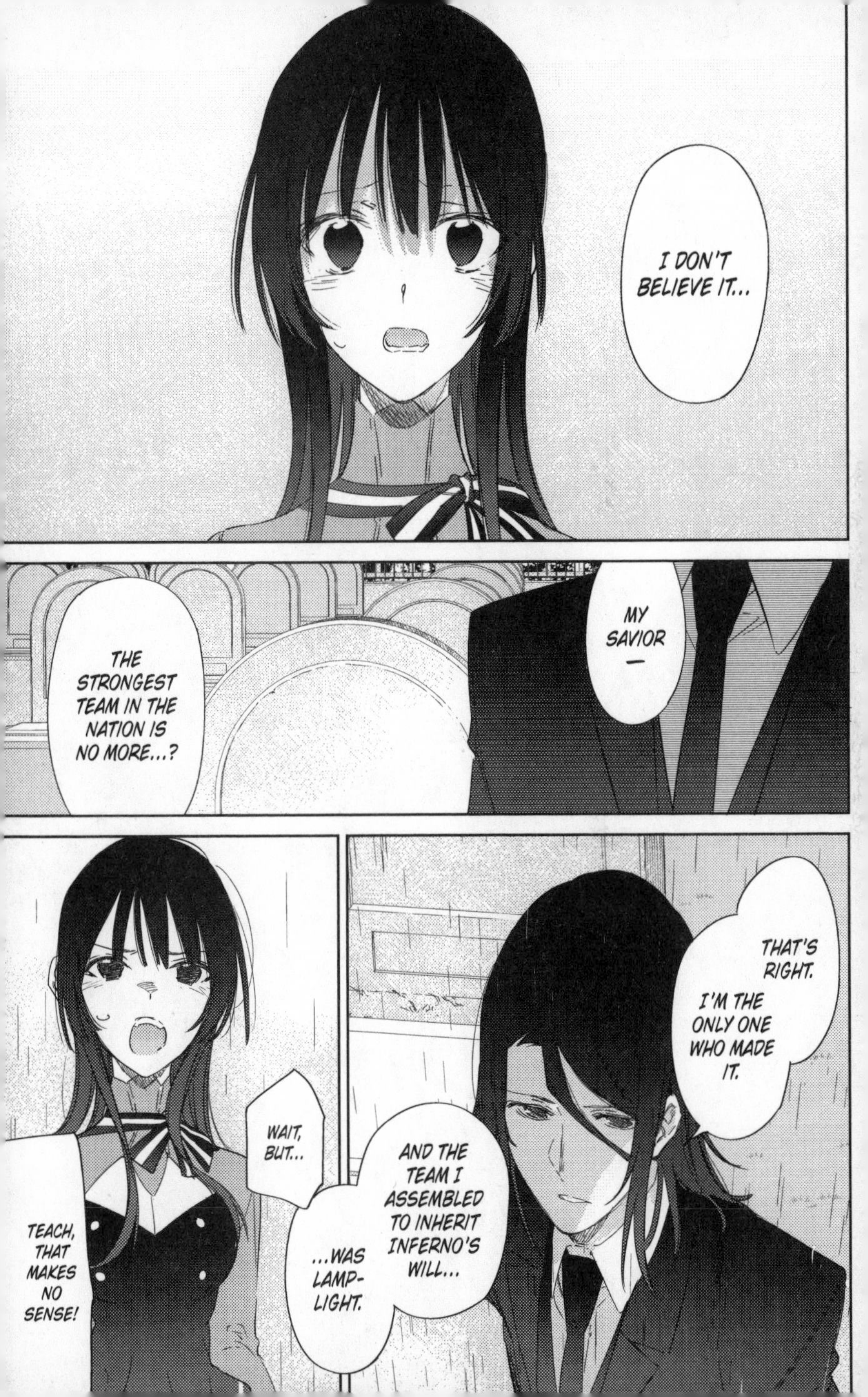
I DON'T BELIEVE IT...
MY SAVIOR —
THE STRONGEST TEAM IN THE NATION IS NO MORE...?
THAT'S RIGHT.
I'M THE ONLY ONE WHO MADE IT.
AND THE TEAM I ASSEMBLED TO INHERIT INFERNO'S WILL...
...WAS LAMPLIGHT.
WAIT, BUT...
TEACH, THAT MAKES NO SENSE!

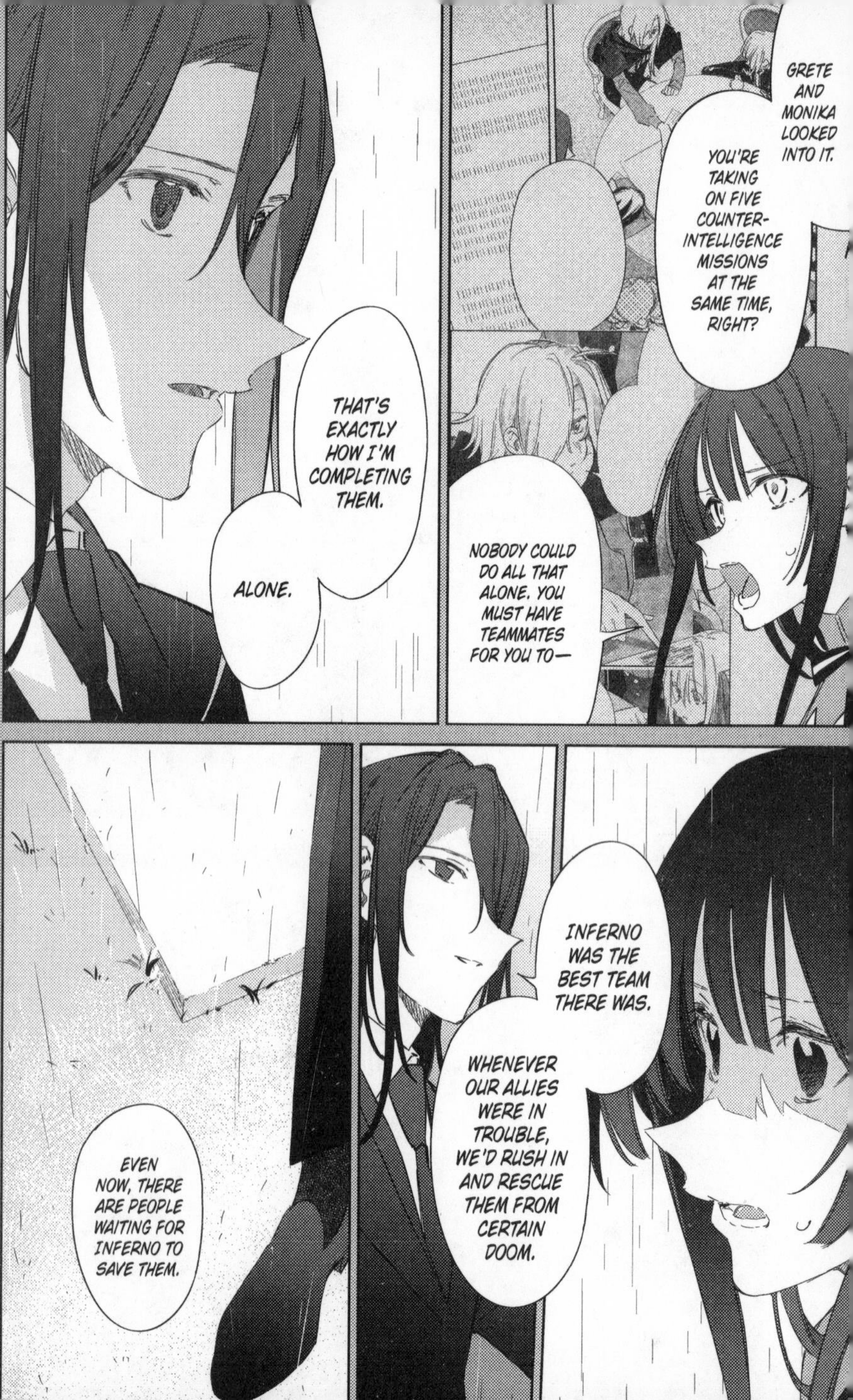
GRETE AND MONIKA LOOKED INTO IT.
YOU'RE TAKING ON FIVE COUNTER-INTELLIGENCE MISSIONS AT THE SAME TIME, RIGHT?
NOBODY COULD DO ALL THAT ALONE. YOU MUST HAVE TEAMMATES FOR YOU TO—
THAT'S EXACTLY HOW I'M COMPLETING THEM.
ALONE.
INFERNO WAS THE BEST TEAM THERE WAS.
WHENEVER OUR ALLIES WERE IN TROUBLE, WE'D RUSH IN AND RESCUE THEM FROM CERTAIN DOOM.
EVEN NOW, THERE ARE PEOPLE WAITING FOR INFERNO TO SAVE THEM.

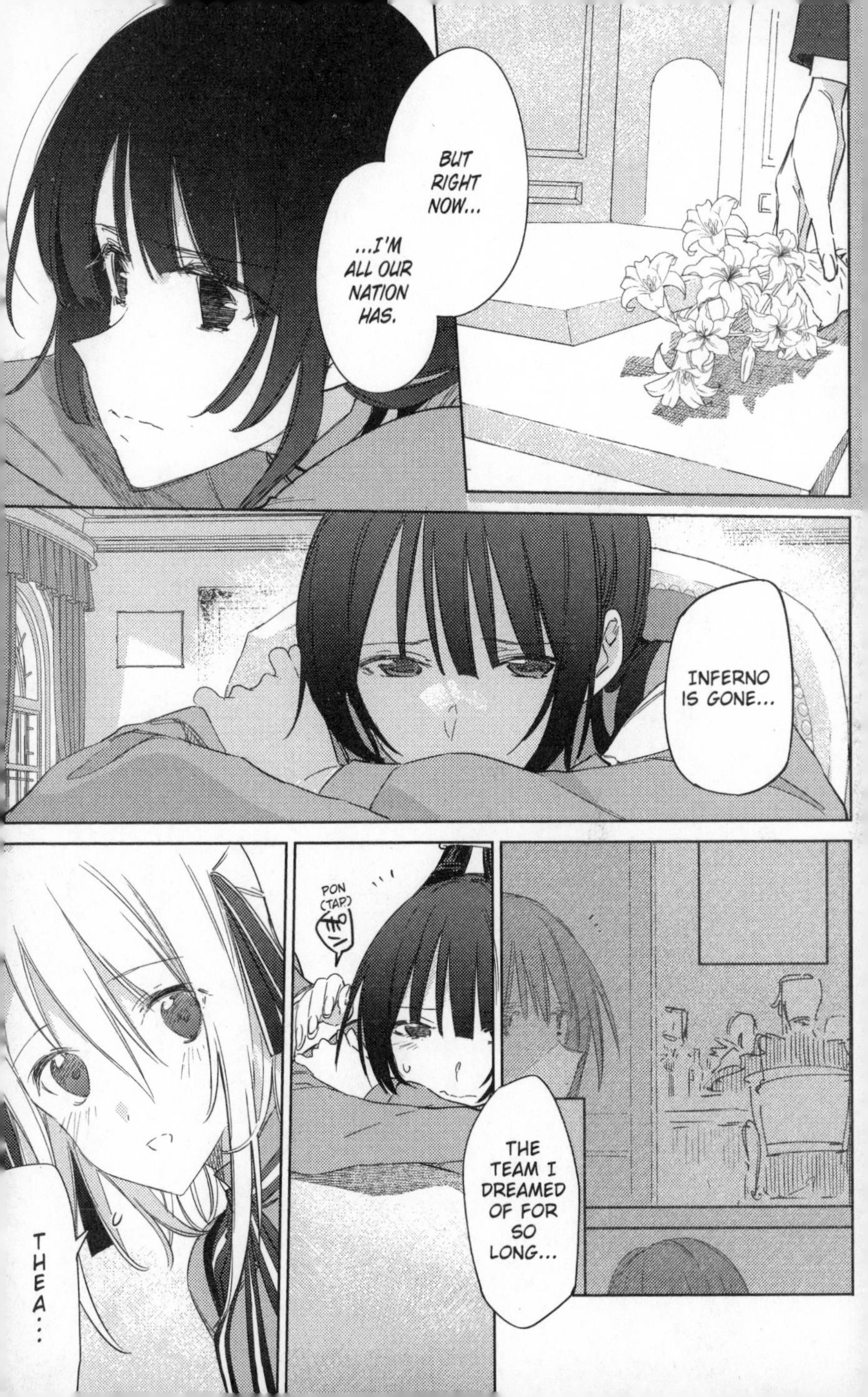
BUT RIGHT NOW...
...I'M ALL OUR NATION HAS.
INFERNO IS GONE...
THE TEAM I DREAMED OF FOR SO LONG...
PON (TAP)
THEA...

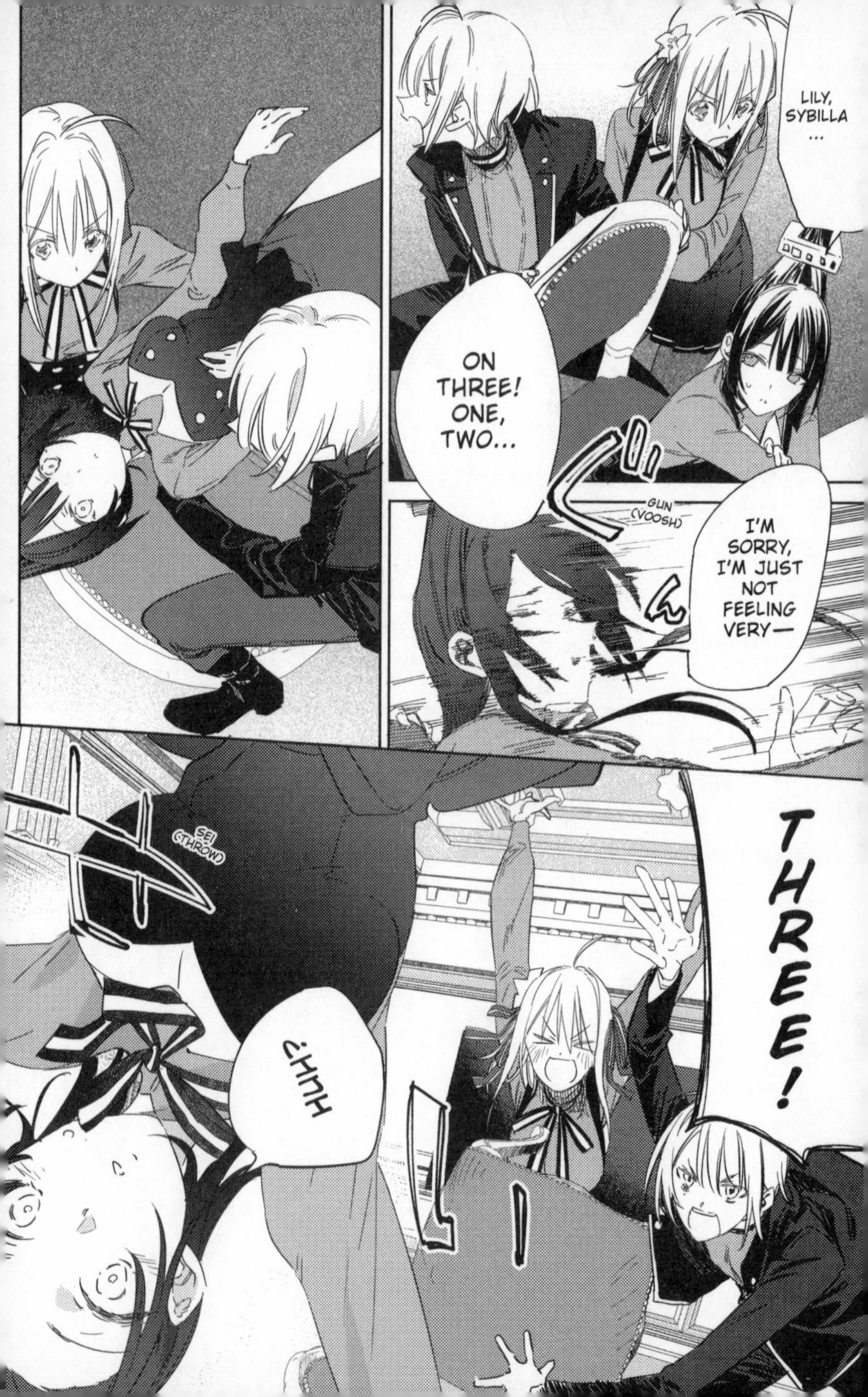

LILY, SYBILLA...
ON THREE! ONE, TWO...
GUN (VOOSH)
I'M SORRY, I'M JUST NOT FEELING VERY—
THREE!
SEI (THROW)
HUH!?

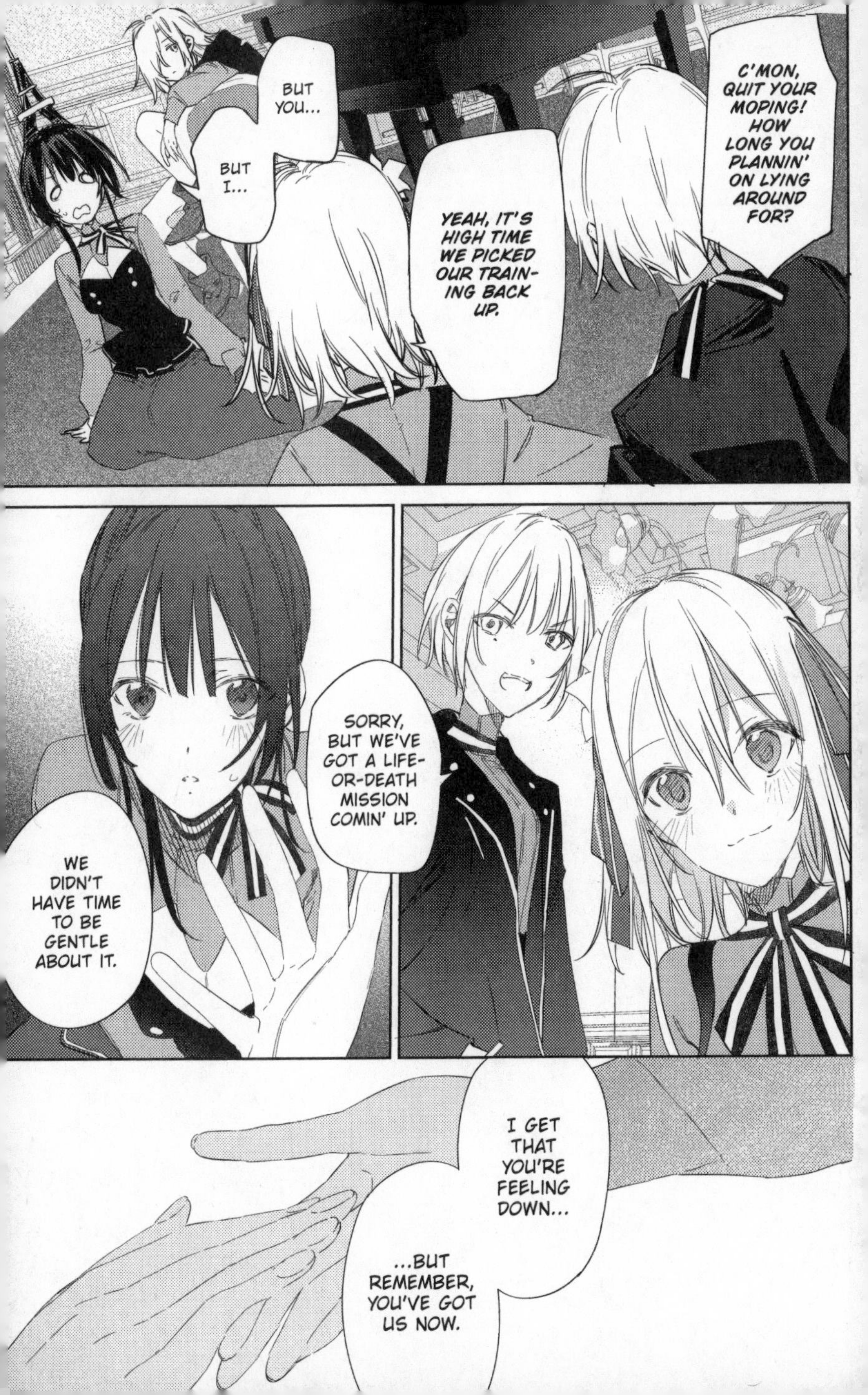
C'MON, QUIT YOUR MOPING! HOW LONG YOU PLANNIN' ON LYING AROUND FOR?
YEAH, IT'S HIGH TIME WE PICKED OUR TRAINING BACK UP.
BUT YOU...
BUT I...
SORRY, BUT WE'VE GOT A LIFE-OR-DEATH MISSION COMIN' UP.
WE DIDN'T HAVE TIME TO BE GENTLE ABOUT IT.
I GET THAT YOU'RE FEELING DOWN...
...BUT REMEMBER, YOU'VE GOT US NOW.

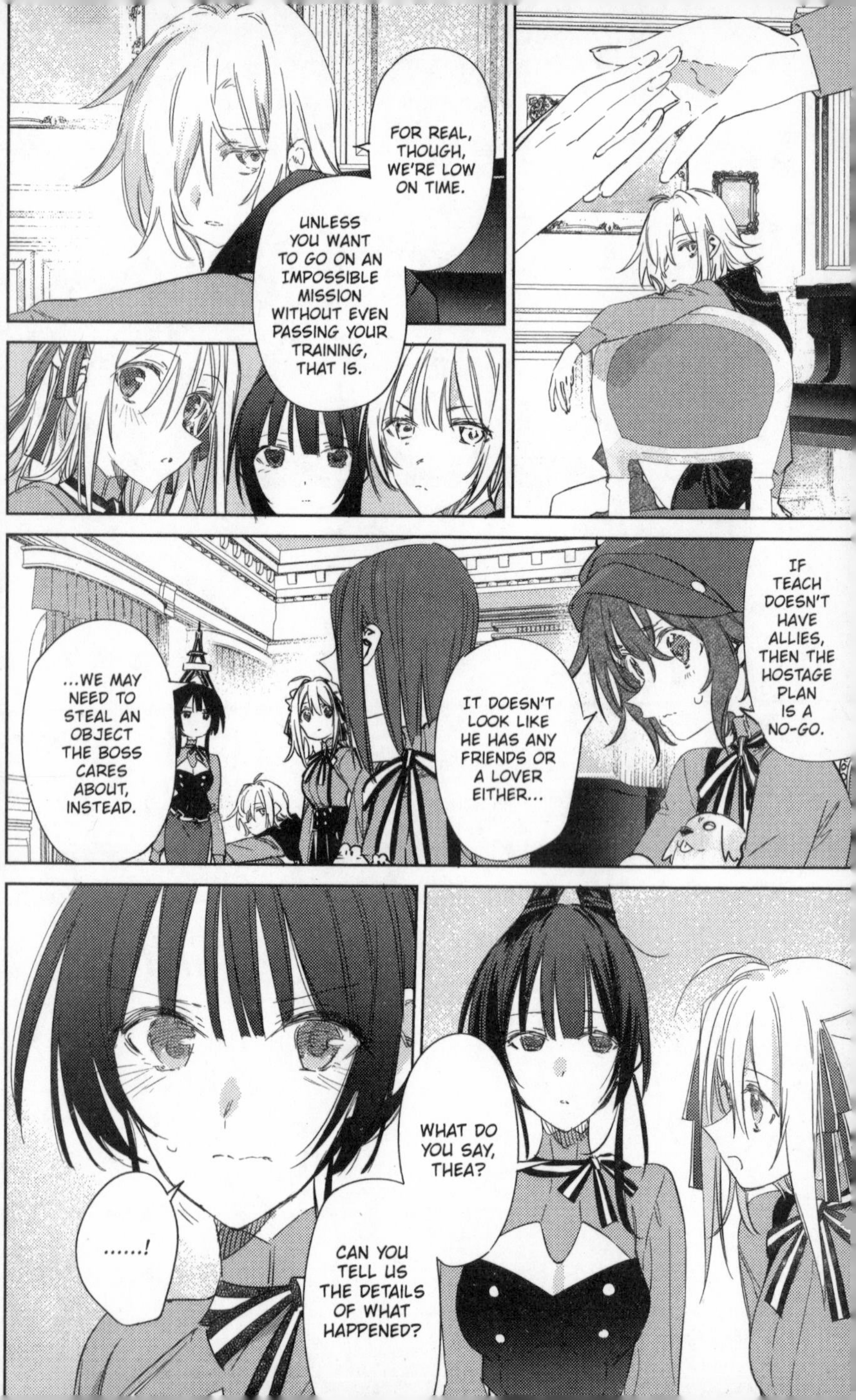
FOR REAL, THOUGH, WE'RE LOW ON TIME.
UNLESS YOU WANT TO GO ON AN IMPOSSIBLE MISSION WITHOUT EVEN PASSING YOUR TRAINING, THAT IS.
IF TEACH DOESN'T HAVE ALLIES, THEN THE HOSTAGE PLAN IS A NO-GO.
IT DOESN'T LOOK LIKE HE HAS ANY FRIENDS OR A LOVER EITHER...
...WE MAY NEED TO STEAL AN OBJECT THE BOSS CARES ABOUT, INSTEAD.
WHAT DO YOU SAY, THEA?
CAN YOU TELL US THE DETAILS OF WHAT HAPPENED?
......!

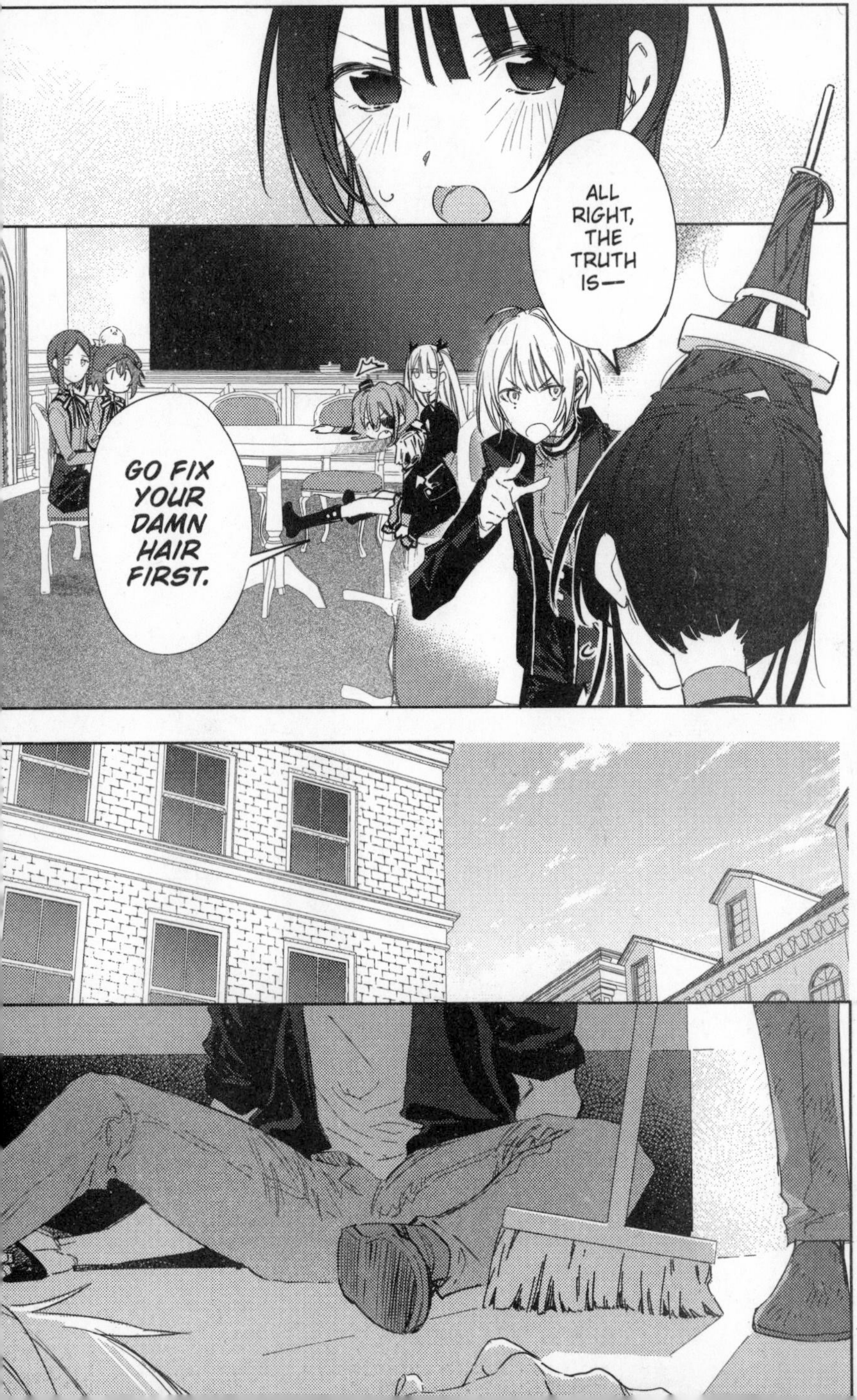
ALL RIGHT, THE TRUTH IS—
GO FIX YOUR DAMN HAIR FIRST.

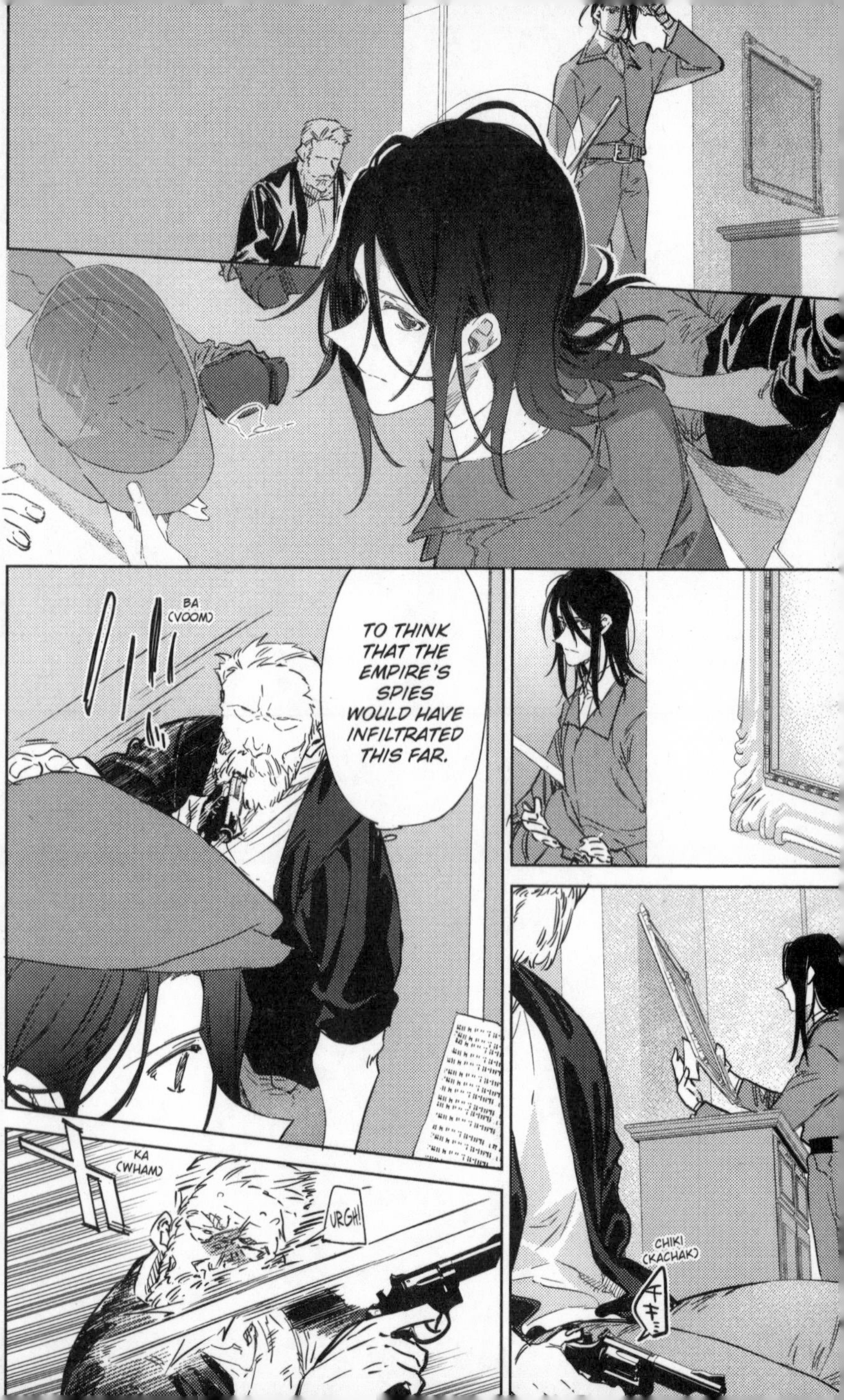
BA (VOOM)
TO THINK THAT THE EMPIRE'S SPIES WOULD HAVE INFILTRATED THIS FAR.
CHIKI (KACHAK)
KA (WHAM)
URGH!

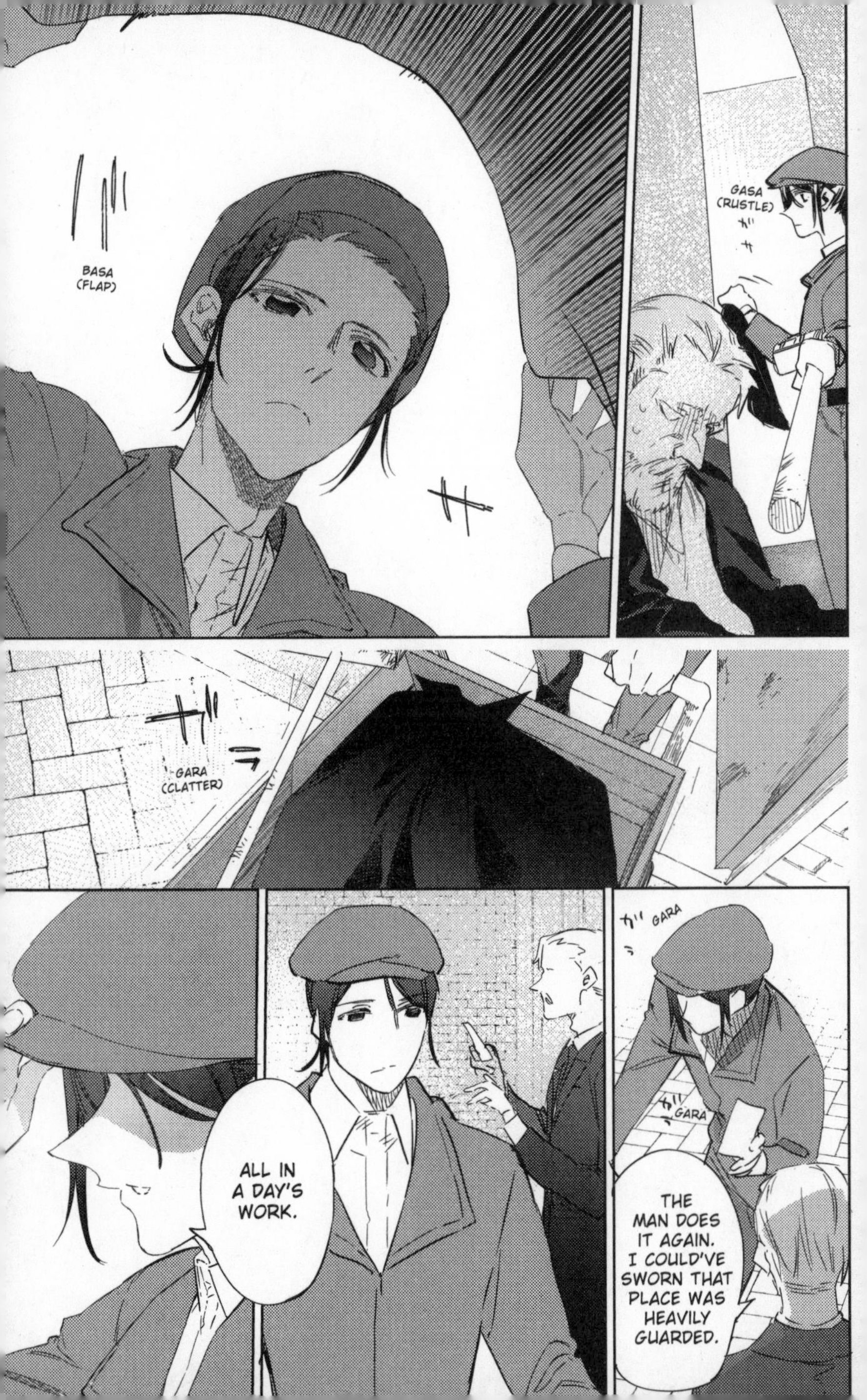
GASA (RUSTLE)
BASA (FLAP)
GARA (CLATTER)
GARA
GARA
THE MAN DOES IT AGAIN. I COULD'VE SWORN THAT PLACE WAS HEAVILY GUARDED.
ALL IN A DAY'S WORK.

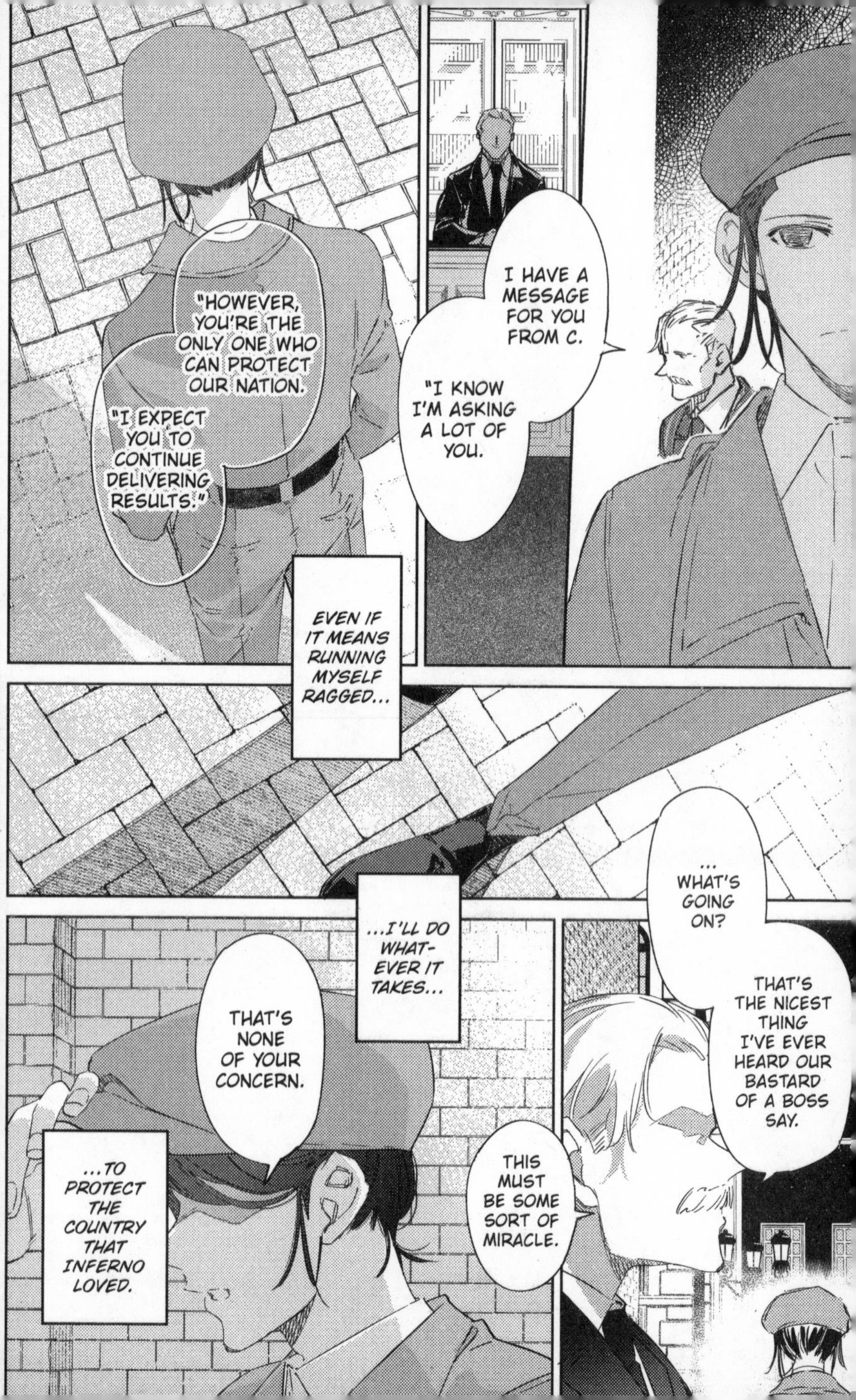
I HAVE A MESSAGE FOR YOU FROM C.
"I KNOW I'M ASKING A LOT OF YOU.
"HOWEVER, YOU'RE THE ONLY ONE WHO CAN PROTECT OUR NATION.
"I EXPECT YOU TO CONTINUE DELIVERING RESULTS."
EVEN IF IT MEANS RUNNING MYSELF RAGGED...
... WHAT'S GOING ON?
...I'LL DO WHAT-EVER IT TAKES...
THAT'S THE NICEST THING I'VE EVER HEARD OUR BASTARD OF A BOSS SAY.
THIS MUST BE SOME SORT OF MIRACLE.
THAT'S NONE OF YOUR CONCERN.
...TO PROTECT THE COUNTRY THAT INFERNO LOVED.

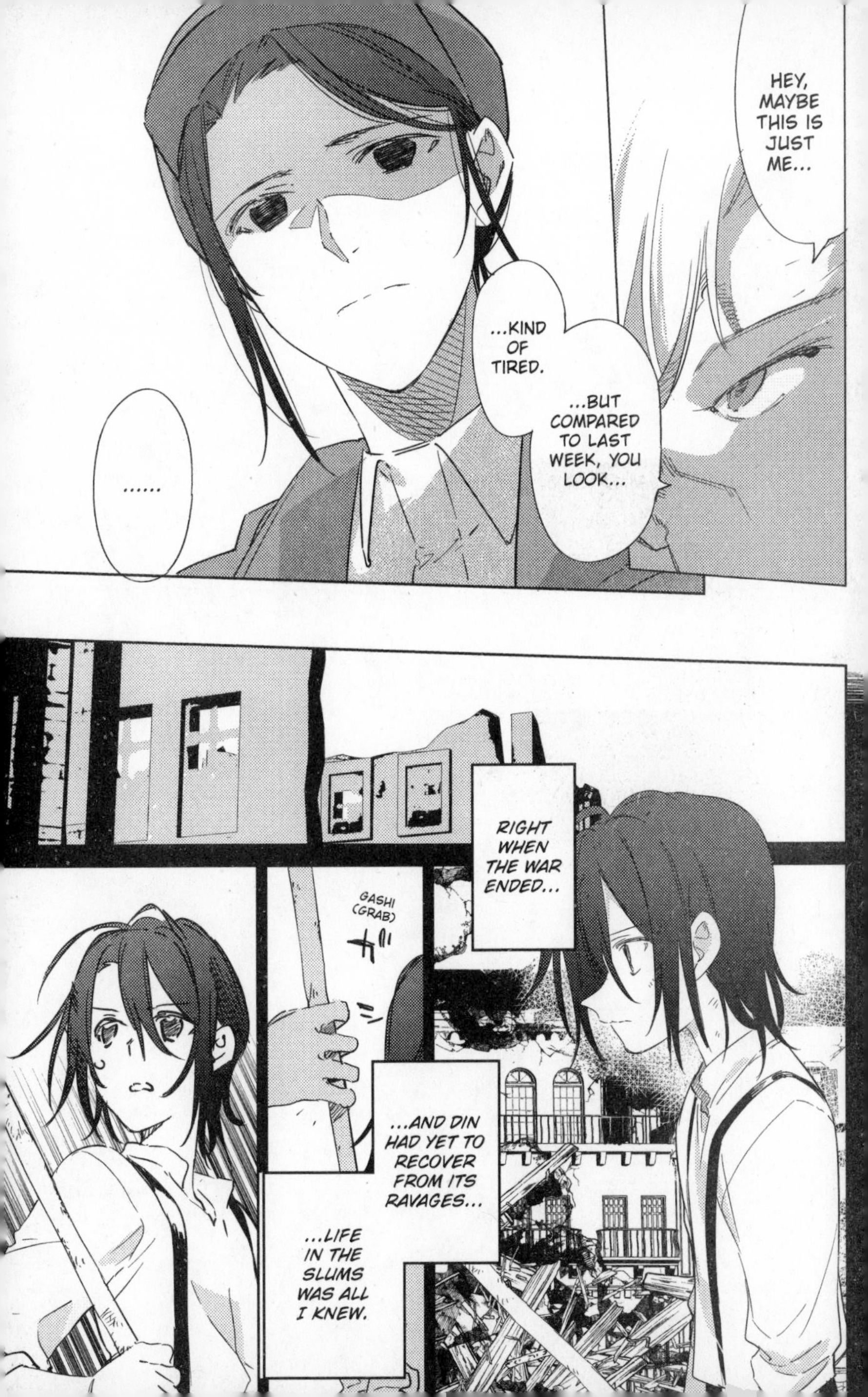
HEY, MAYBE THIS IS JUST ME...
...KIND OF TIRED.
...BUT COMPARED TO LAST WEEK, YOU LOOK...
......
RIGHT WHEN THE WAR ENDED...
GASHI (GRAB)
...AND DIN HAD YET TO RECOVER FROM ITS RAVAGES...
...LIFE IN THE SLUMS WAS ALL I KNEW.

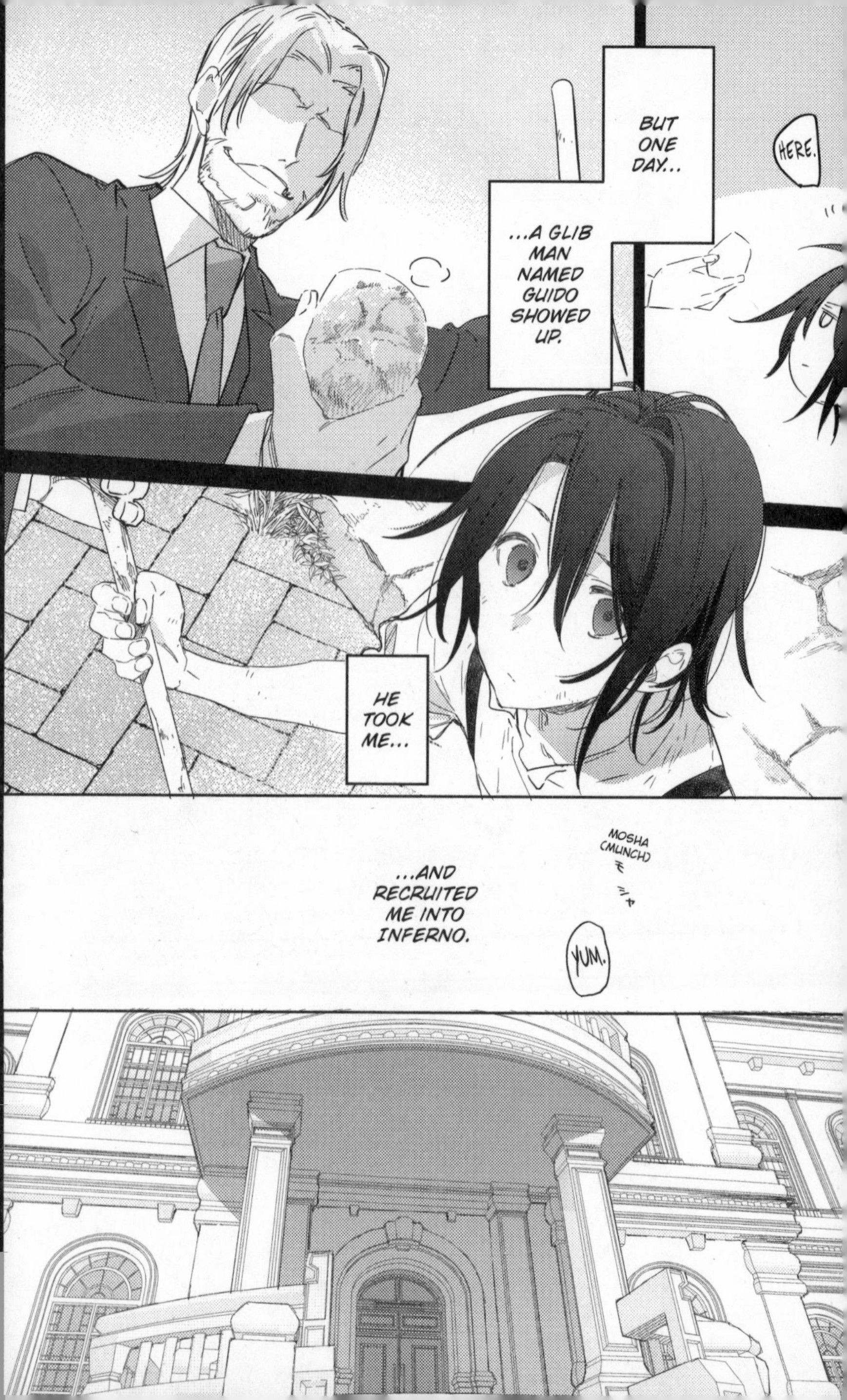
HERE.
BUT ONE DAY...
...A GLIB MAN NAMED GUIDO SHOWED UP.
HE TOOK ME...
MOSHA (MUNCH)
YUM.
...AND RECRUITED ME INTO INFERNO.

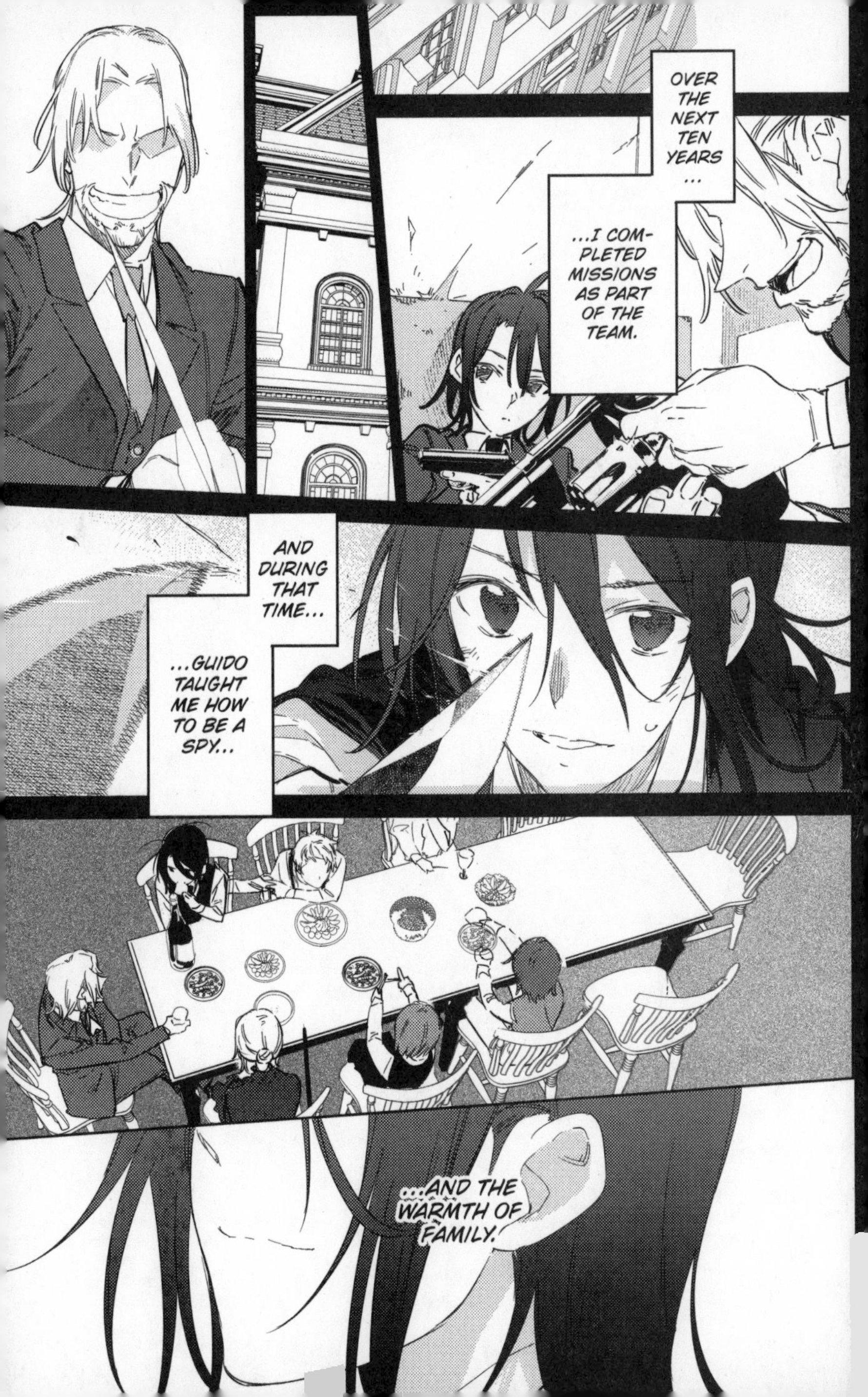
OVER THE NEXT TEN YEARS...
...I COMPLETED MISSIONS AS PART OF THE TEAM.
AND DURING THAT TIME...
...GUIDO TAUGHT ME HOW TO BE A SPY...
...AND THE WARMTH OF FAMILY.

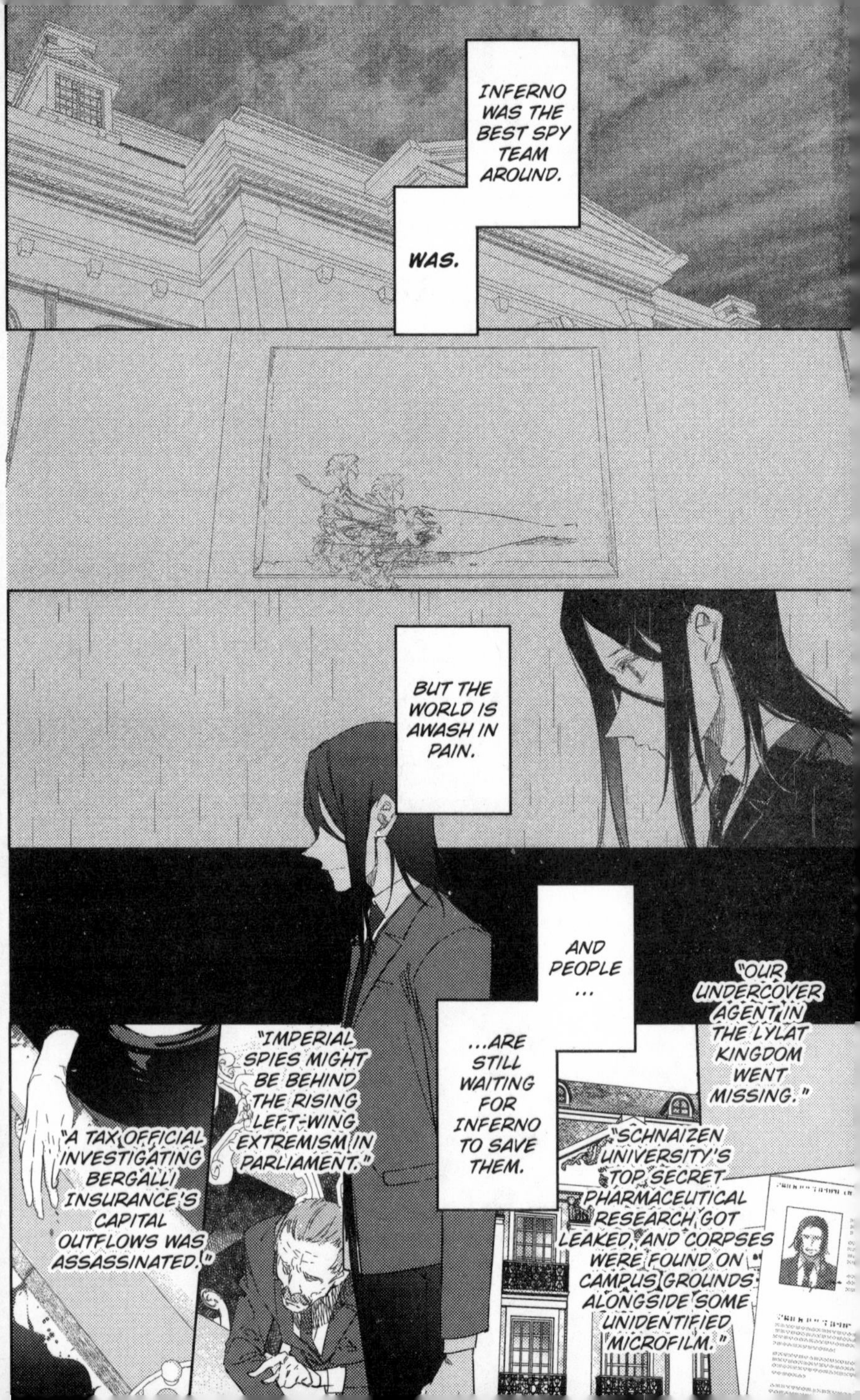
INFERNO WAS THE BEST SPY TEAM AROUND.
WAS.
BUT THE WORLD IS AWASH IN PAIN.
"OUR UNDERCOVER AGENT IN THE LYLAT KINGDOM WENT MISSING."
AND PEOPLE...
...ARE STILL WAITING FOR INFERNO TO SAVE THEM.
"SCHNAIZEN UNIVERSITY'S TOP SECRET PHARMACEUTICAL RESEARCH GOT LEAKED, AND CORPSES WERE FOUND ON CAMPUS GROUNDS ALONGSIDE SOME UNIDENTIFIED MICROFILM."
"IMPERIAL SPIES MIGHT BE BEHIND THE RISING LEFT-WING EXTREMISM IN PARLIAMENT."
"A TAX OFFICIAL INVESTIGATING BERGALLI INSURANCE'S CAPITAL OUTFLOWS WAS ASSASSINATED!"

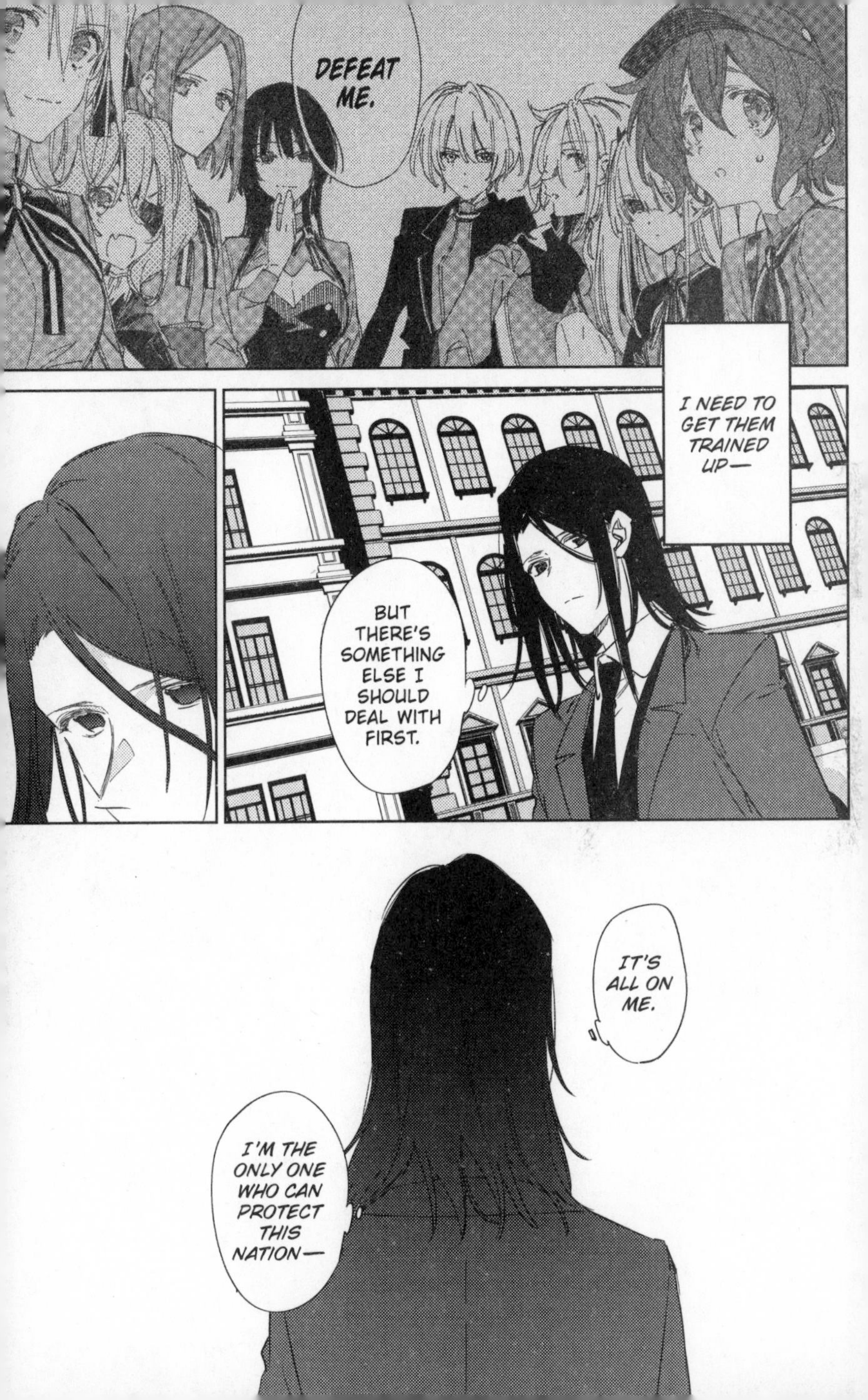
DEFEAT ME.
I NEED TO GET THEM TRAINED UP—
BUT THERE'S SOMETHING ELSE I SHOULD DEAL WITH FIRST.
IT'S ALL ON ME.
I'M THE ONLY ONE WHO CAN PROTECT THIS NATION—

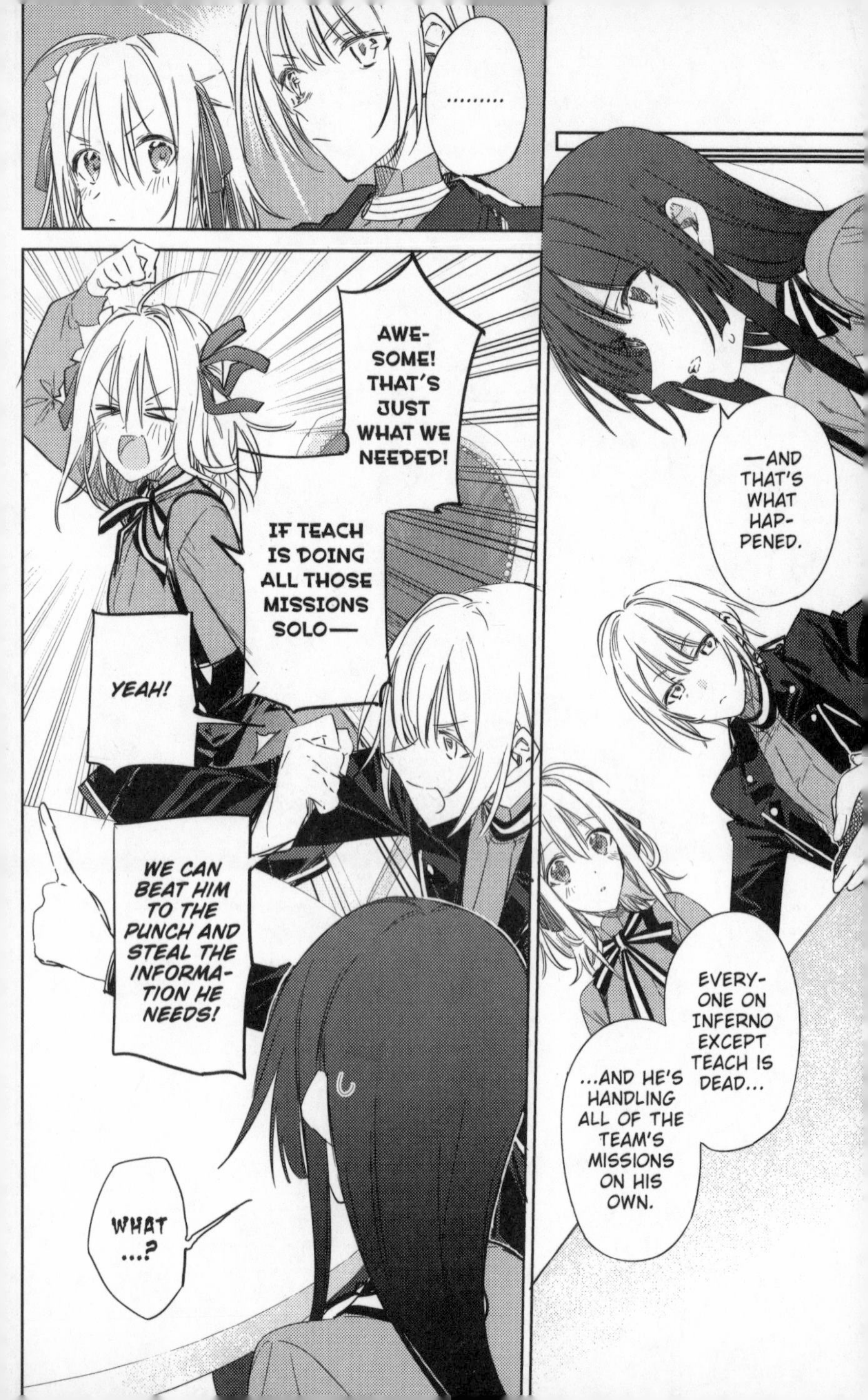
—AND THAT'S WHAT HAPPENED.
EVERYONE ON INFERNO EXCEPT TEACH IS DEAD...
...AND HE'S HANDLING ALL OF THE TEAM'S MISSIONS ON HIS OWN.
....
AWESOME! THAT'S JUST WHAT WE NEEDED!
IF TEACH IS DOING ALL THOSE MISSIONS SOLO—
YEAH!
WE CAN BEAT HIM TO THE PUNCH AND STEAL THE INFORMATION HE NEEDS!
WHAT...?

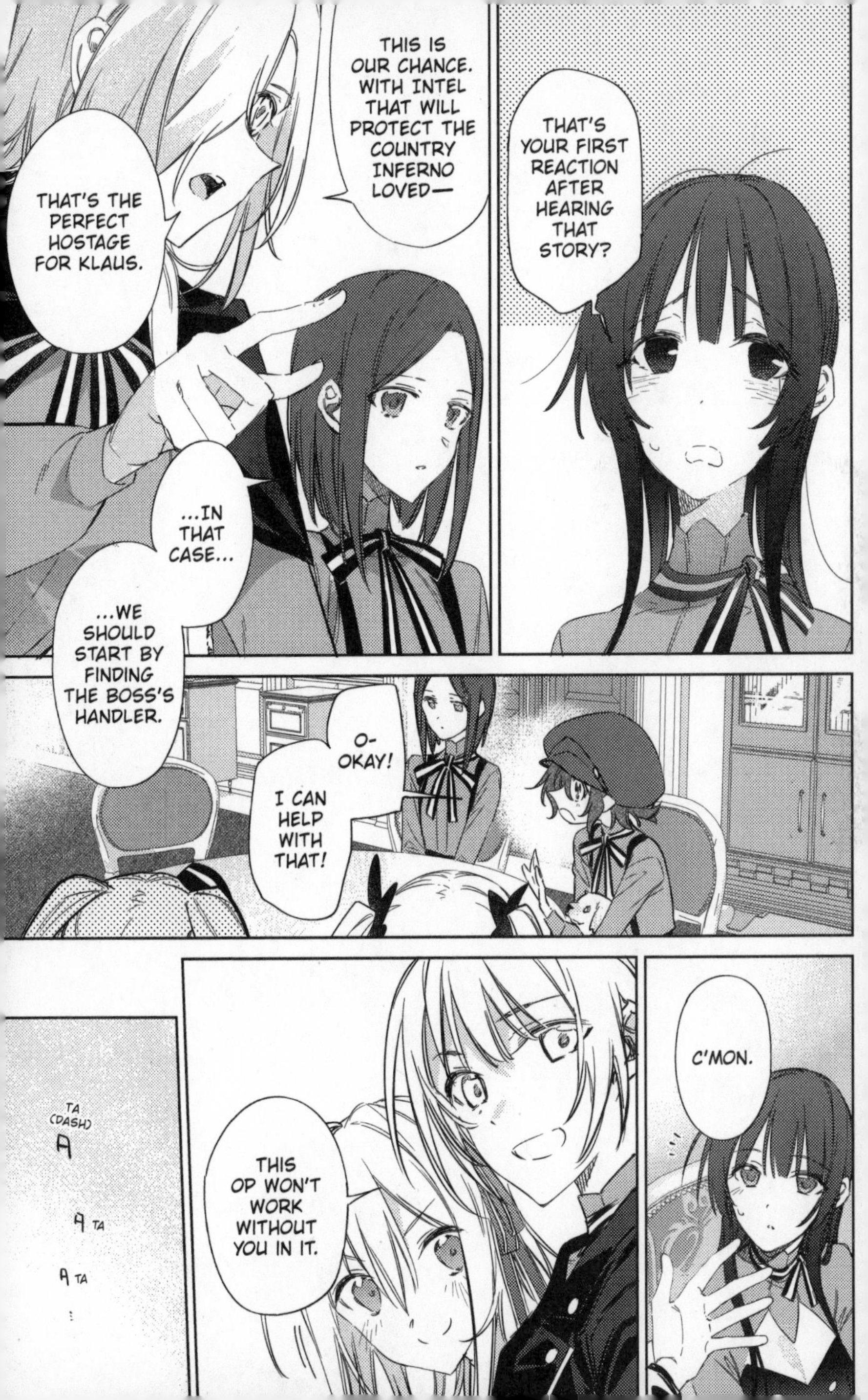
THAT'S YOUR FIRST REACTION AFTER HEARING THAT STORY?
THIS IS OUR CHANCE. WITH INTEL THAT WILL PROTECT THE COUNTRY INFERNO LOVED—
THAT'S THE PERFECT HOSTAGE FOR KLAUS.
...IN THAT CASE...
...WE SHOULD START BY FINDING THE BOSS'S HANDLER.
O-OKAY!
I CAN HELP WITH THAT!
C'MON.
THIS OP WON'T WORK WITHOUT YOU IN IT.
TA (DASH)
TA
TA

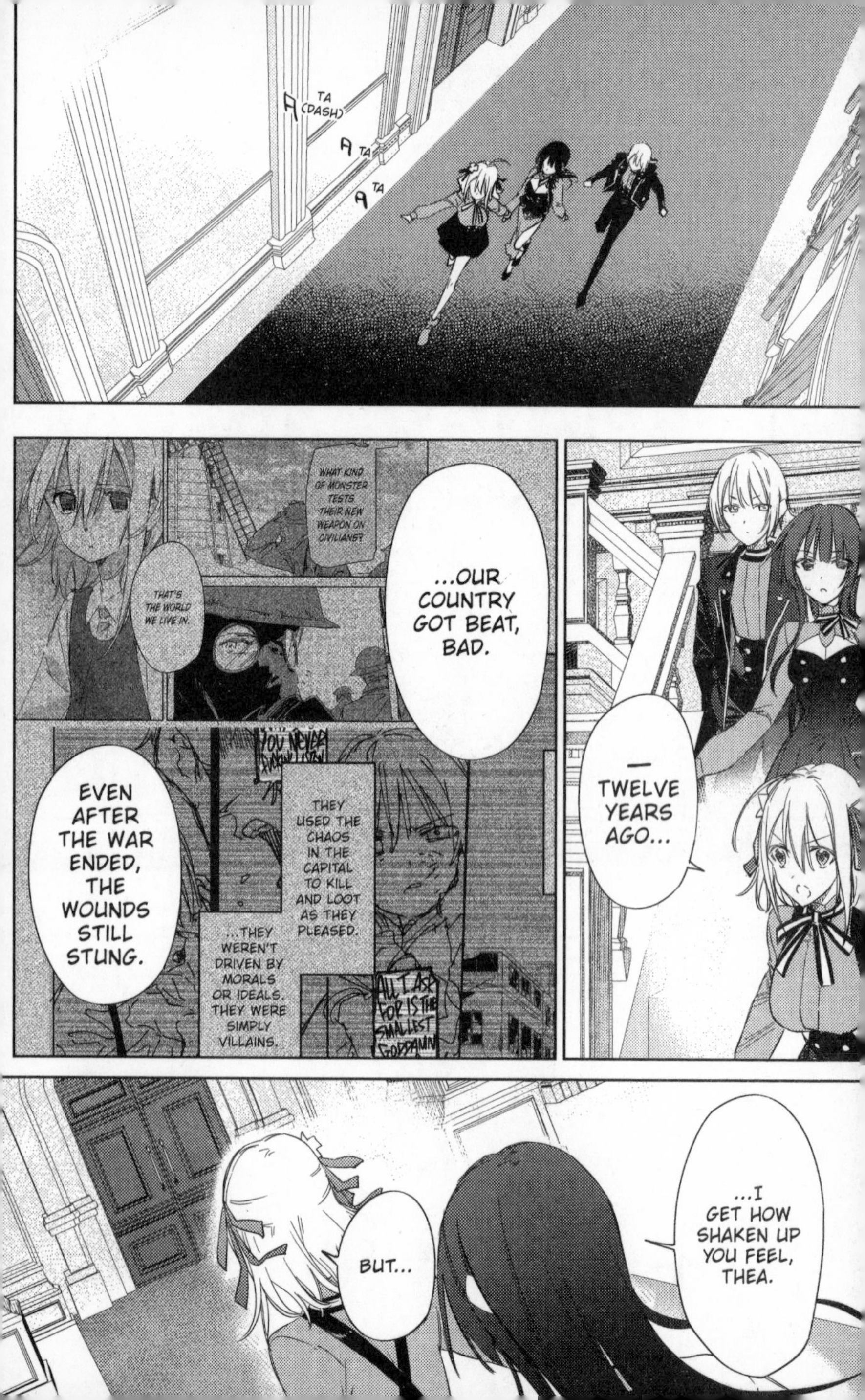
TA (DASH)
TA
TA
— TWELVE YEARS AGO...
...OUR COUNTRY GOT BEAT, BAD.
WHAT KIND OF MONSTER TESTS THEIR NEW WEAPON ON CIVILIANS?
THAT'S THE WORLD WE LIVE IN.
THEY USED THE CHAOS IN THE CAPITAL TO KILL AND LOOT AS THEY PLEASED.
ALL I ASK FOR IS THE SMALLEST GODDAMN
...THEY WEREN'T DRIVEN BY MORALS OR IDEALS. THEY WERE SIMPLY VILLAINS.
EVEN AFTER THE WAR ENDED, THE WOUNDS STILL STUNG.
...I GET HOW SHAKEN UP YOU FEEL, THEA.
BUT...

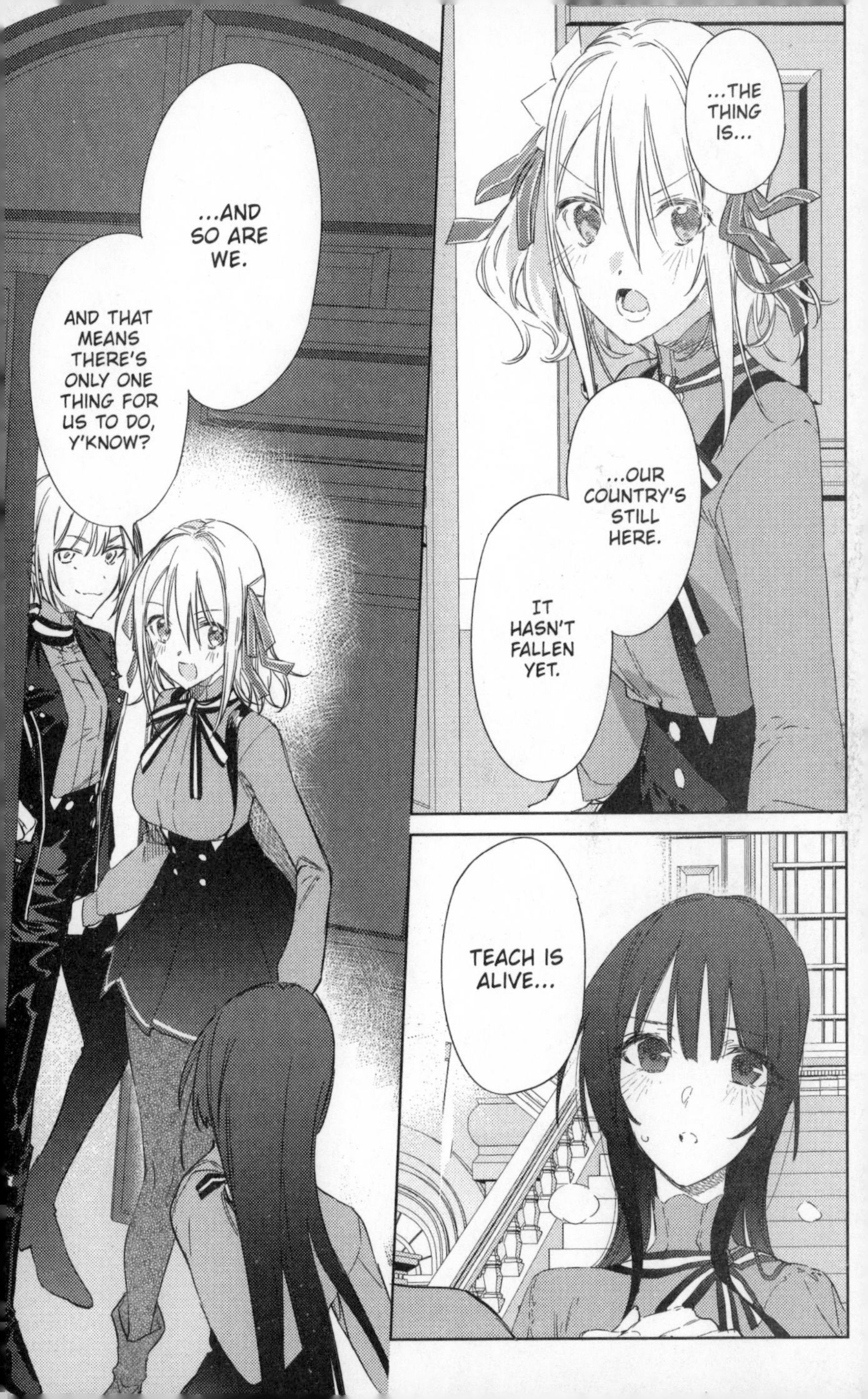
…THE THING IS…
…OUR COUNTRY'S STILL HERE.
IT HASN'T FALLEN YET.
TEACH IS ALIVE…
…AND SO ARE WE.
AND THAT MEANS THERE'S ONLY ONE THING FOR US TO DO, Y'KNOW?

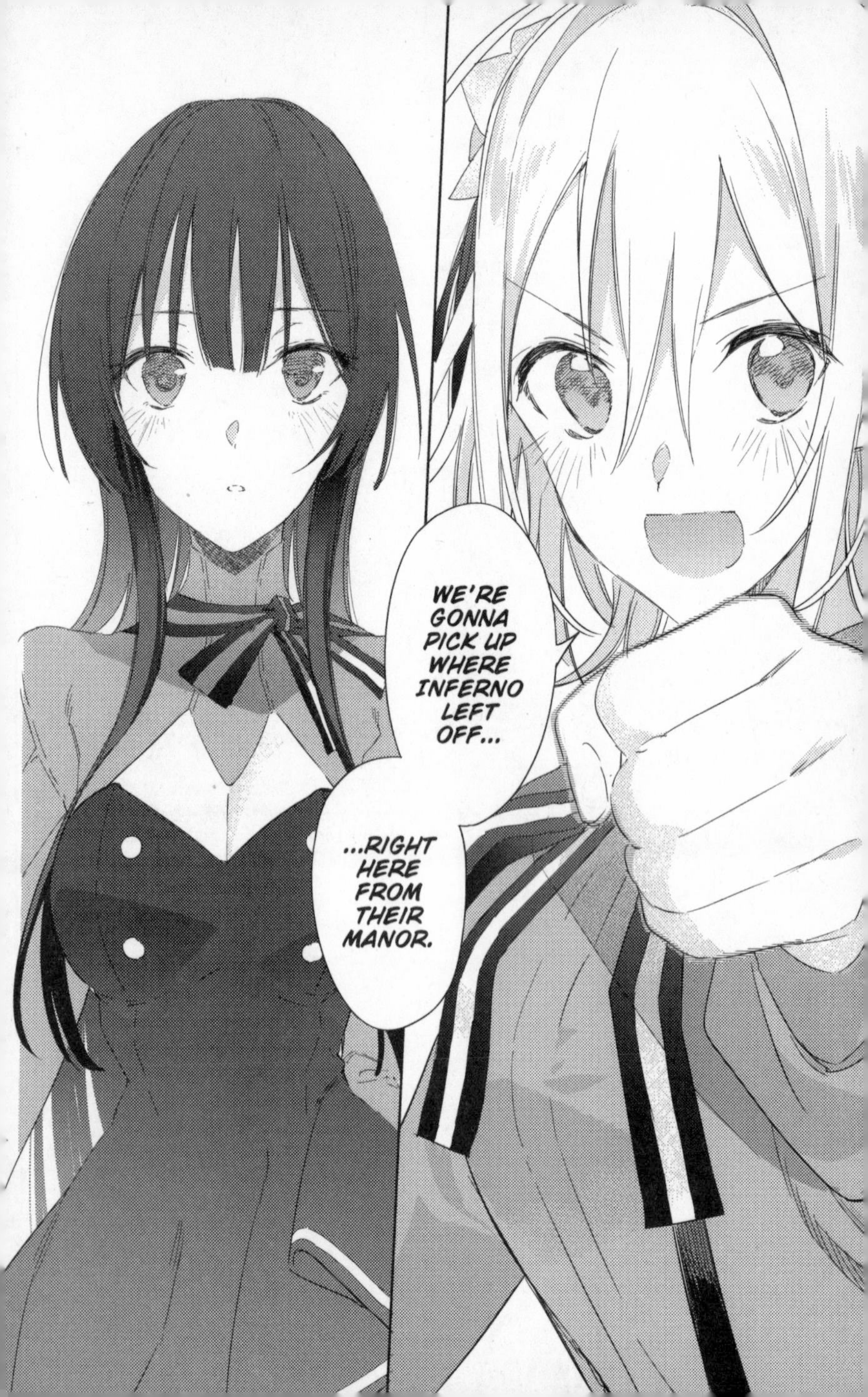
WE'RE GONNA PICK UP WHERE INFERNO LEFT OFF...
...RIGHT HERE FROM THEIR MANOR.

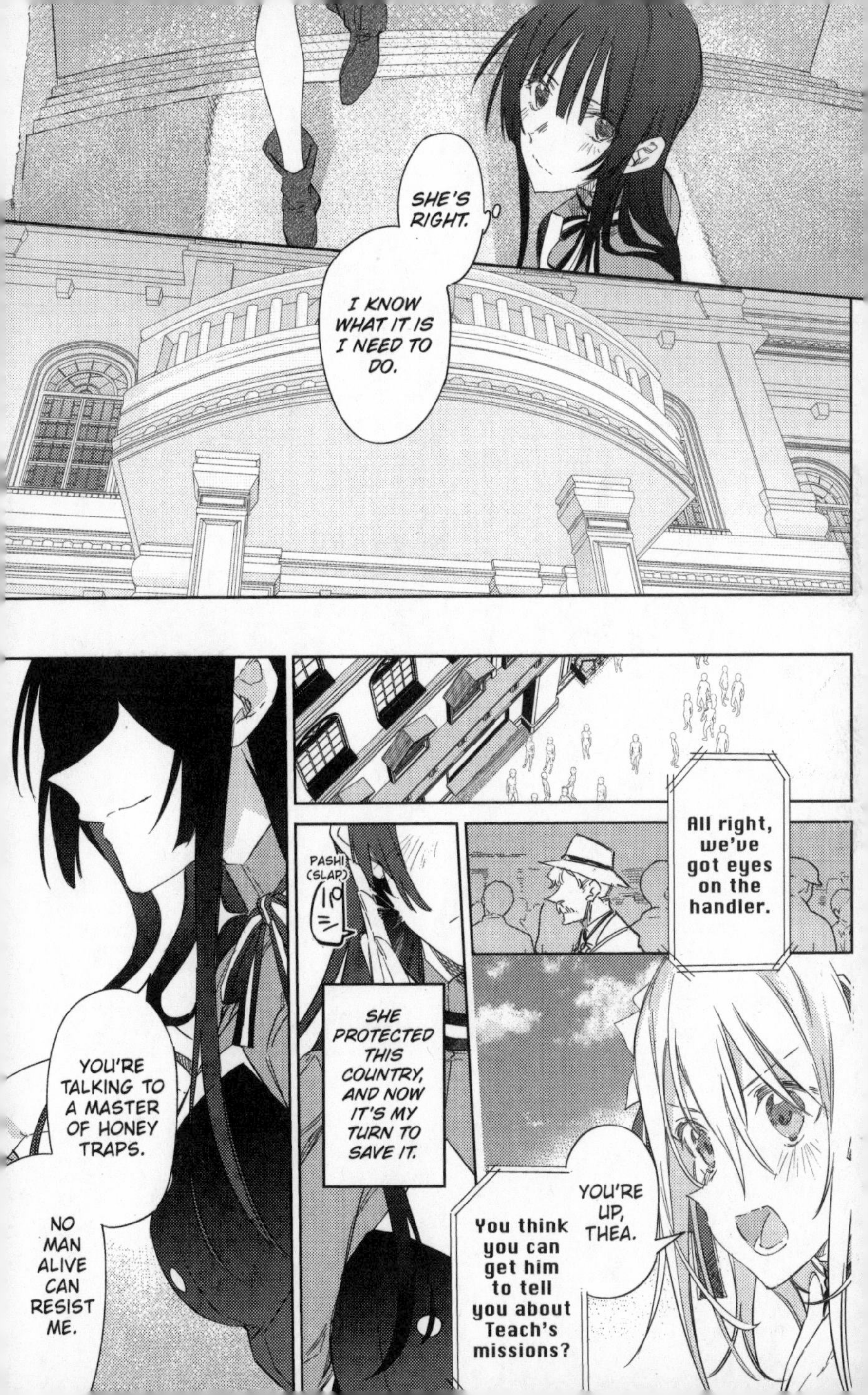

SHE'S RIGHT.
I KNOW WHAT IT IS I NEED TO DO.
All right, we've got eyes on the handler.
PASHI (SLAP)
SHE PROTECTED THIS COUNTRY, AND NOW IT'S MY TURN TO SAVE IT.
YOU'RE UP, THEA.
You think you can get him to tell you about Teach's missions?
YOU'RE TALKING TO A MASTER OF HONEY TRAPS.
NO MAN ALIVE CAN RESIST ME.

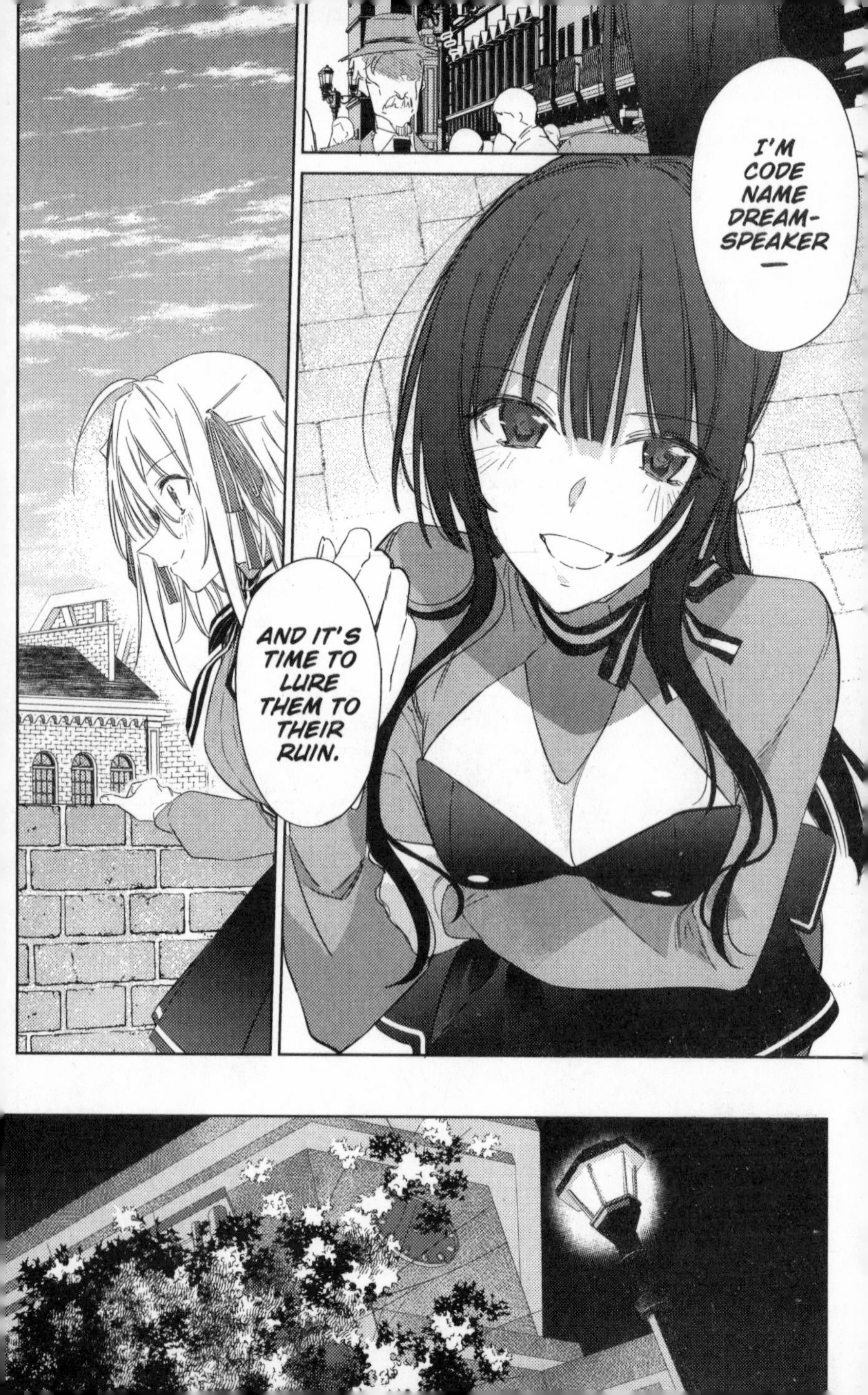
I'M CODE NAME DREAM-SPEAKER —
AND IT'S TIME TO LURE THEM TO THEIR RUIN.

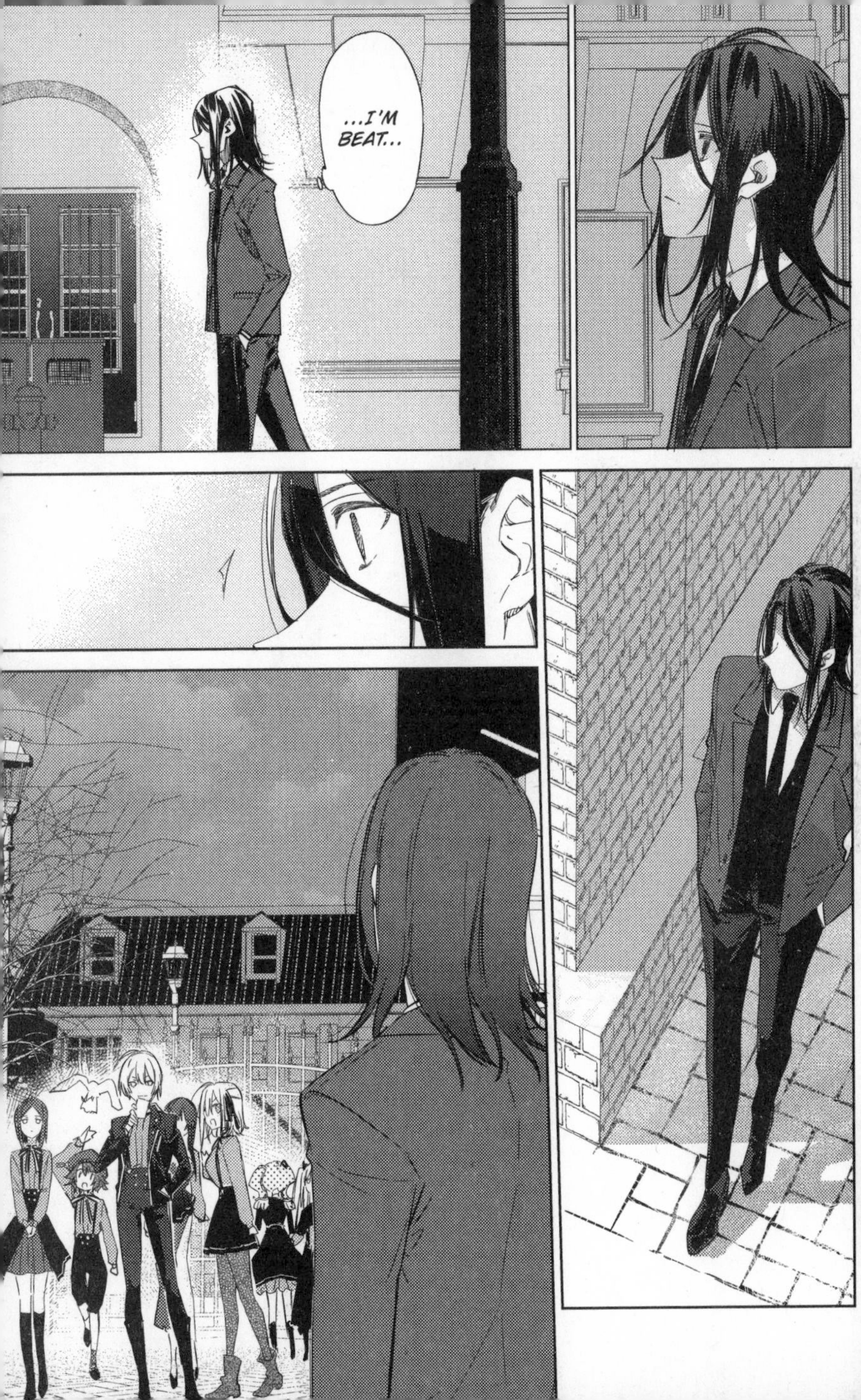
...I'M BEAT...

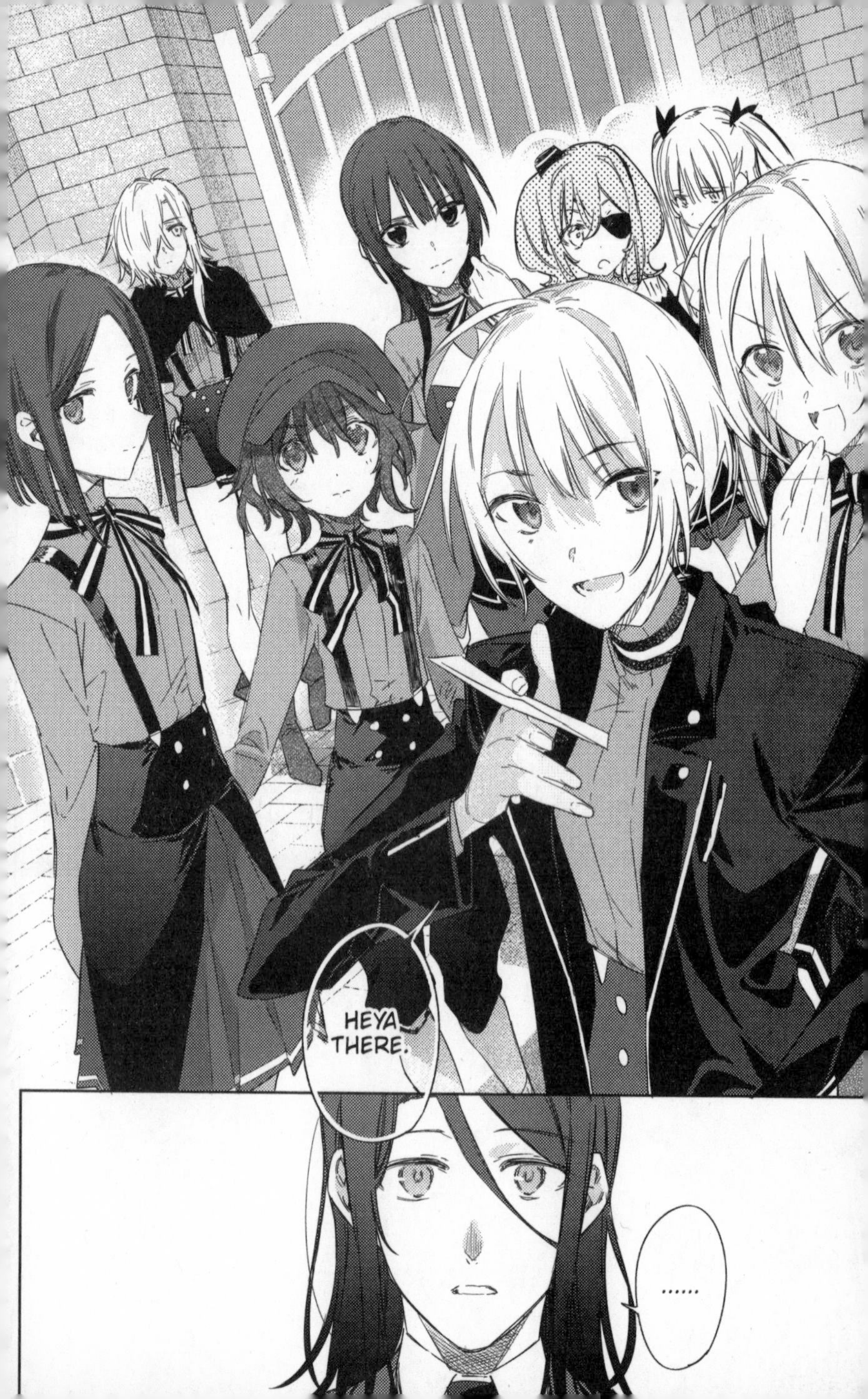
HEYA THERE.
......

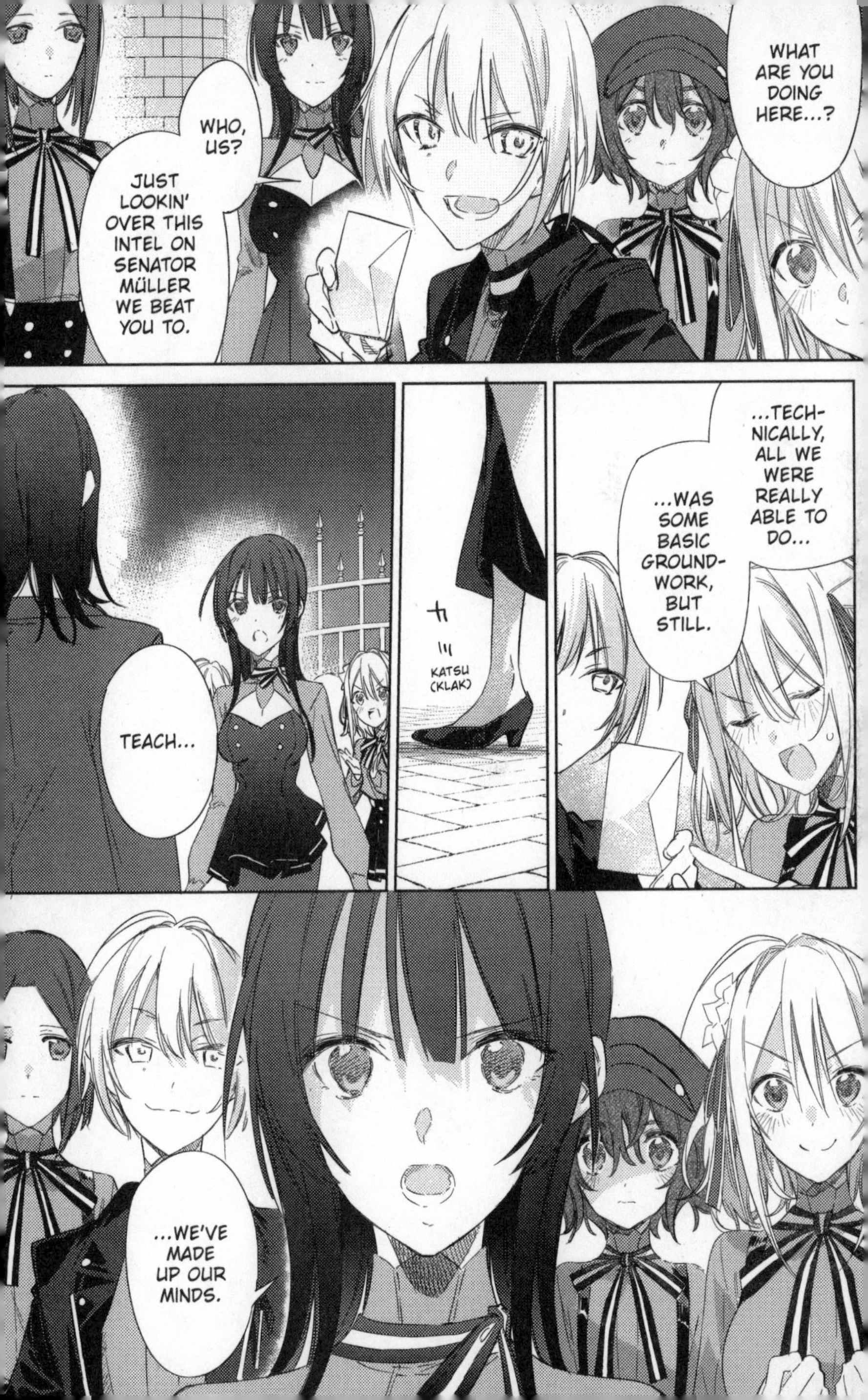
WHAT ARE YOU DOING HERE...?
WHO, US?
JUST LOOKIN' OVER THIS INTEL ON SENATOR MÜLLER WE BEAT YOU TO.
...TECHNICALLY, ALL WE WERE REALLY ABLE TO DO...
...WAS SOME BASIC GROUNDWORK, BUT STILL.
カツ
KATSU (KLAK)
TEACH...
...WE'VE MADE UP OUR MINDS.

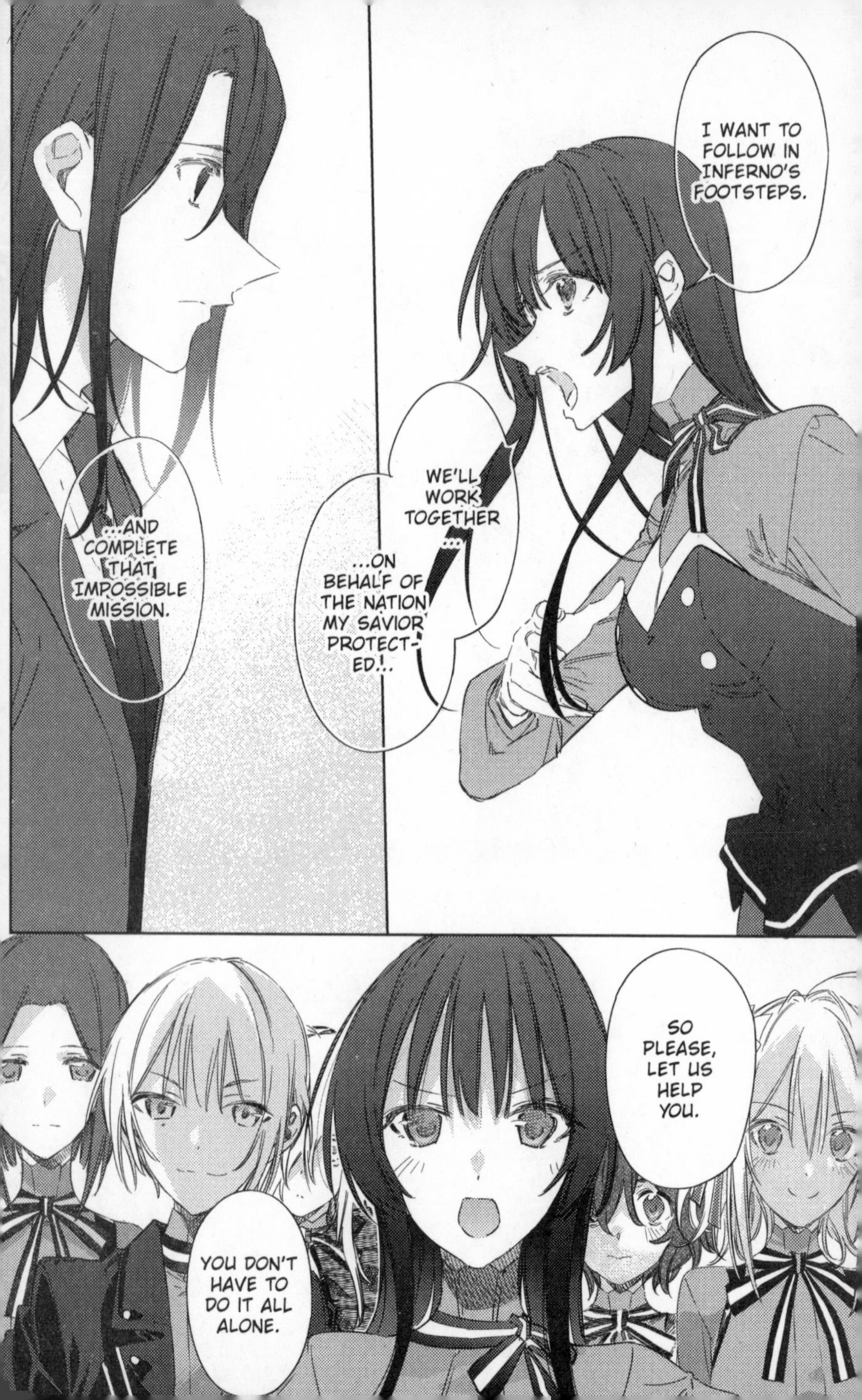
I WANT TO FOLLOW IN INFERNO'S FOOTSTEPS.
WE'LL WORK TOGETHER ...
...ON BEHALF OF THE NATION MY SAVIOR PROTECT-ED!..
...AND COMPLETE THAT IMPOSSIBLE MISSION.
SO PLEASE, LET US HELP YOU.
YOU DON'T HAVE TO DO IT ALL ALONE.

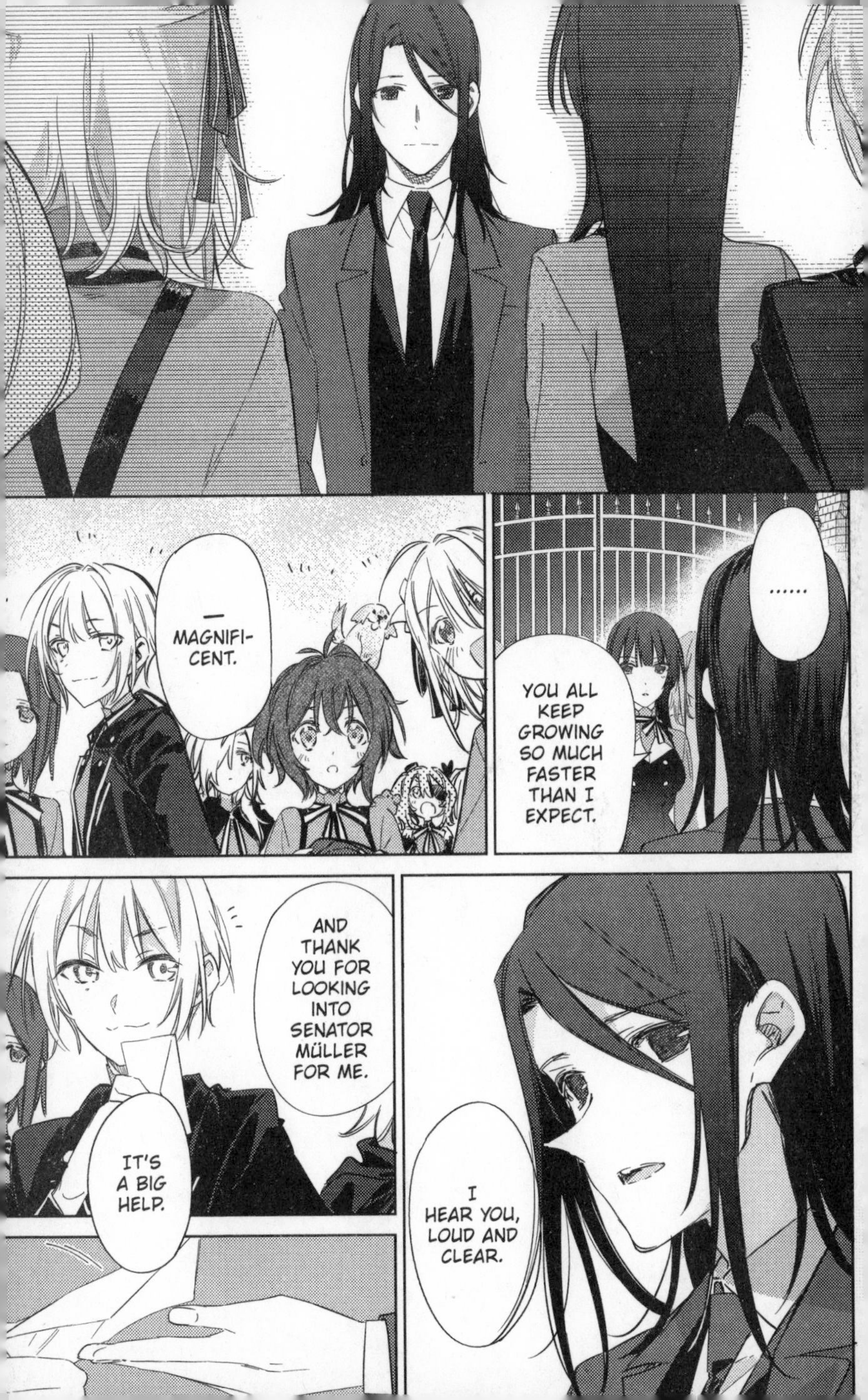
……
YOU ALL KEEP GROWING SO MUCH FASTER THAN I EXPECT.
—MAGNIFI-CENT.
I HEAR YOU, LOUD AND CLEAR.
AND THANK YOU FOR LOOKING INTO SENATOR MÜLLER FOR ME.
IT'S A BIG HELP.

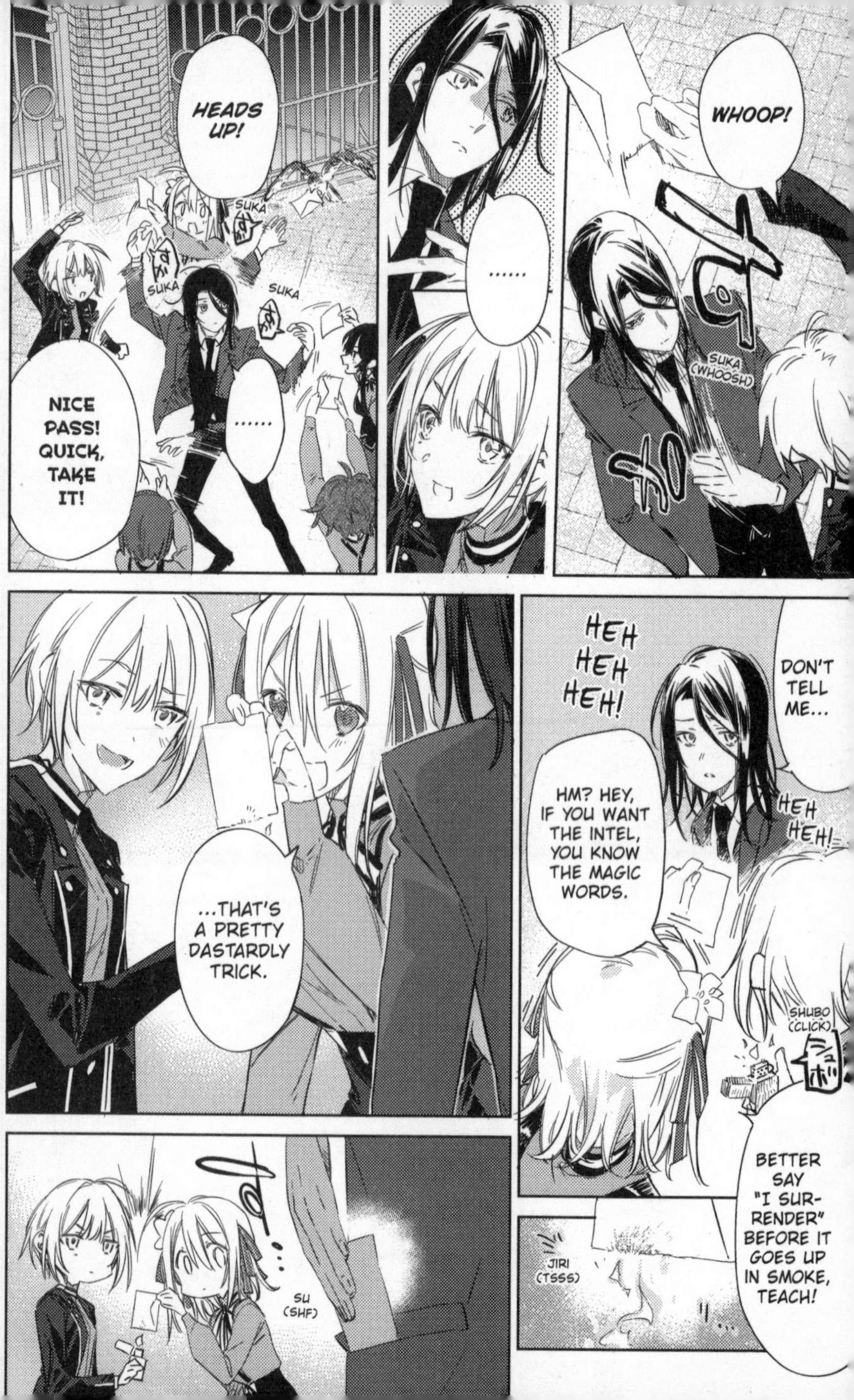
WHOOP!
SUKA (WHOOSH)
......
HEADS UP!
SUKA
SUKA
SUKA
NICE PASS! QUICK, TAKE IT!
......
DON'T TELL ME...
HEH HEH HEH!
HM? HEY, IF YOU WANT THE INTEL, YOU KNOW THE MAGIC WORDS.
HEH HEH!
SHUBO (CLICK)
BETTER SAY "I SURRENDER" BEFORE IT GOES UP IN SMOKE, TEACH!
...THAT'S A PRETTY DASTARDLY TRICK.
JIRI (TSSS)
!...
SU (SHF)

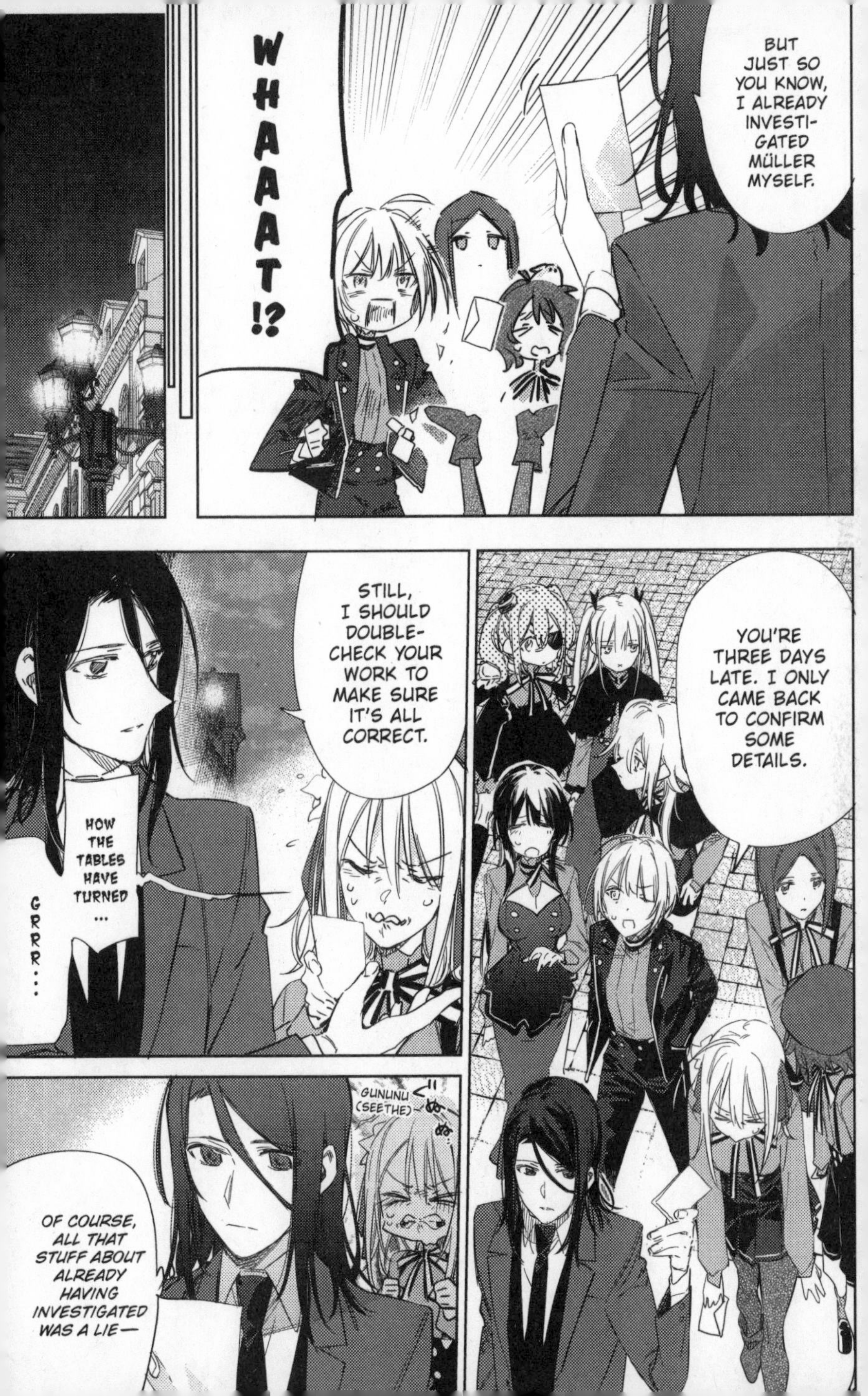
BUT JUST SO YOU KNOW, I ALREADY INVESTI-GATED MÜLLER MYSELF.
WHAAAAT!?
YOU'RE THREE DAYS LATE. I ONLY CAME BACK TO CONFIRM SOME DETAILS.
STILL, I SHOULD DOUBLE-CHECK YOUR WORK TO MAKE SURE IT'S ALL CORRECT.
HOW THE TABLES HAVE TURNED...
GRRR...
GUNUNU (SEETHE)
OF COURSE, ALL THAT STUFF ABOUT ALREADY HAVING INVESTIGATED WAS A LIE—

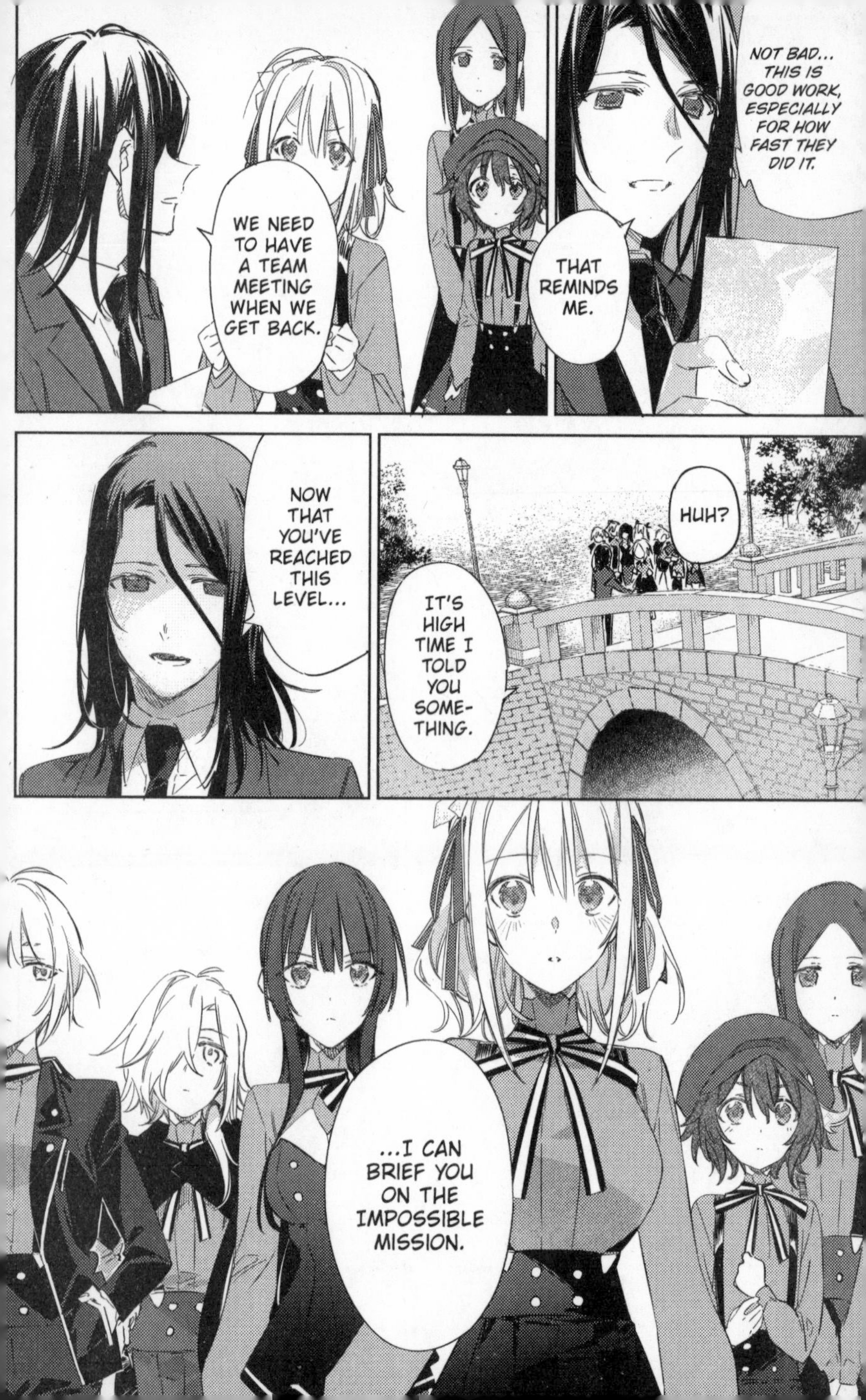
NOT BAD... THIS IS GOOD WORK, ESPECIALLY FOR HOW FAST THEY DID IT.
THAT REMINDS ME.
WE NEED TO HAVE A TEAM MEETING WHEN WE GET BACK.
HUH?
IT'S HIGH TIME I TOLD YOU SOMETHING.
NOW THAT YOU'VE REACHED THIS LEVEL...
...I CAN BRIEF YOU ON THE IMPOSSIBLE MISSION.

Chapter 9 — Situation

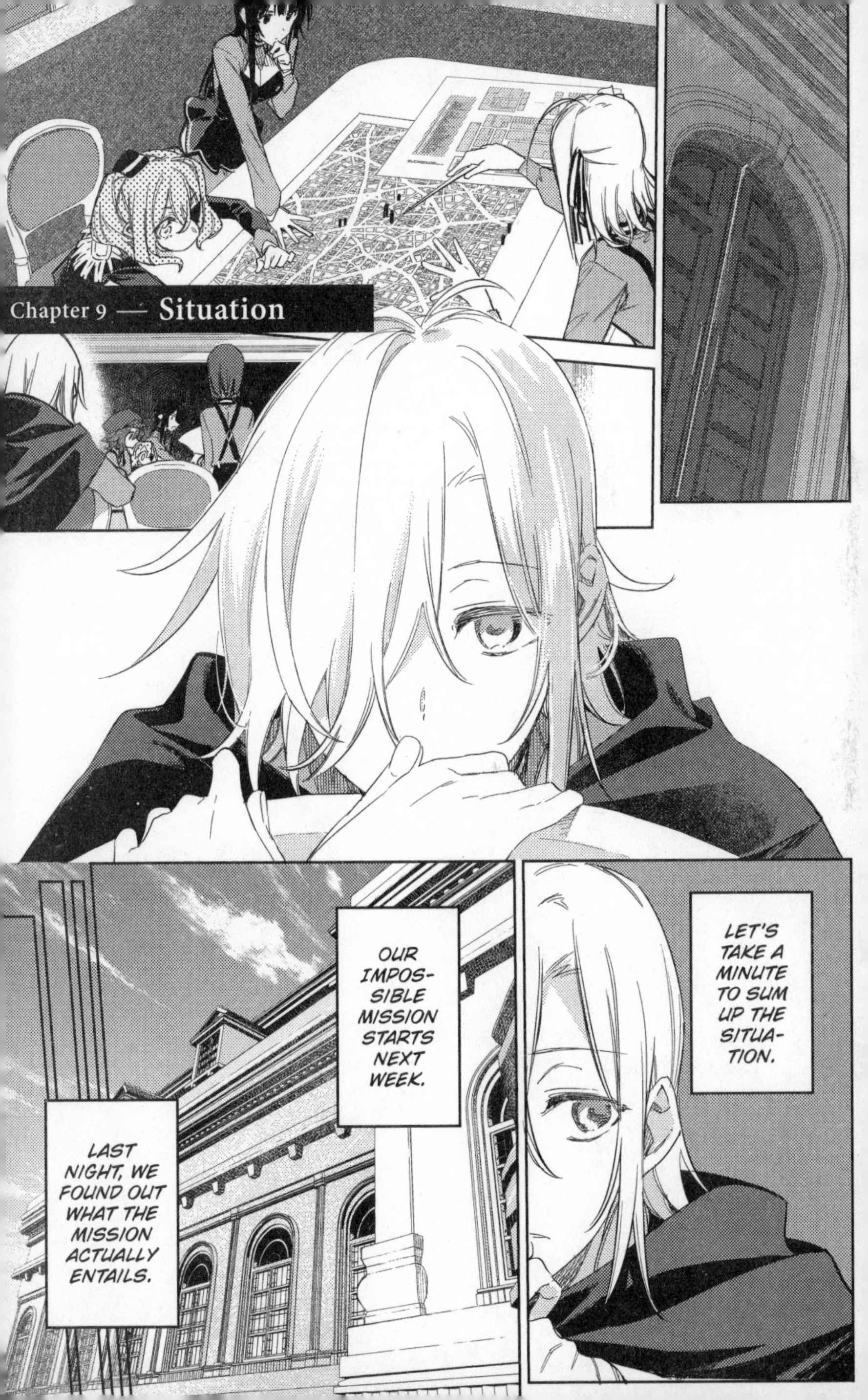

LET'S TAKE A MINUTE TO SUM UP THE SITUA-TION.
OUR IMPOS-SIBLE MISSION STARTS NEXT WEEK.
LAST NIGHT, WE FOUND OUT WHAT THE MISSION ACTUALLY ENTAILS.

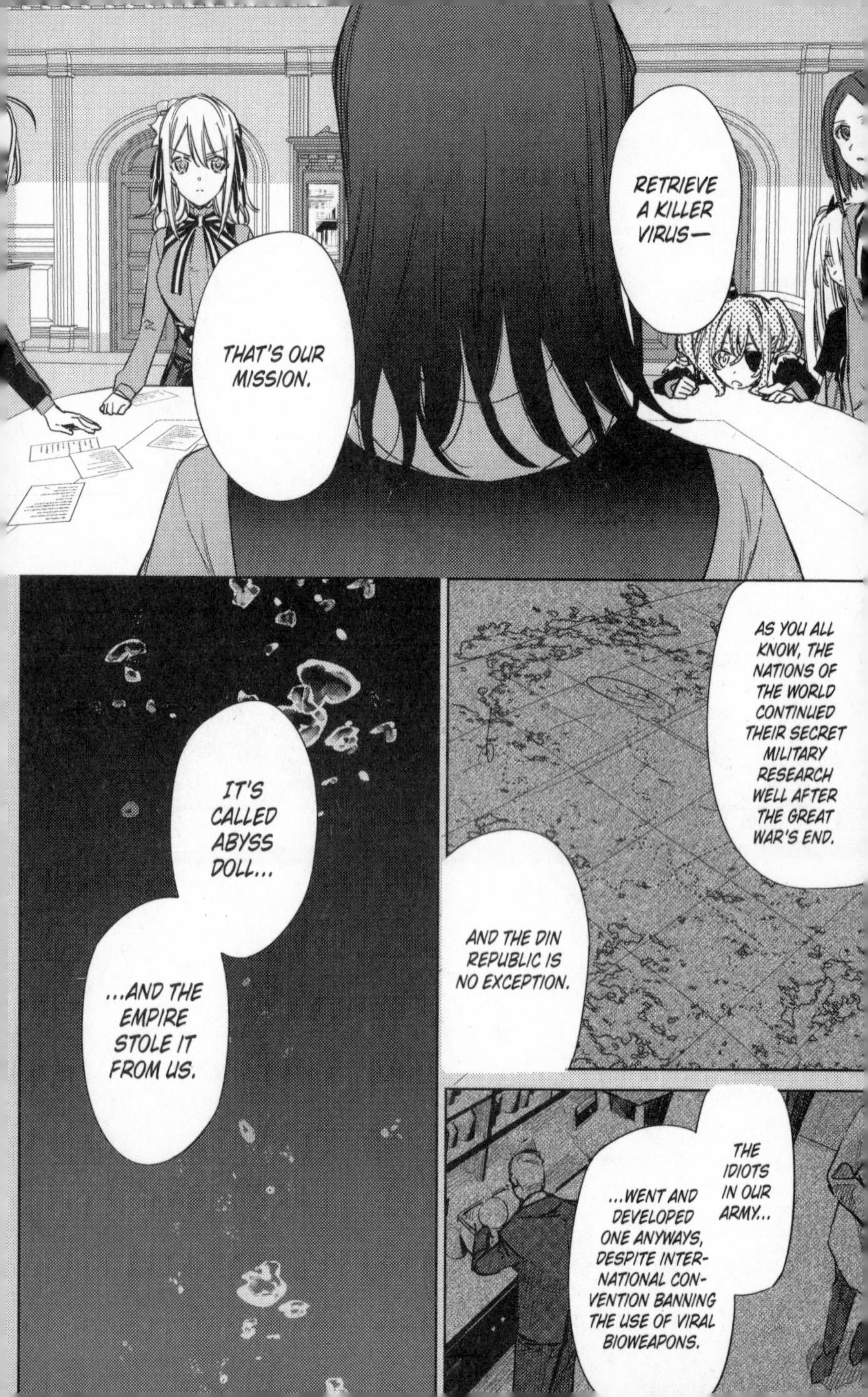
RETRIEVE A KILLER VIRUS—
THAT'S OUR MISSION.
AS YOU ALL KNOW, THE NATIONS OF THE WORLD CONTINUED THEIR SECRET MILITARY RESEARCH WELL AFTER THE GREAT WAR'S END.
AND THE DIN REPUBLIC IS NO EXCEPTION.
THE IDIOTS IN OUR ARMY...
...WENT AND DEVELOPED ONE ANYWAYS, DESPITE INTER-NATIONAL CON-VENTION BANNING THE USE OF VIRAL BIOWEAPONS.
IT'S CALLED ABYSS DOLL...
...AND THE EMPIRE STOLE IT FROM US.

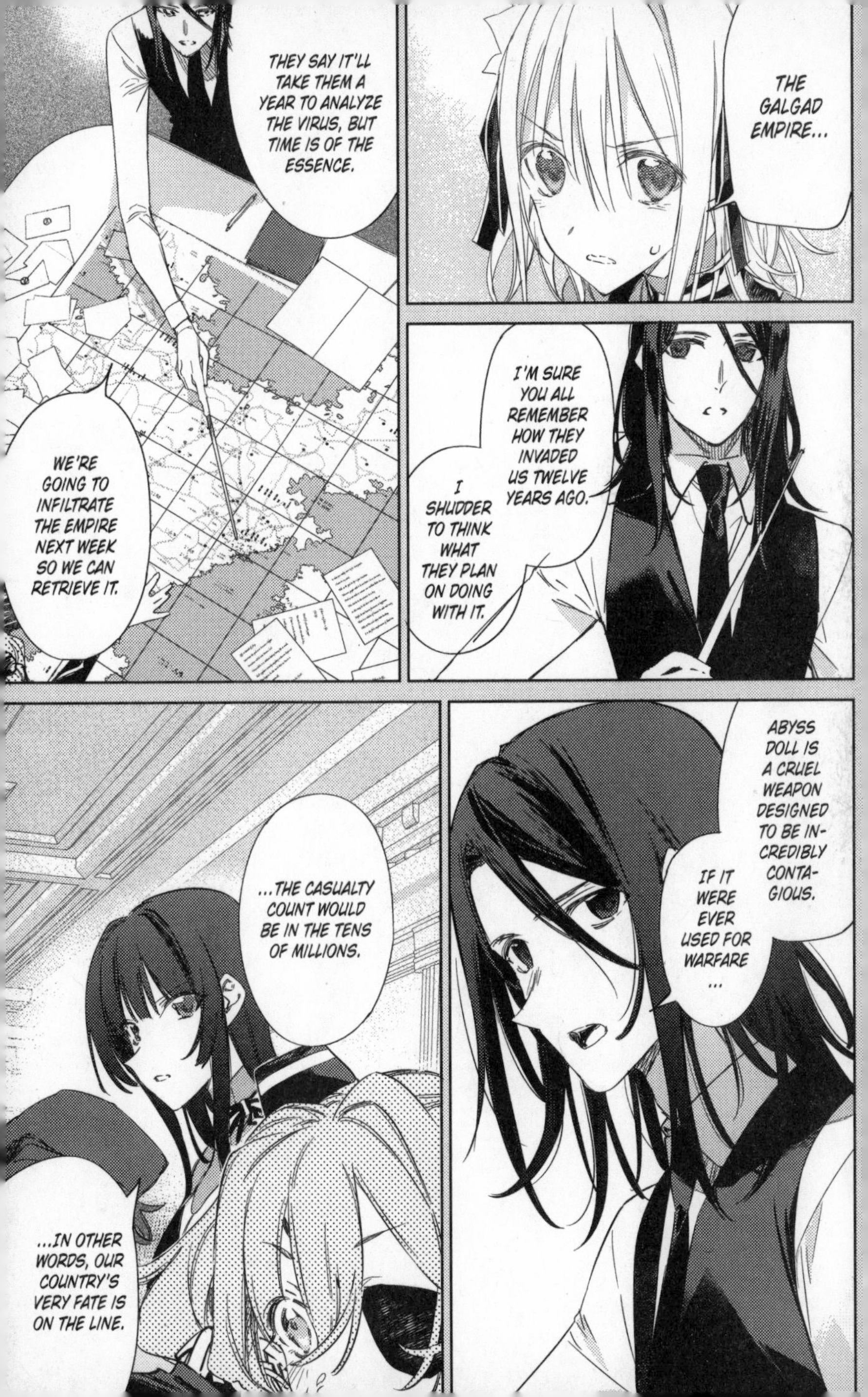
THE GALGAD EMPIRE...
I'M SURE YOU ALL REMEMBER HOW THEY INVADED US TWELVE YEARS AGO.
I SHUDDER TO THINK WHAT THEY PLAN ON DOING WITH IT.
THEY SAY IT'LL TAKE THEM A YEAR TO ANALYZE THE VIRUS, BUT TIME IS OF THE ESSENCE.
WE'RE GOING TO INFILTRATE THE EMPIRE NEXT WEEK SO WE CAN RETRIEVE IT.
ABYSS DOLL IS A CRUEL WEAPON DESIGNED TO BE IN-CREDIBLY CONTA-GIOUS.
IF IT WERE EVER USED FOR WARFARE...
...THE CASUALTY COUNT WOULD BE IN THE TENS OF MILLIONS.
...IN OTHER WORDS, OUR COUNTRY'S VERY FATE IS ON THE LINE.

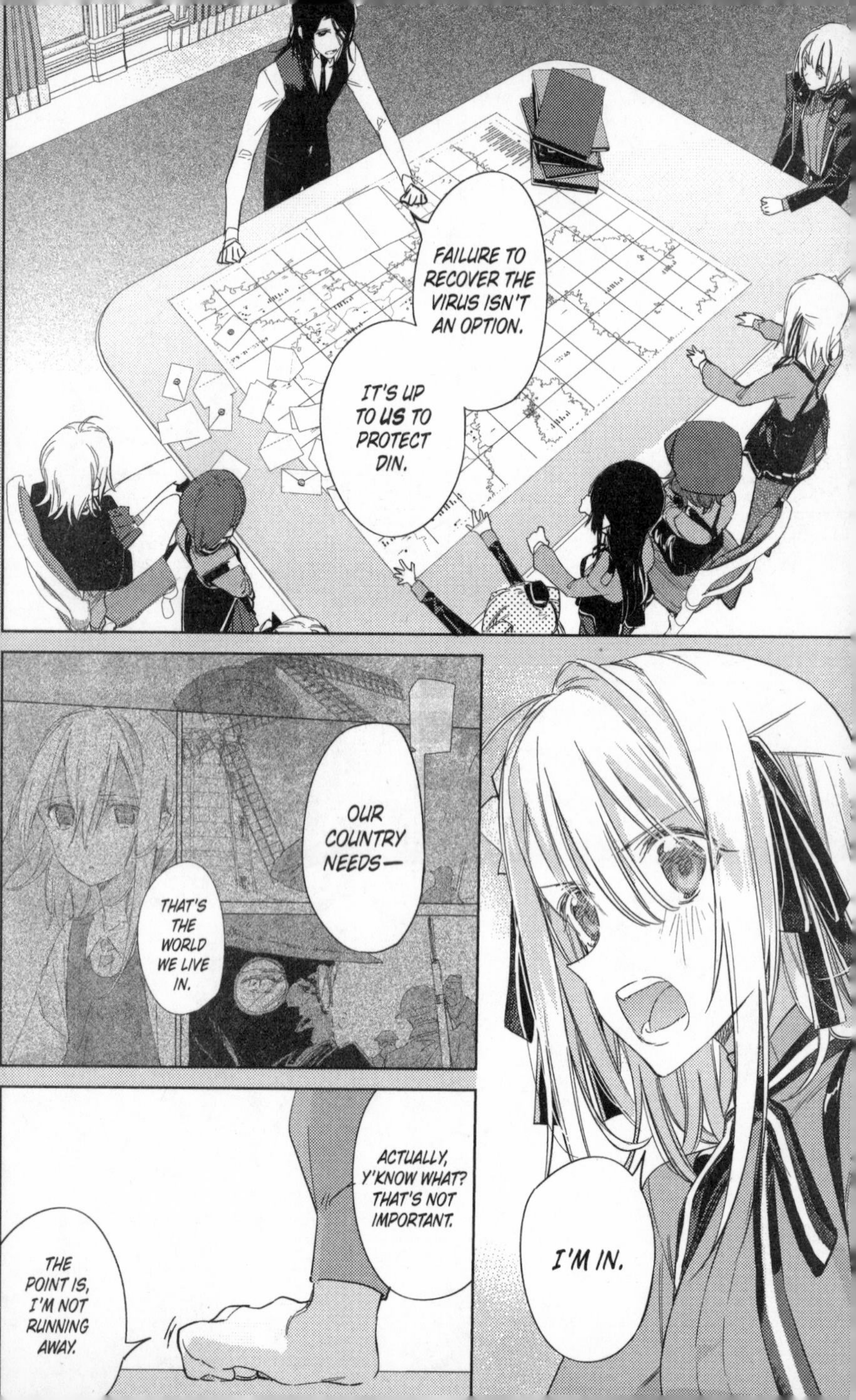
FAILURE TO RECOVER THE VIRUS ISN'T AN OPTION.
IT'S UP TO **US** TO PROTECT DIN.
I'M IN.
OUR COUNTRY NEEDS—
THAT'S THE WORLD WE LIVE IN.
ACTUALLY, Y'KNOW WHAT? THAT'S NOT IMPORTANT.
THE POINT IS, I'M NOT RUNNING AWAY.

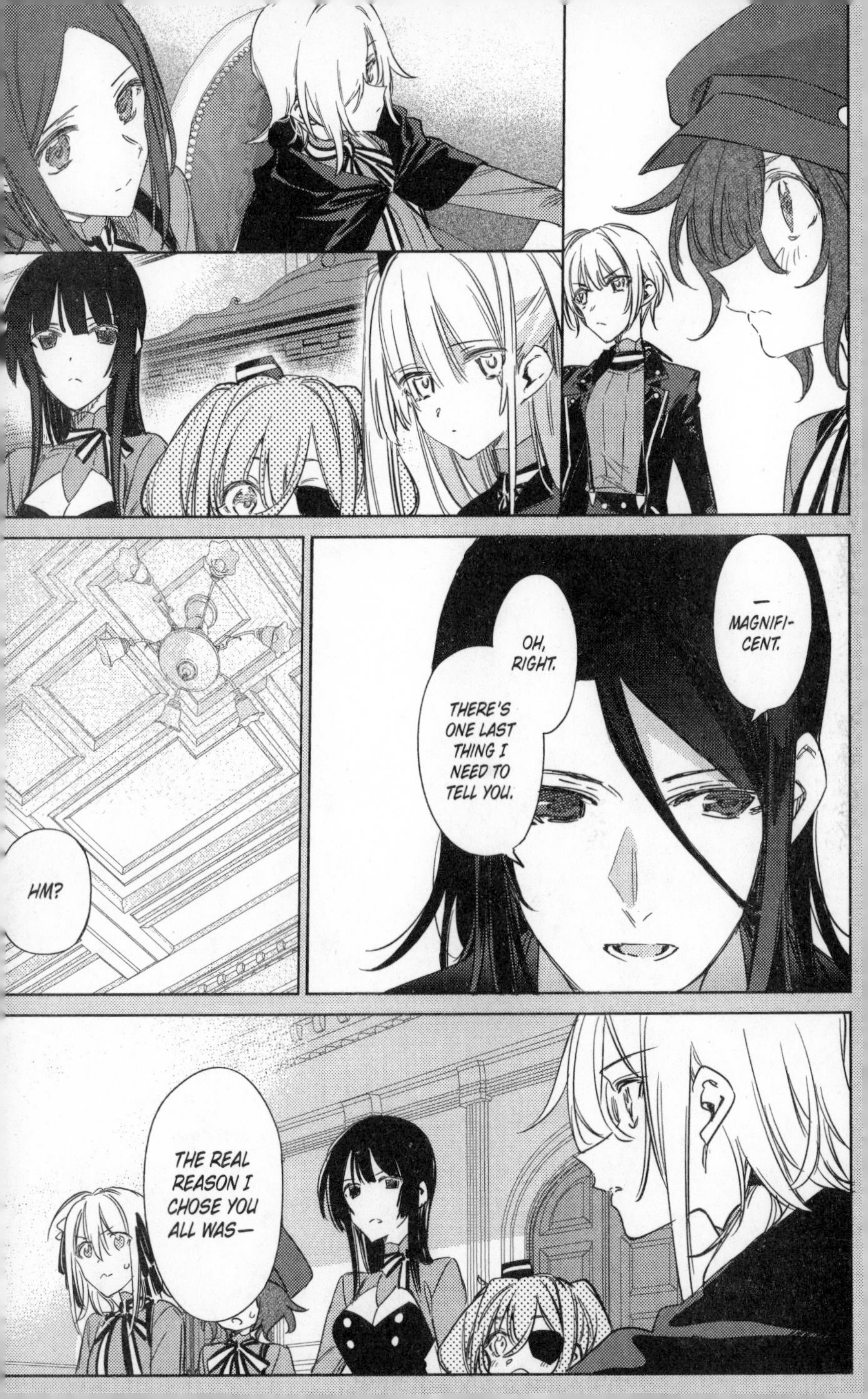
—MAGNIFICENT.
OH, RIGHT.
THERE'S ONE LAST THING I NEED TO TELL YOU.
HM?
THE REAL REASON I CHOSE YOU ALL WAS—

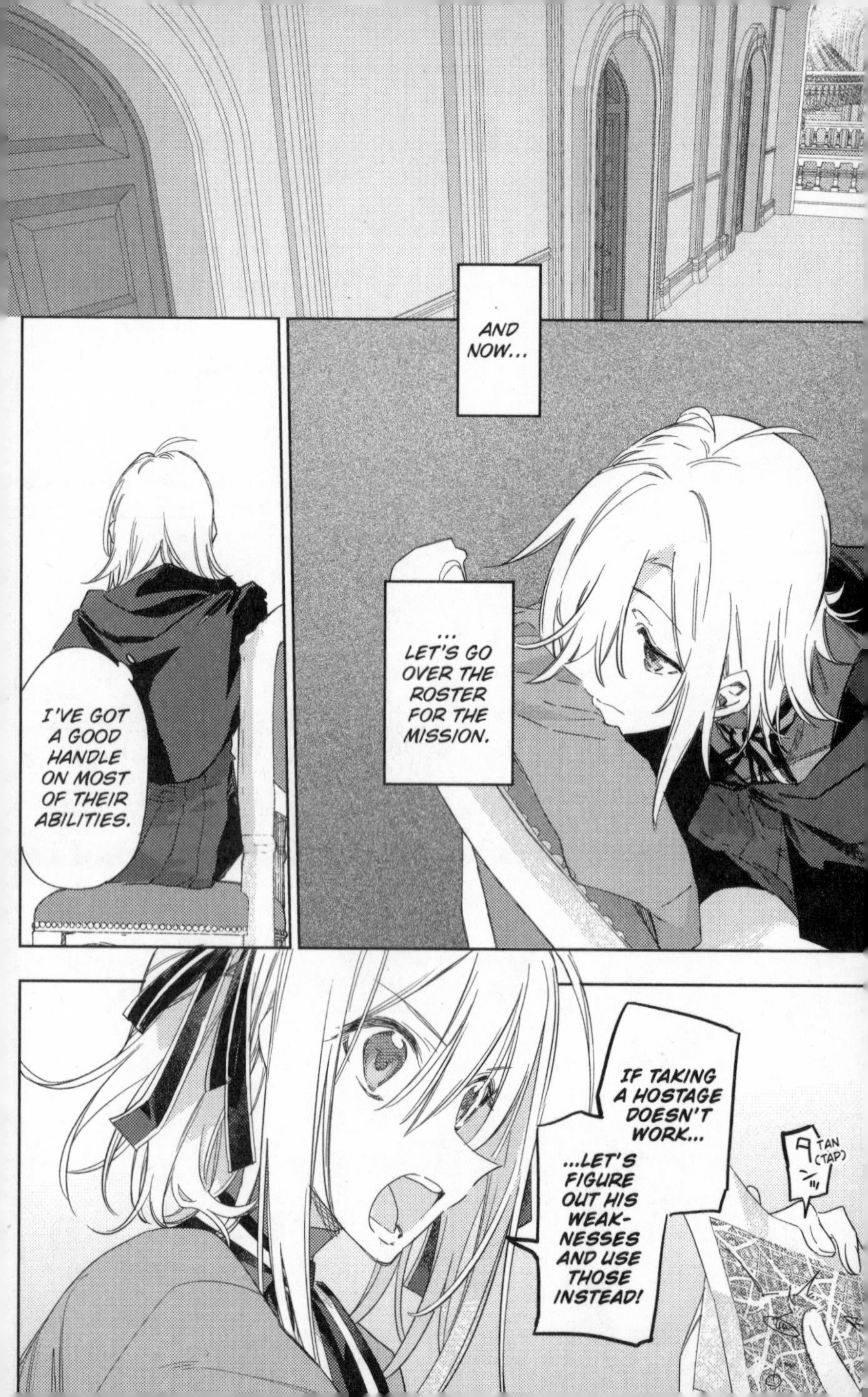
AND NOW...
... LET'S GO OVER THE ROSTER FOR THE MISSION.
I'VE GOT A GOOD HANDLE ON MOST OF THEIR ABILITIES.
IF TAKING A HOSTAGE DOESN'T WORK...
...LET'S FIGURE OUT HIS WEAK-NESSES AND USE THOSE INSTEAD!
TAN (TAP)

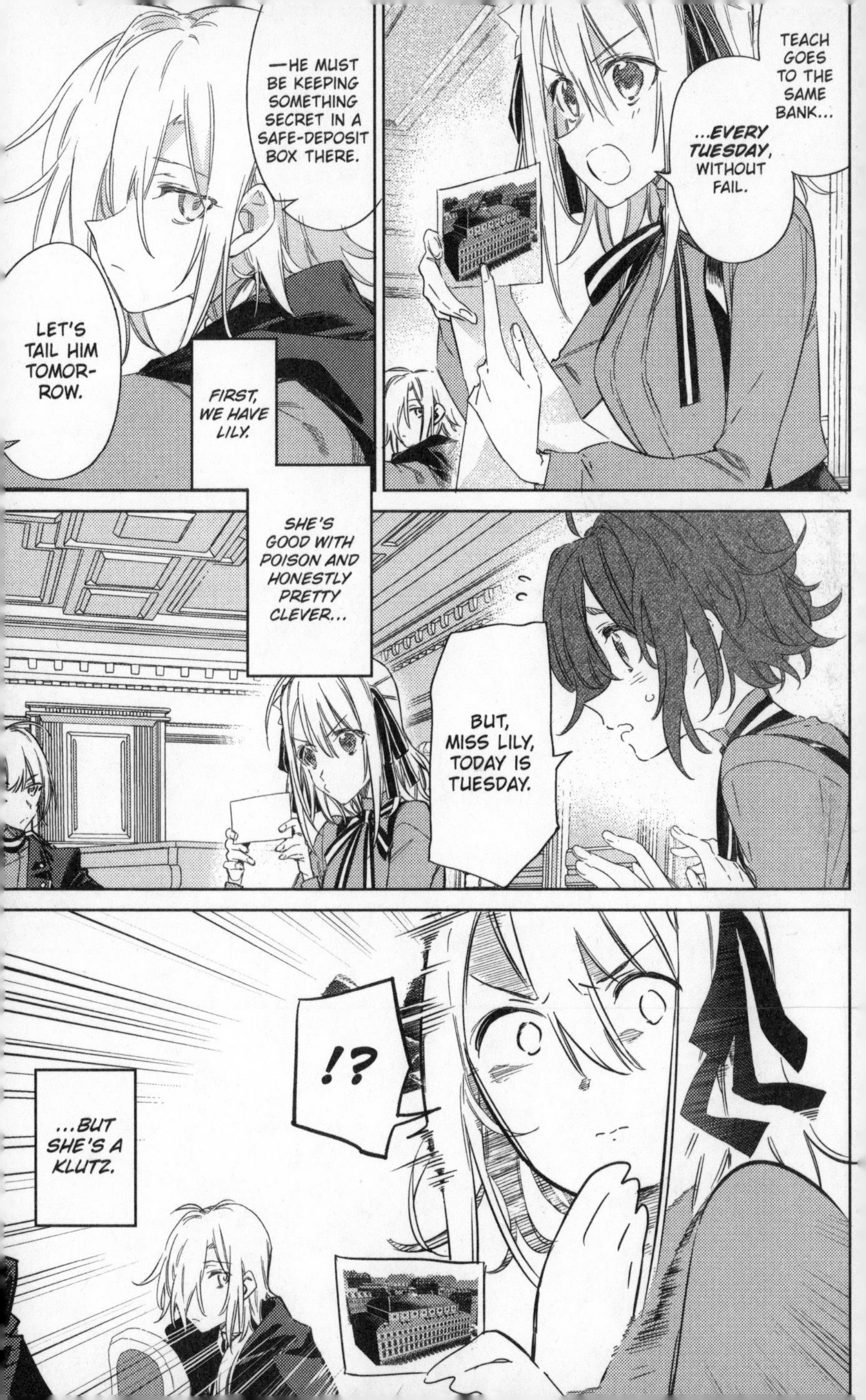
TEACH GOES TO THE SAME BANK...
...EVERY TUESDAY, WITHOUT FAIL.
—HE MUST BE KEEPING SOMETHING SECRET IN A SAFE-DEPOSIT BOX THERE.
LET'S TAIL HIM TOMOR-ROW.
FIRST, WE HAVE LILY.
SHE'S GOOD WITH POISON AND HONESTLY PRETTY CLEVER...
BUT, MISS LILY, TODAY IS TUESDAY.
!?
...BUT SHE'S A KLUTZ.

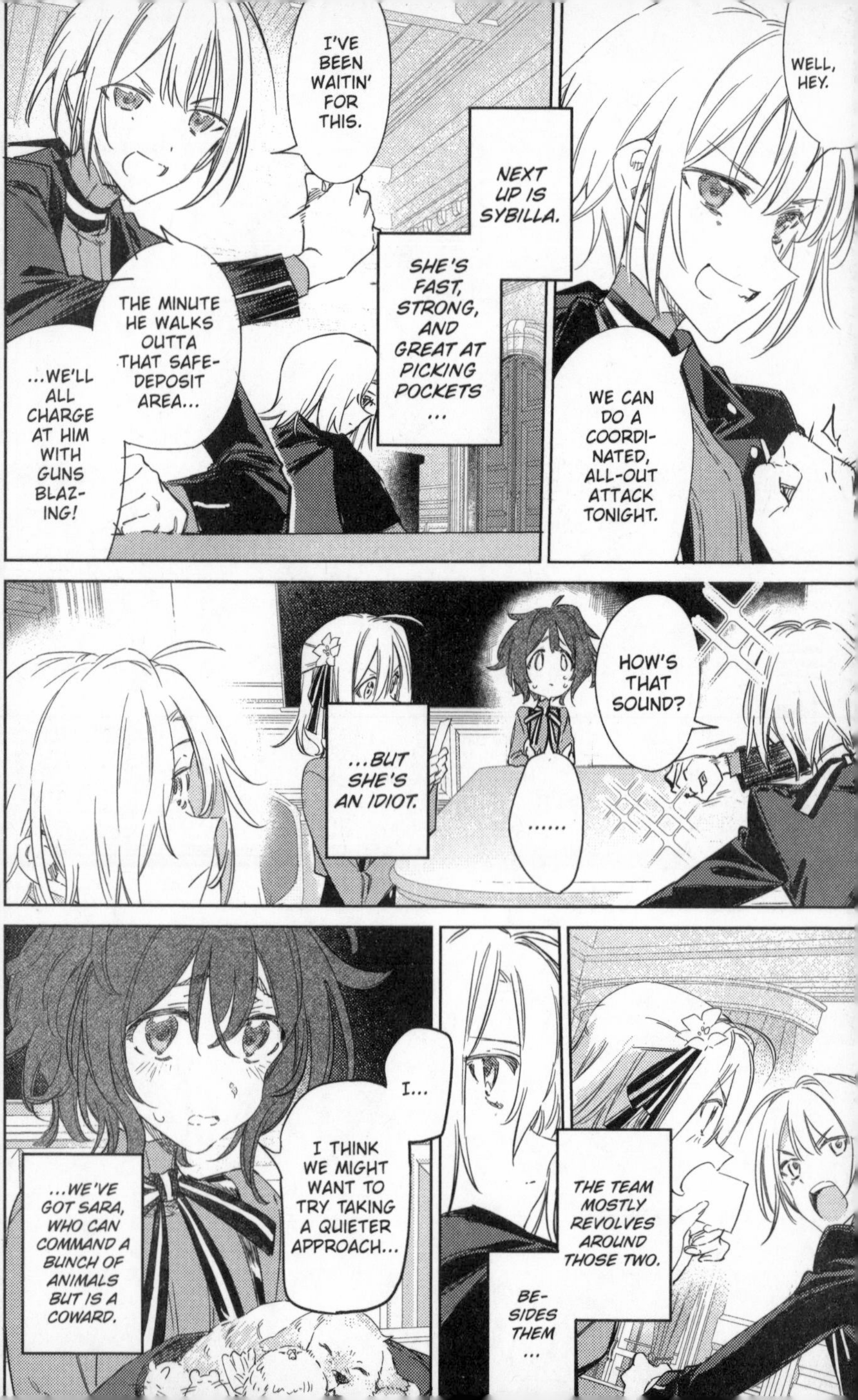
WELL, HEY.
NEXT UP IS SYBILLA.
SHE'S FAST, STRONG, AND GREAT AT PICKING POCKETS...
WE CAN DO A COORDINATED, ALL-OUT ATTACK TONIGHT.
I'VE BEEN WAITIN' FOR THIS.
THE MINUTE HE WALKS OUTTA THAT SAFE-DEPOSIT AREA...
...WE'LL ALL CHARGE AT HIM WITH GUNS BLAZING!
HOW'S THAT SOUND?
......
...BUT SHE'S AN IDIOT.
THE TEAM MOSTLY REVOLVES AROUND THOSE TWO.
BESIDES THEM...
I...
I THINK WE MIGHT WANT TO TRY TAKING A QUIETER APPROACH...
...WE'VE GOT SARA, WHO CAN COMMAND A BUNCH OF ANIMALS BUT IS A COWARD.

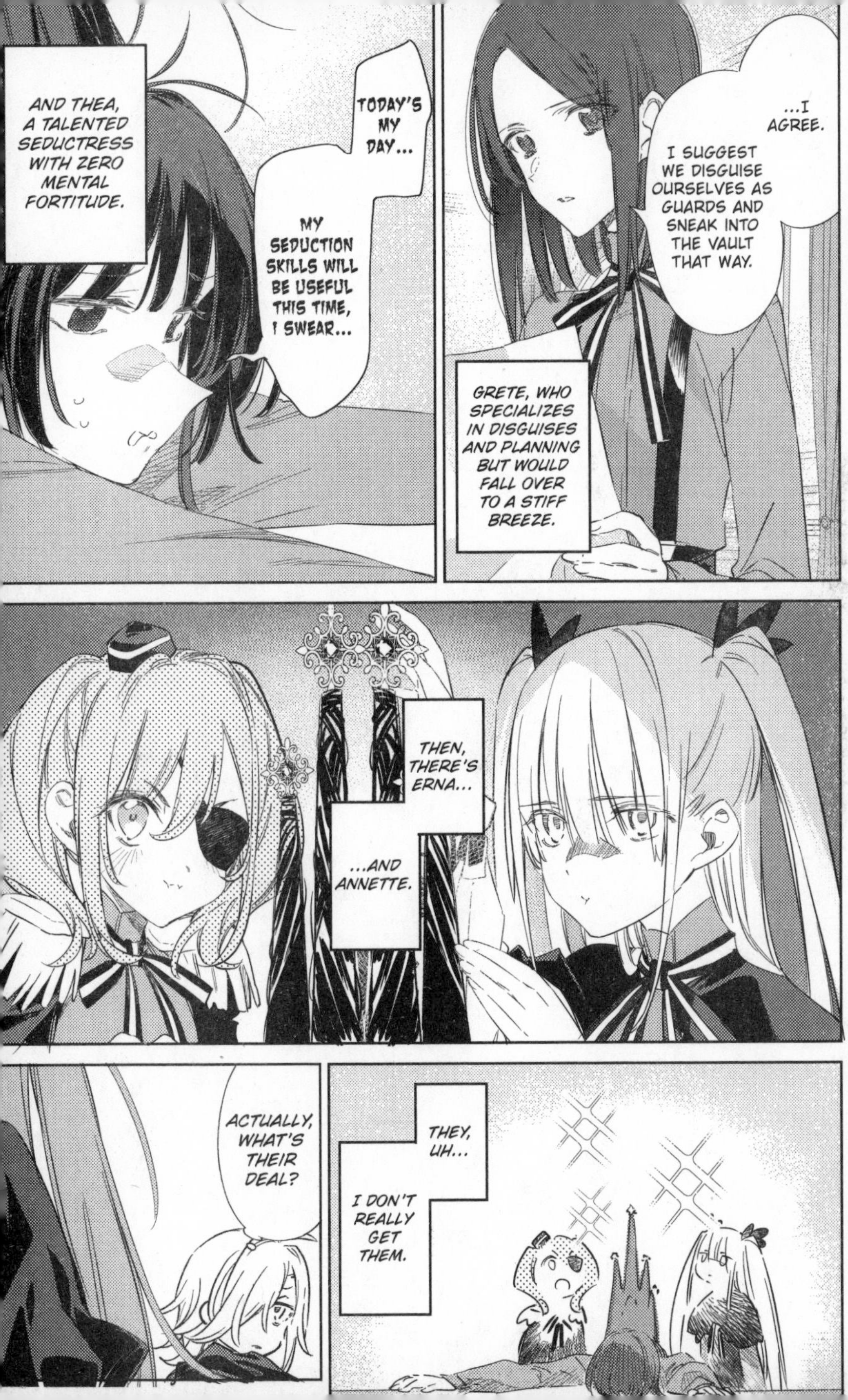

...I AGREE.
I SUGGEST WE DISGUISE OURSELVES AS GUARDS AND SNEAK INTO THE VAULT THAT WAY.
GRETE, WHO SPECIALIZES IN DISGUISES AND PLANNING BUT WOULD FALL OVER TO A STIFF BREEZE.
TODAY'S MY DAY...
MY SEDUCTION SKILLS WILL BE USEFUL THIS TIME, I SWEAR...
AND THEA, A TALENTED SEDUCTRESS WITH ZERO MENTAL FORTITUDE.
THEN, THERE'S ERNA...
...AND ANNETTE.
THEY, UH...
I DON'T REALLY GET THEM.
ACTUALLY, WHAT'S THEIR DEAL?

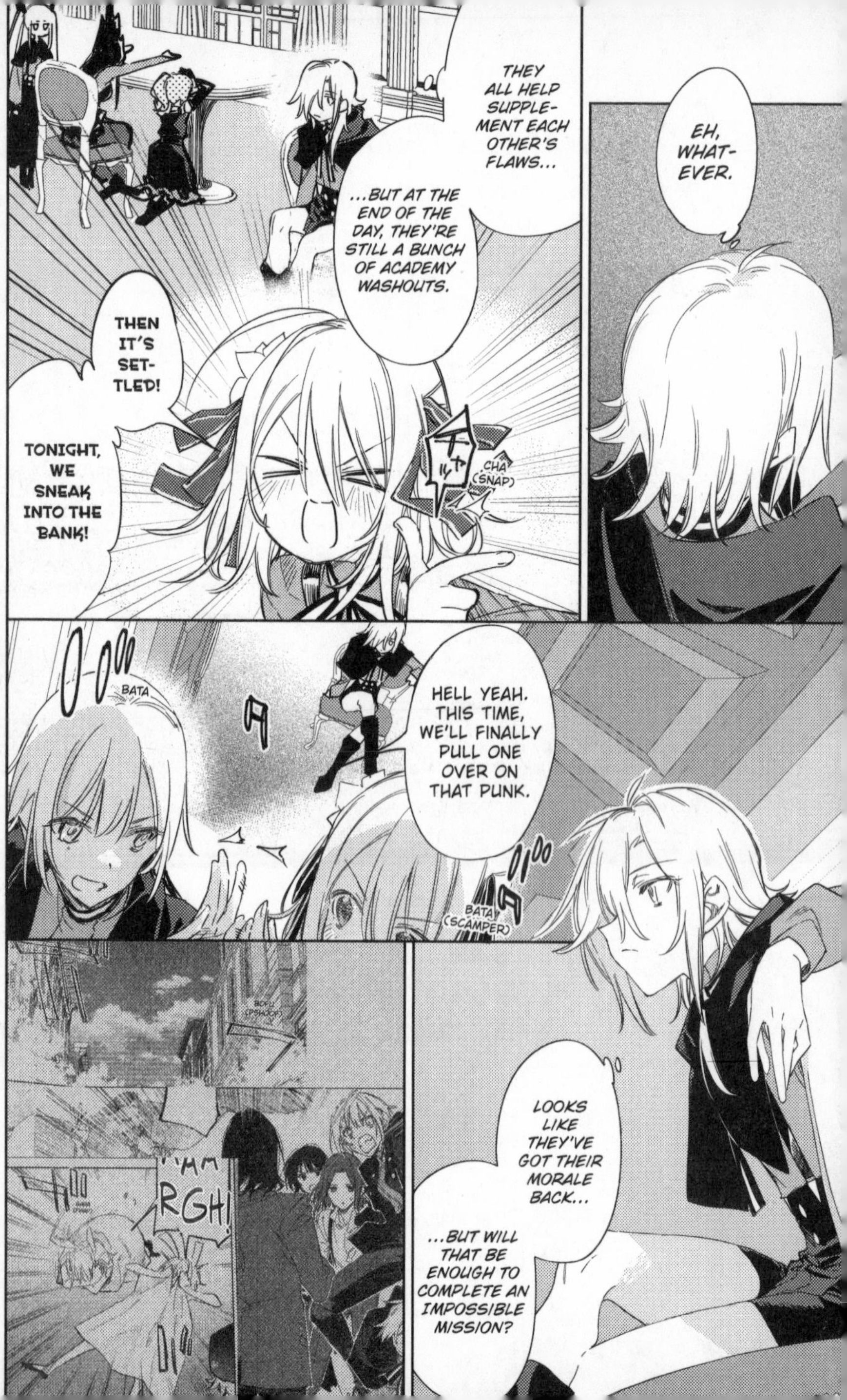
EH, WHATEVER.
THEY ALL HELP SUPPLEMENT EACH OTHER'S FLAWS...
...BUT AT THE END OF THE DAY, THEY'RE STILL A BUNCH OF ACADEMY WASHOUTS.
CHA (SNAP)
THEN IT'S SETTLED!
TONIGHT, WE SNEAK INTO THE BANK!
HELL YEAH. THIS TIME, WE'LL FINALLY PULL ONE OVER ON THAT PUNK.
BATA (SCAMPER)
BATA
LOOKS LIKE THEY'VE GOT THEIR MORALE BACK...
...BUT WILL THAT BE ENOUGH TO COMPLETE AN IMPOSSIBLE MISSION?
BOFU (PSHOOF)
MMRGH!

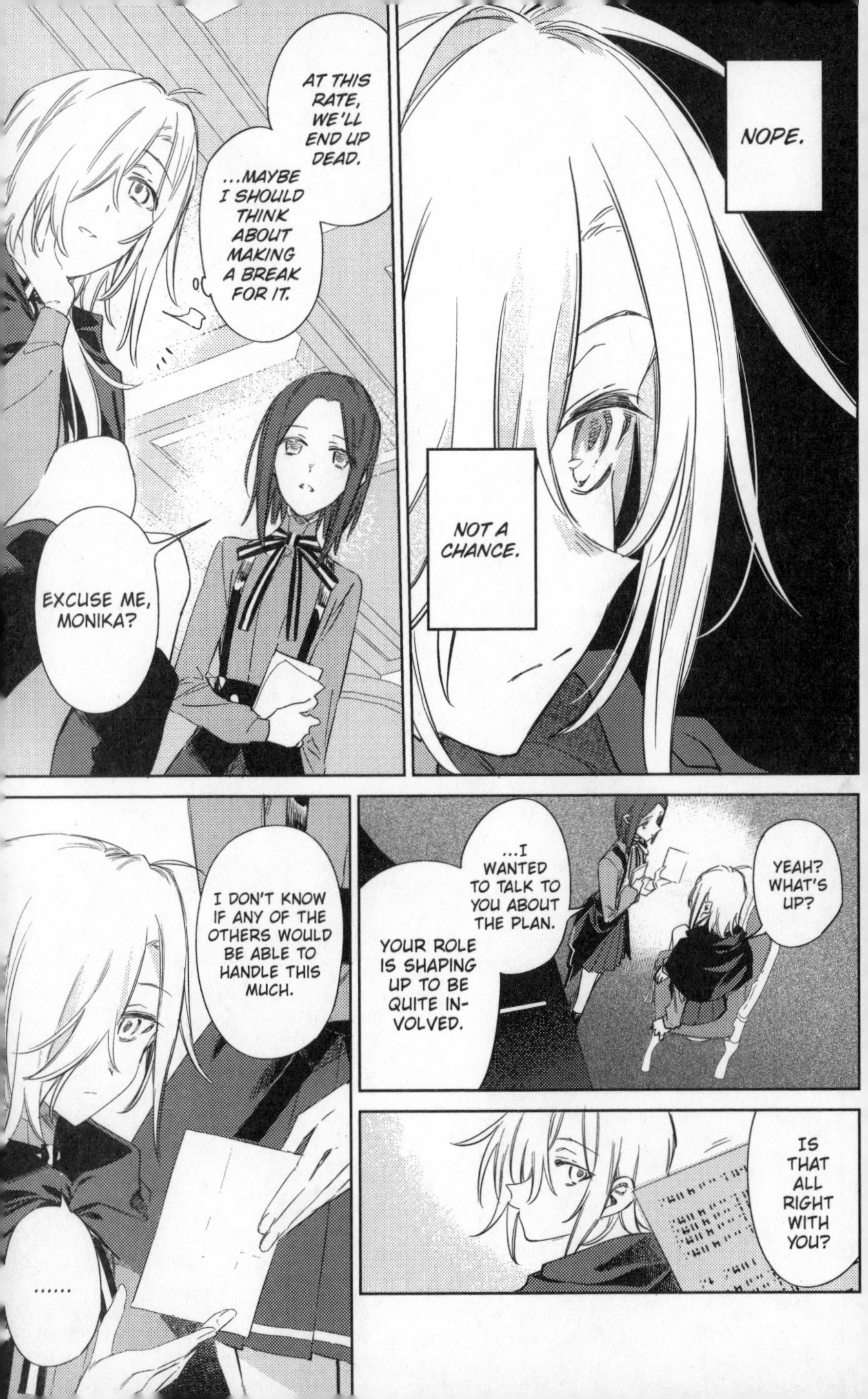
NOPE.
NOT A CHANCE.
AT THIS RATE, WE'LL END UP DEAD.
...MAYBE I SHOULD THINK ABOUT MAKING A BREAK FOR IT.
EXCUSE ME, MONIKA?
YEAH? WHAT'S UP?
...I WANTED TO TALK TO YOU ABOUT THE PLAN.
YOUR ROLE IS SHAPING UP TO BE QUITE INVOLVED.
IS THAT ALL RIGHT WITH YOU?
I DON'T KNOW IF ANY OF THE OTHERS WOULD BE ABLE TO HANDLE THIS MUCH.
......

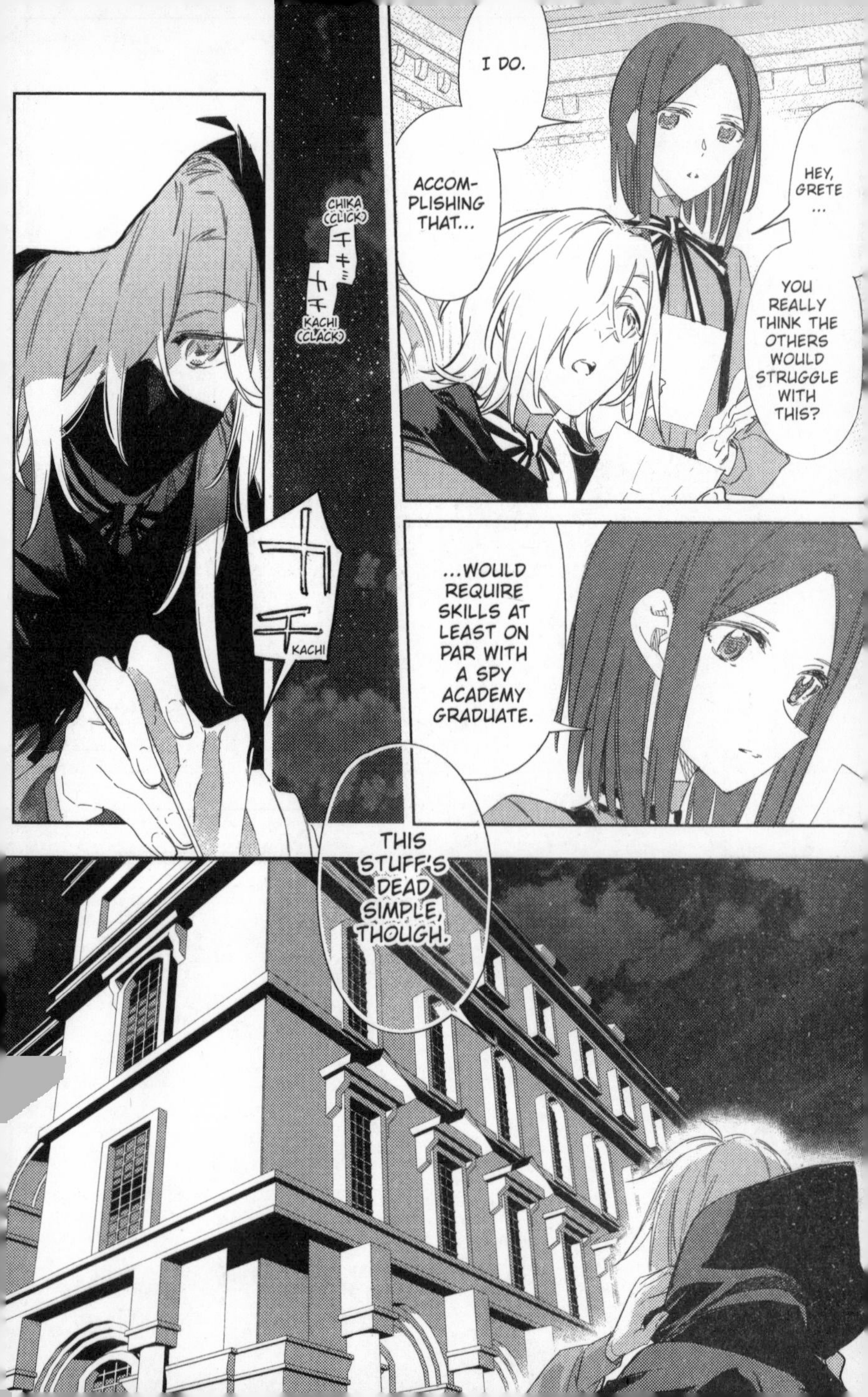
HEY, GRETE...
YOU REALLY THINK THE OTHERS WOULD STRUGGLE WITH THIS?
I DO.
ACCOMPLISHING THAT...
...WOULD REQUIRE SKILLS AT LEAST ON PAR WITH A SPY ACADEMY GRADUATE.
CHIKA (CLICK)
KACHI (CLACK)
KACHI
THIS STUFF'S DEAD SIMPLE, THOUGH.

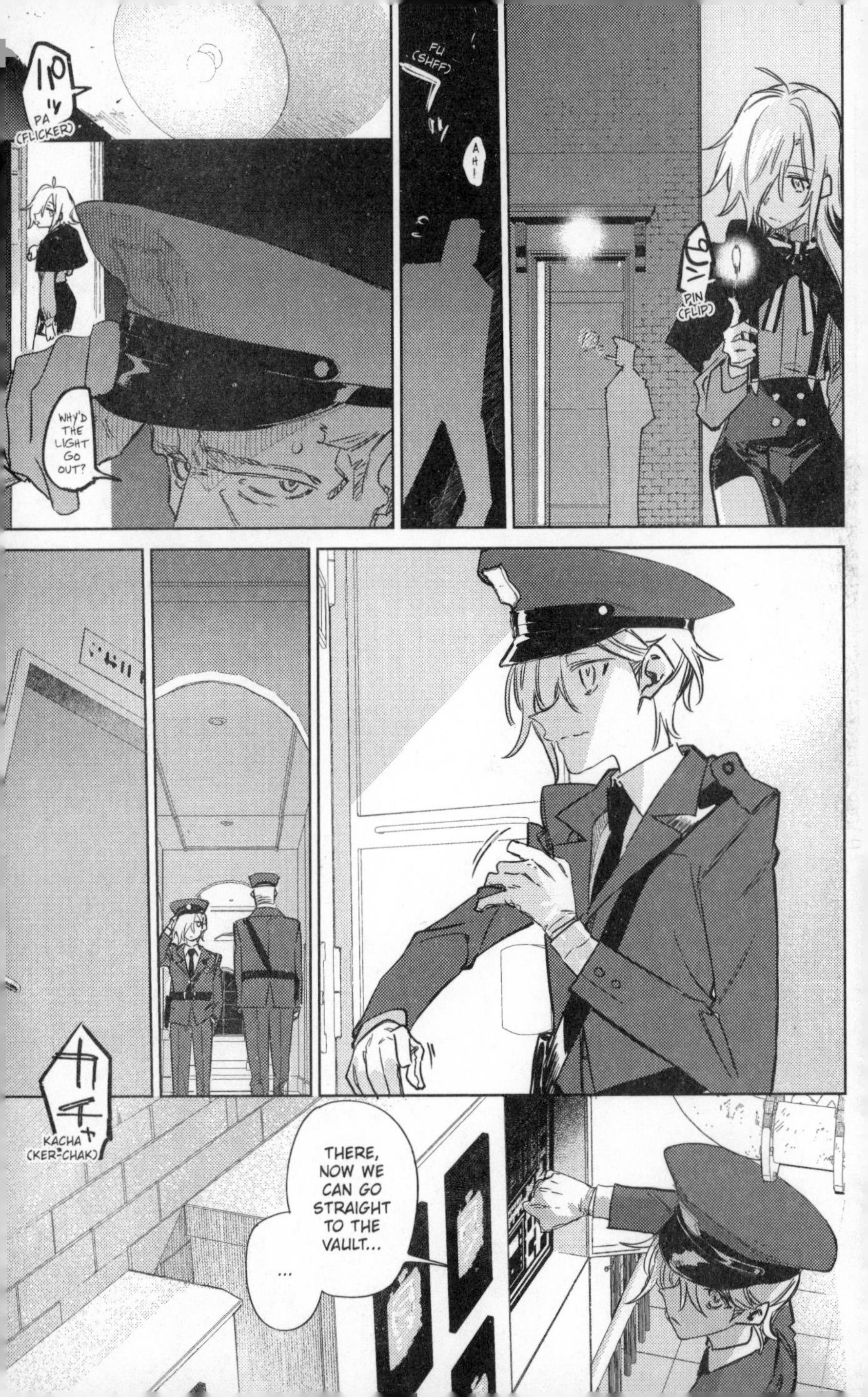
PIN (FLIP)
FU (SHFF)
AH!
PA (FLICKER)
WHY'D THE LIGHT GO OUT?
KACHA (KER-CHAK)
THERE, NOW WE CAN GO STRAIGHT TO THE VAULT...
...

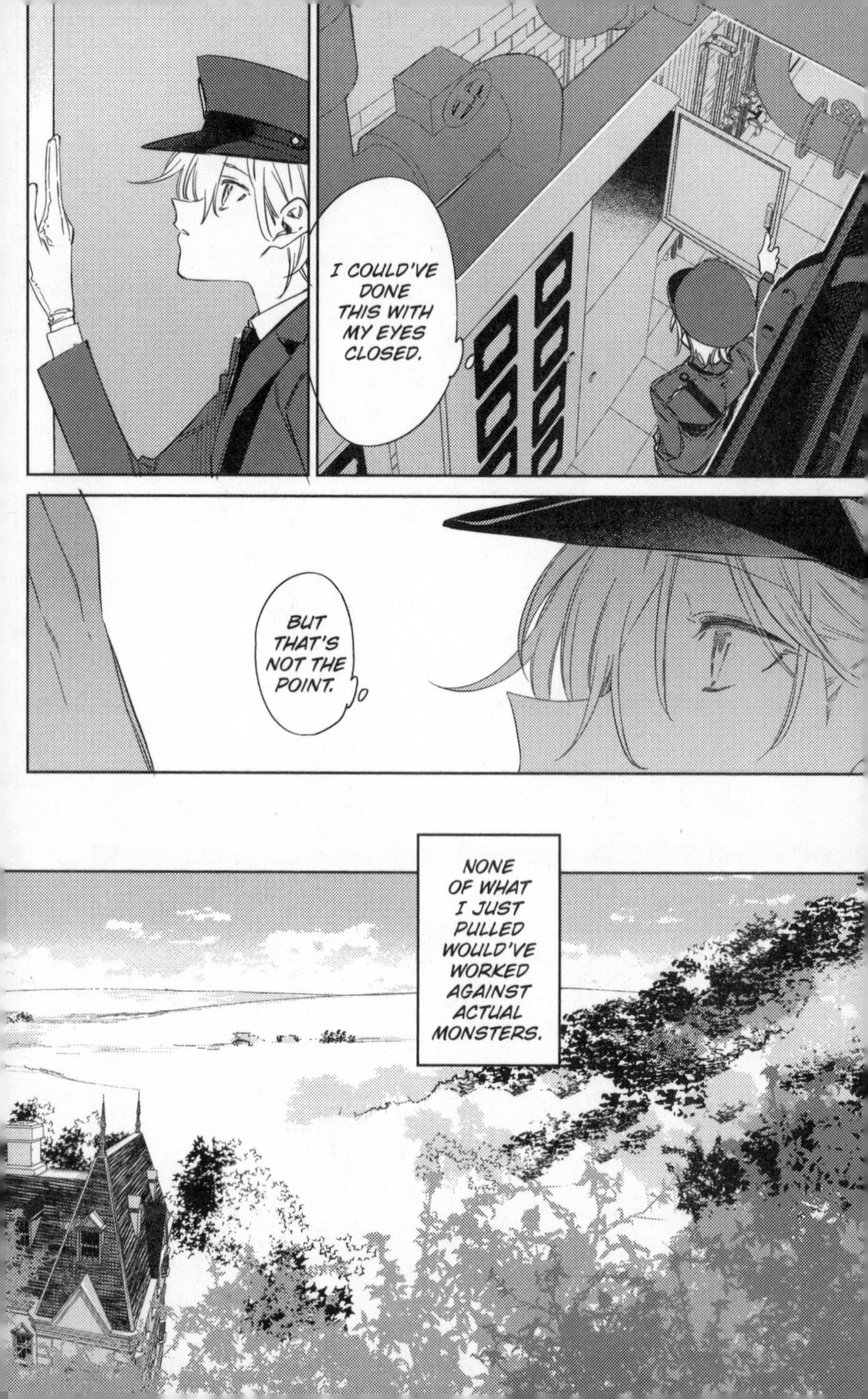
I COULD'VE DONE THIS WITH MY EYES CLOSED.
BUT THAT'S NOT THE POINT.
NONE OF WHAT I JUST PULLED WOULD'VE WORKED AGAINST ACTUAL MONSTERS.

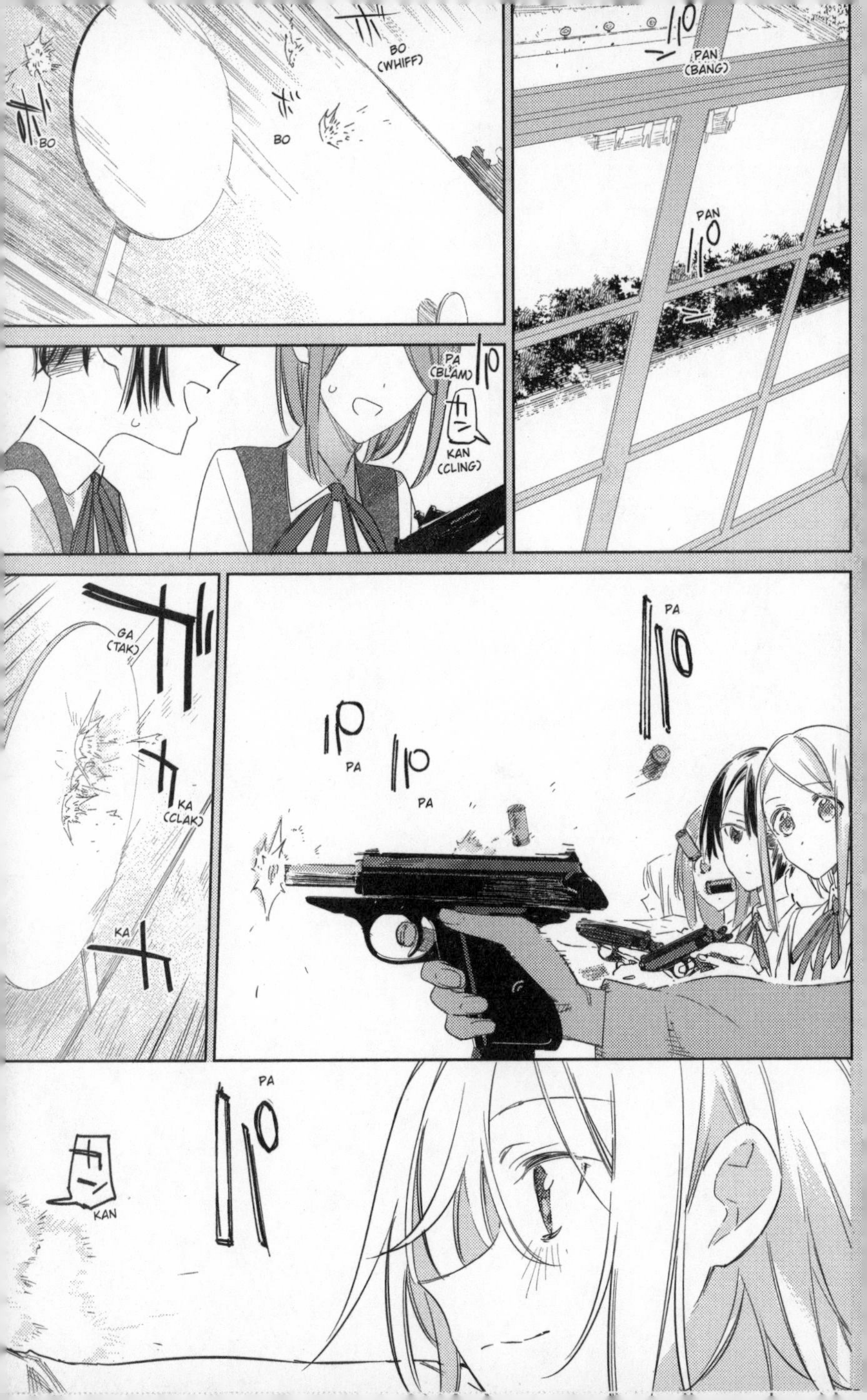
PAN (BANG)
PAN
BO (WHIFF)
BO
BO
PA (BLAM)
KAN (CLING)
PA
PA
PA
GA (TAK)
KA (CLAK)
KA
PA
KAN

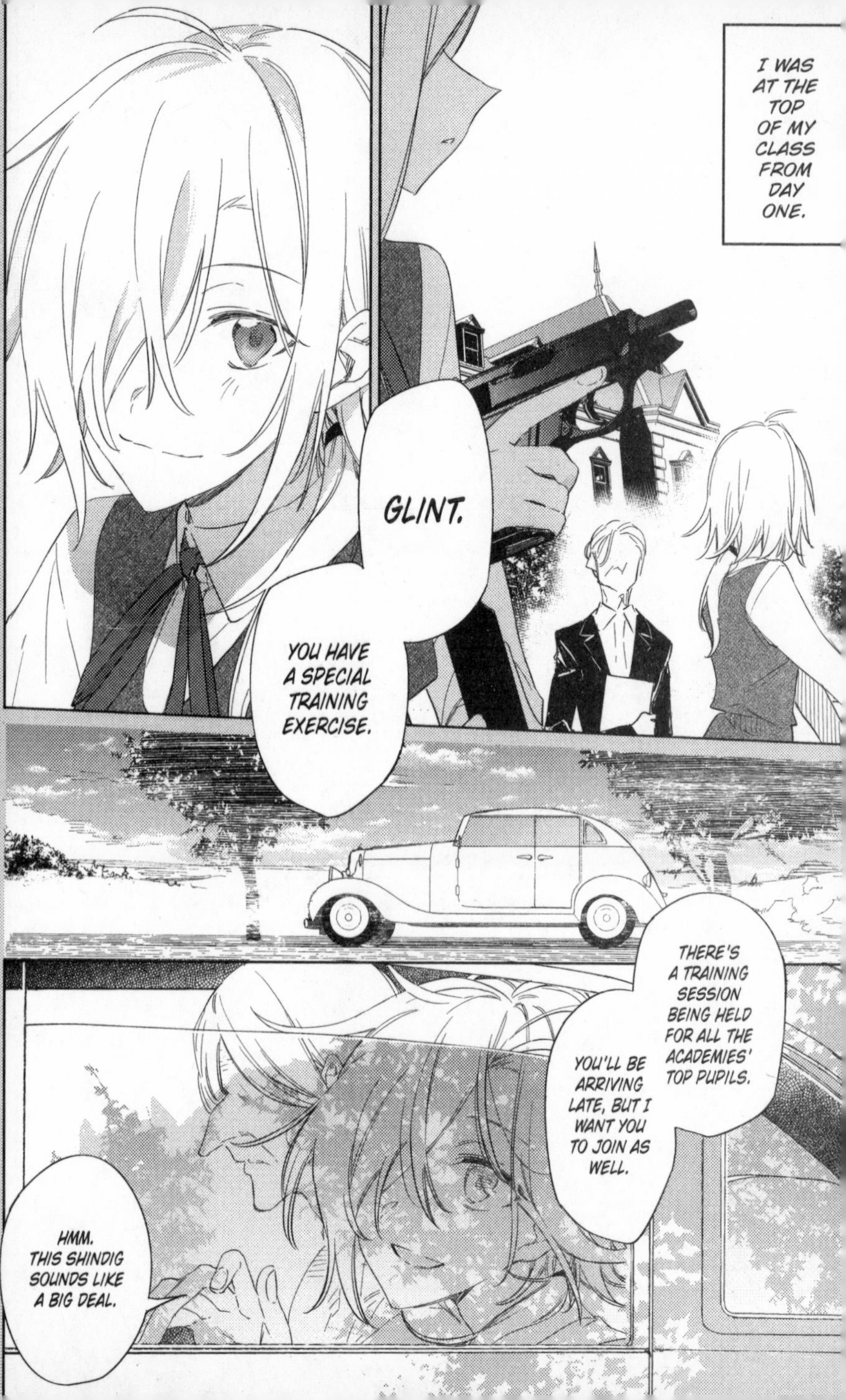
I WAS AT THE TOP OF MY CLASS FROM DAY ONE.
GLINT.
YOU HAVE A SPECIAL TRAINING EXERCISE.
THERE'S A TRAINING SESSION BEING HELD FOR ALL THE ACADEMIES' TOP PUPILS.
YOU'LL BE ARRIVING LATE, BUT I WANT YOU TO JOIN AS WELL.
HMM. THIS SHINDIG SOUNDS LIKE A BIG DEAL.

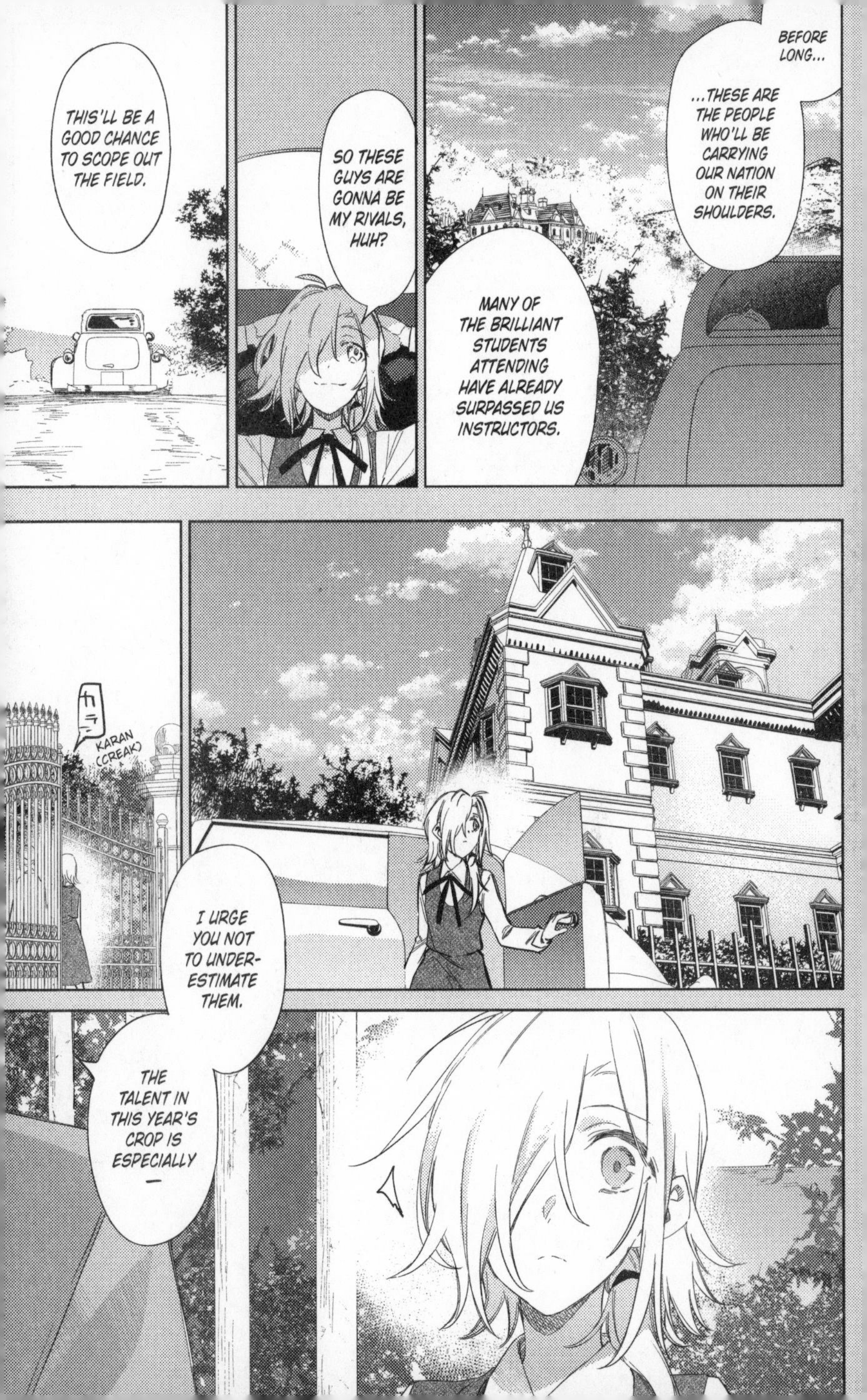
BEFORE LONG...
...THESE ARE THE PEOPLE WHO'LL BE CARRYING OUR NATION ON THEIR SHOULDERS.
MANY OF THE BRILLIANT STUDENTS ATTENDING HAVE ALREADY SURPASSED US INSTRUCTORS.
SO THESE GUYS ARE GONNA BE MY RIVALS, HUH?
THIS'LL BE A GOOD CHANCE TO SCOPE OUT THE FIELD.
I URGE YOU NOT TO UNDER-ESTIMATE THEM.
KARAN (CREAK)
THE TALENT IN THIS YEAR'S CROP IS ESPECIALLY —

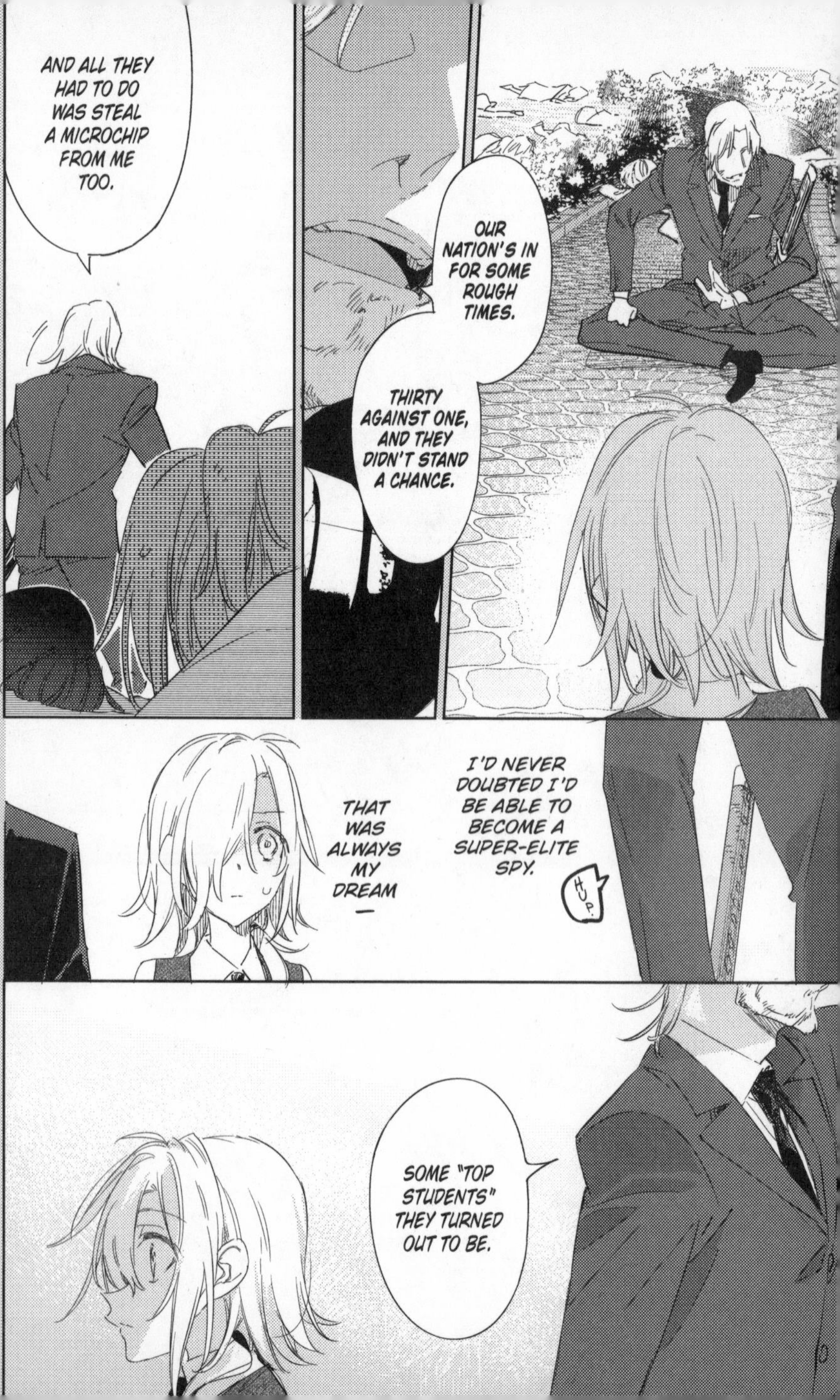
OUR NATION'S IN FOR SOME ROUGH TIMES.
THIRTY AGAINST ONE, AND THEY DIDN'T STAND A CHANCE.
AND ALL THEY HAD TO DO WAS STEAL A MICROCHIP FROM ME TOO.
HUP.
I'D NEVER DOUBTED I'D BE ABLE TO BECOME A SUPER-ELITE SPY.
THAT WAS ALWAYS MY DREAM—
SOME "TOP STUDENTS" THEY TURNED OUT TO BE.

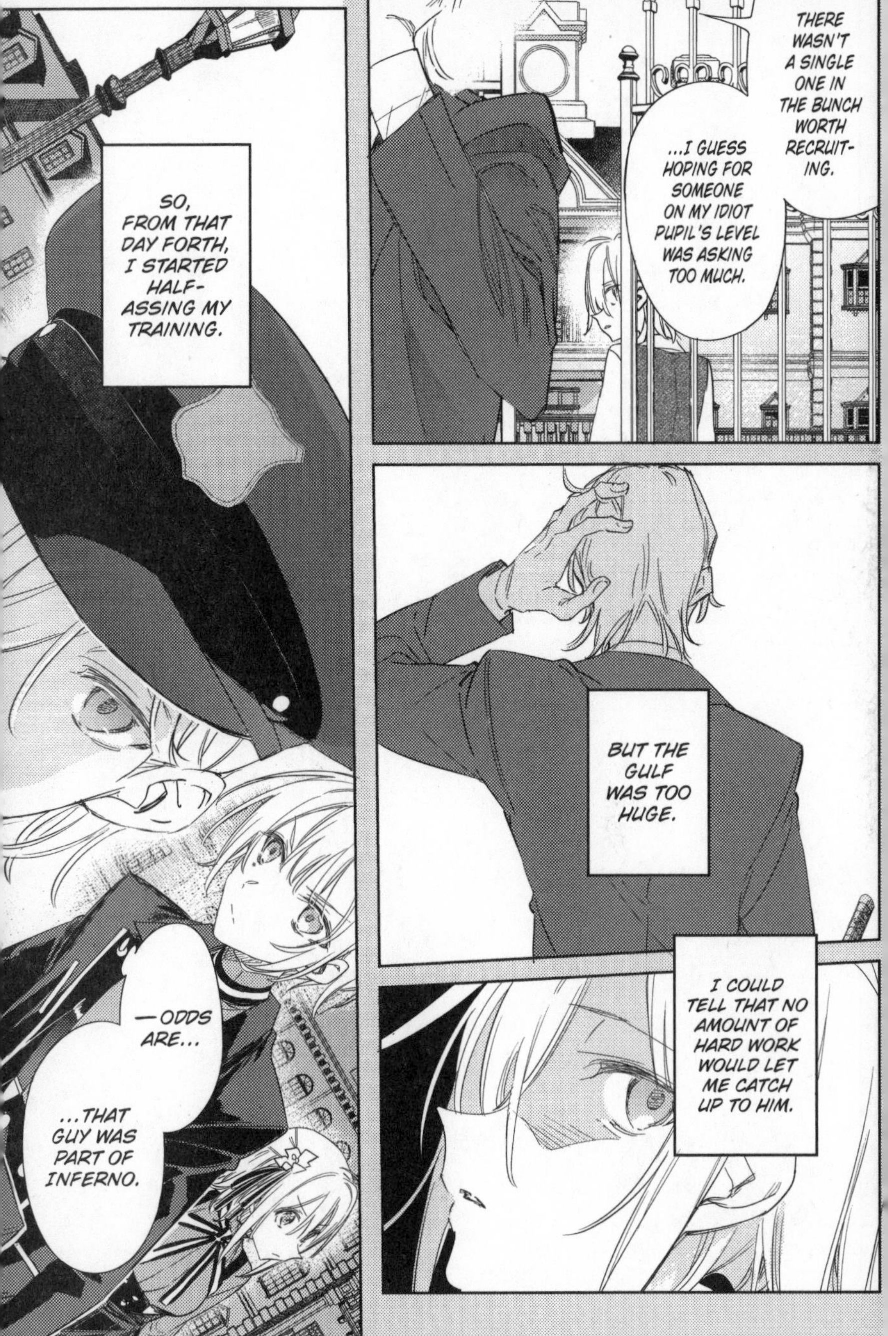
THERE WASN'T A SINGLE ONE IN THE BUNCH WORTH RECRUIT-ING.
...I GUESS HOPING FOR SOMEONE ON MY IDIOT PUPIL'S LEVEL WAS ASKING TOO MUCH.
BUT THE GULF WAS TOO HUGE.
I COULD TELL THAT NO AMOUNT OF HARD WORK WOULD LET ME CATCH UP TO HIM.
SO, FROM THAT DAY FORTH, I STARTED HALF-ASSING MY TRAINING.
—ODDS ARE...
...THAT GUY WAS PART OF INFERNO.

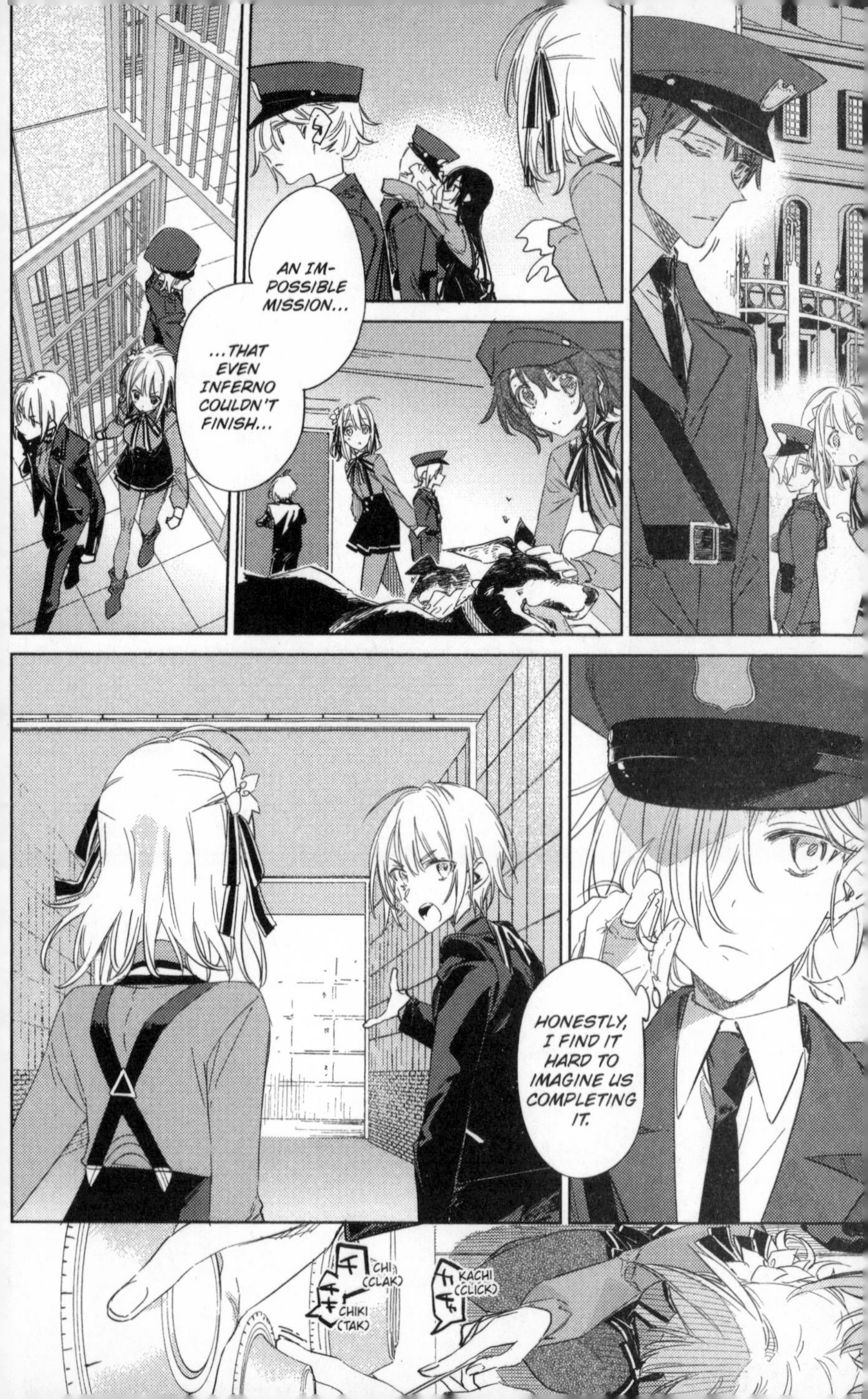
AN IM-POSSIBLE MISSION...
...THAT EVEN INFERNO COULDN'T FINISH...
HONESTLY, I FIND IT HARD TO IMAGINE US COMPLETING IT.
KACHI (CLICK)
CHI (CLAK)
CHIKI (TAK)

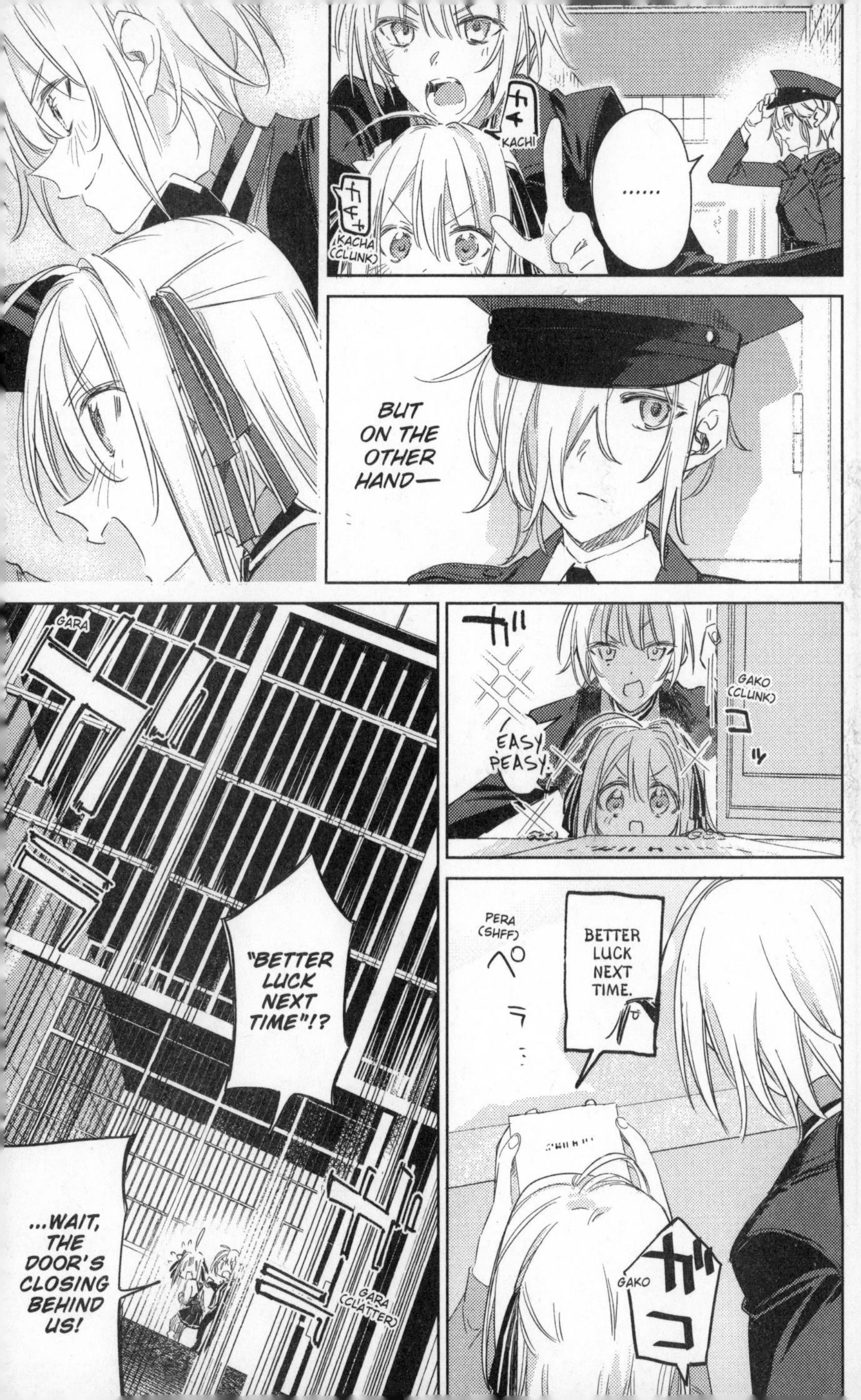
KACHI
KACHA (CLUNK)
......
BUT ON THE OTHER HAND—
GAKO (CLUNK)
EASY PEASY.
PERA (SHFF)
BETTER LUCK NEXT TIME.
GAKO
GARA
"BETTER LUCK NEXT TIME"!?
GARA (CLATTER)
...WAIT, THE DOOR'S CLOSING BEHIND US!

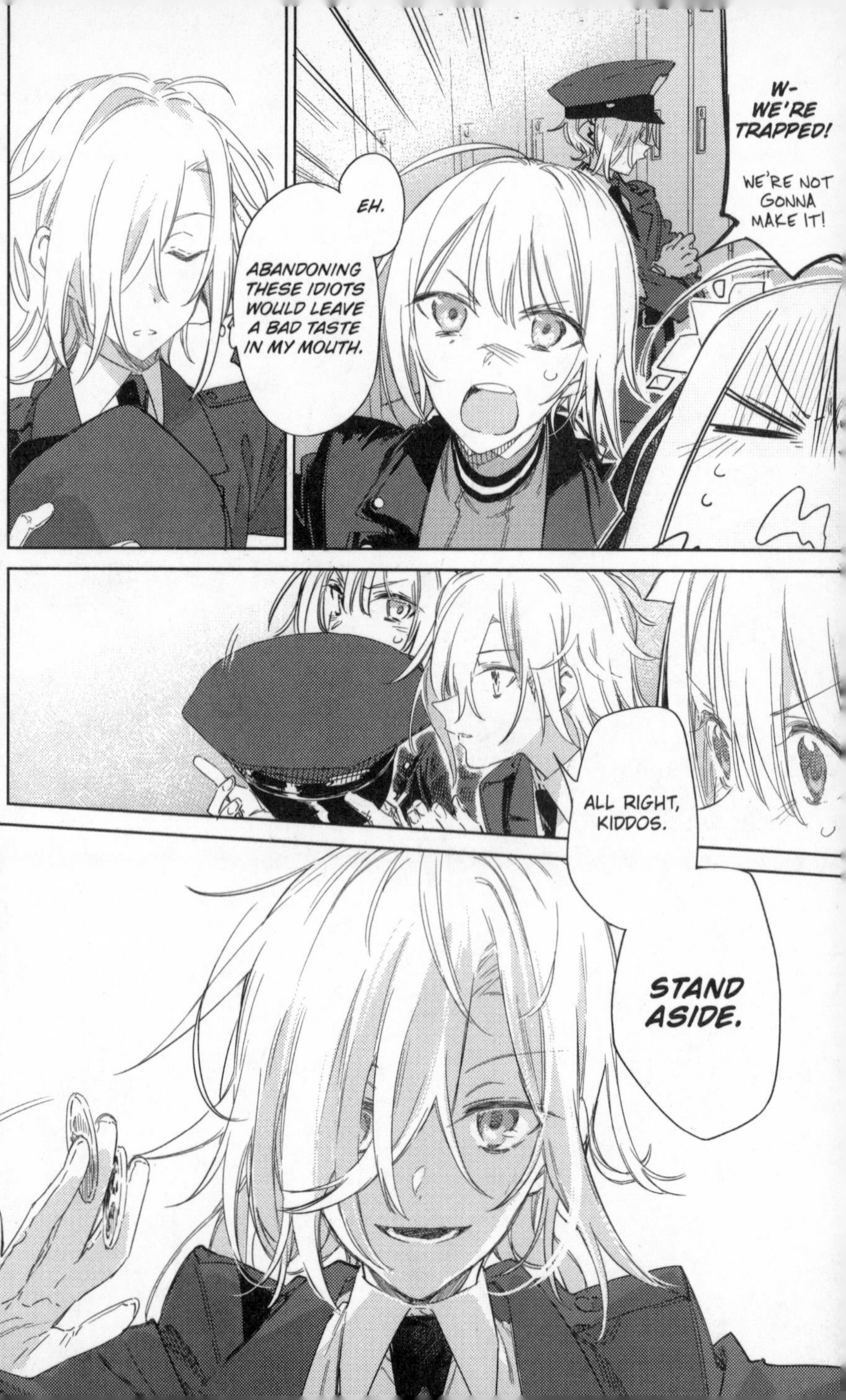
W- WE'RE TRAPPED!
WE'RE NOT GONNA MAKE IT!
EH.
ABANDONING THESE IDIOTS WOULD LEAVE A BAD TASTE IN MY MOUTH.
ALL RIGHT, KIDDOS.
STAND ASIDE.

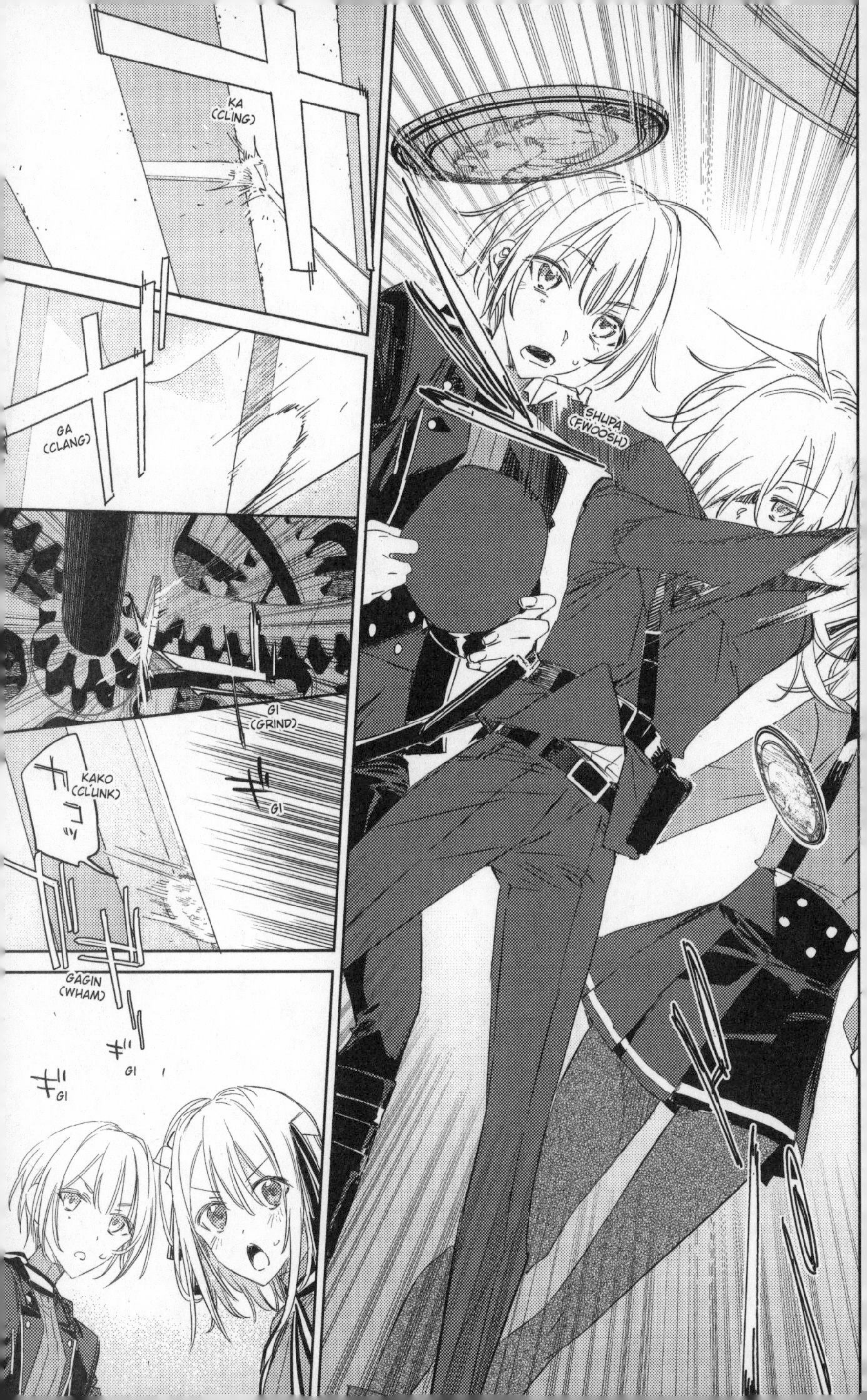
SHUPA (FWOOSH)
KA (CLING)
GA (CLANG)
GI (GRIND)
KAKO (CLUNK)
GI
GAGIN (WHAM)
GI
GI

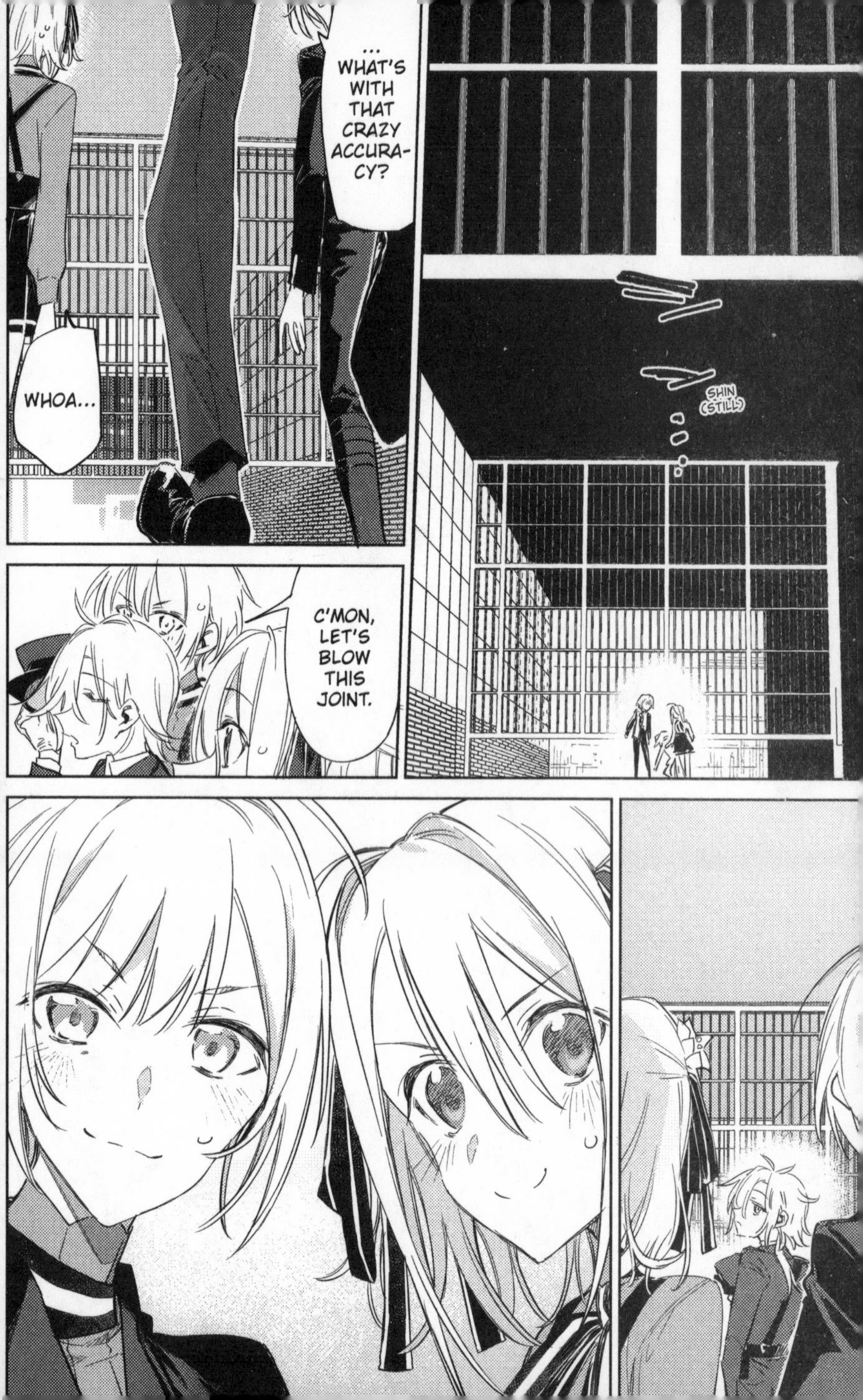
SHIN (STILL)
... WHAT'S WITH THAT CRAZY ACCURA-CY?
WHOA...
C'MON, LET'S BLOW THIS JOINT.

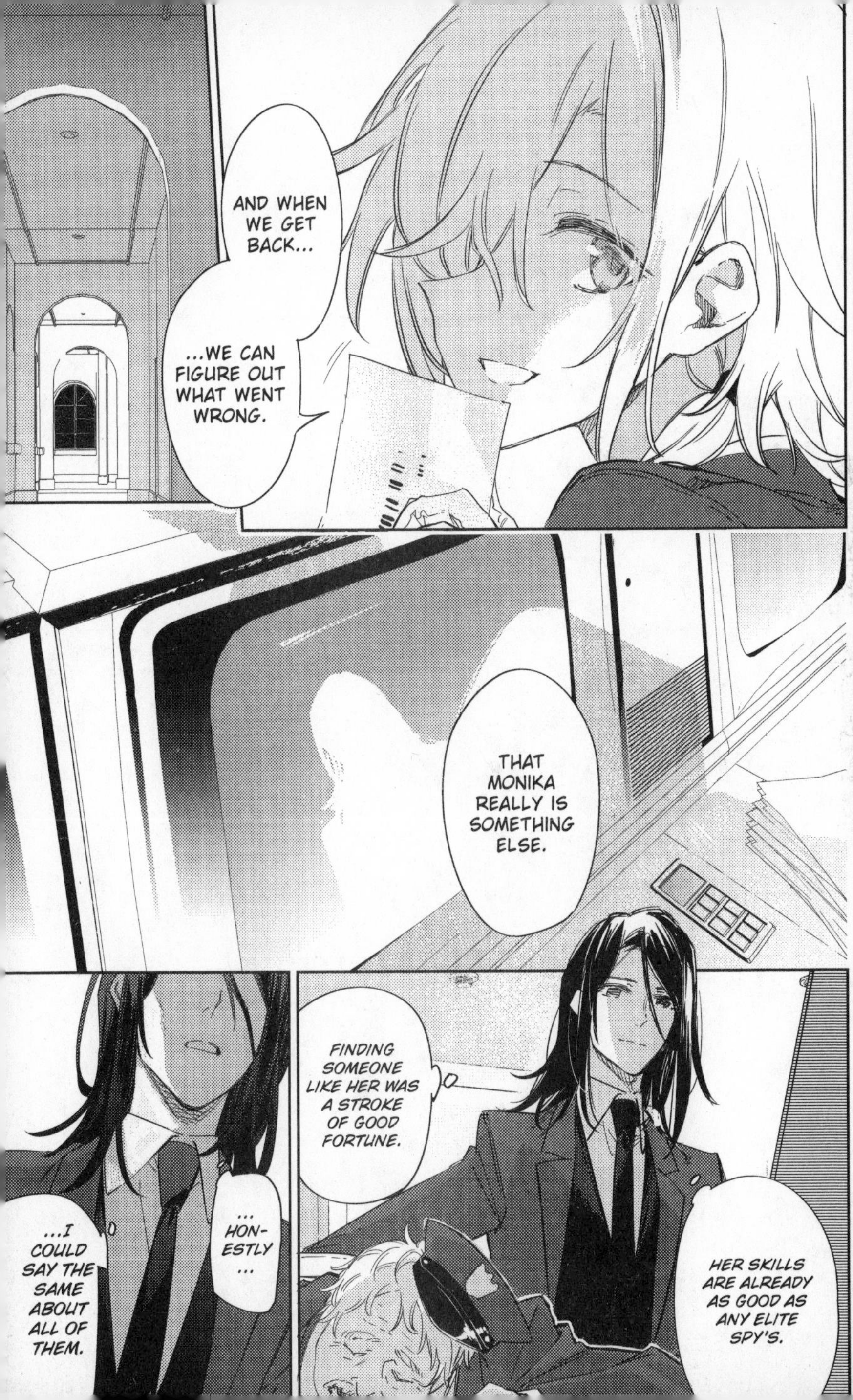
AND WHEN WE GET BACK...
...WE CAN FIGURE OUT WHAT WENT WRONG.
THAT MONIKA REALLY IS SOMETHING ELSE.
FINDING SOMEONE LIKE HER WAS A STROKE OF GOOD FORTUNE.
HER SKILLS ARE ALREADY AS GOOD AS ANY ELITE SPY'S.
...HON-ESTLY...
...I COULD SAY THE SAME ABOUT ALL OF THEM.

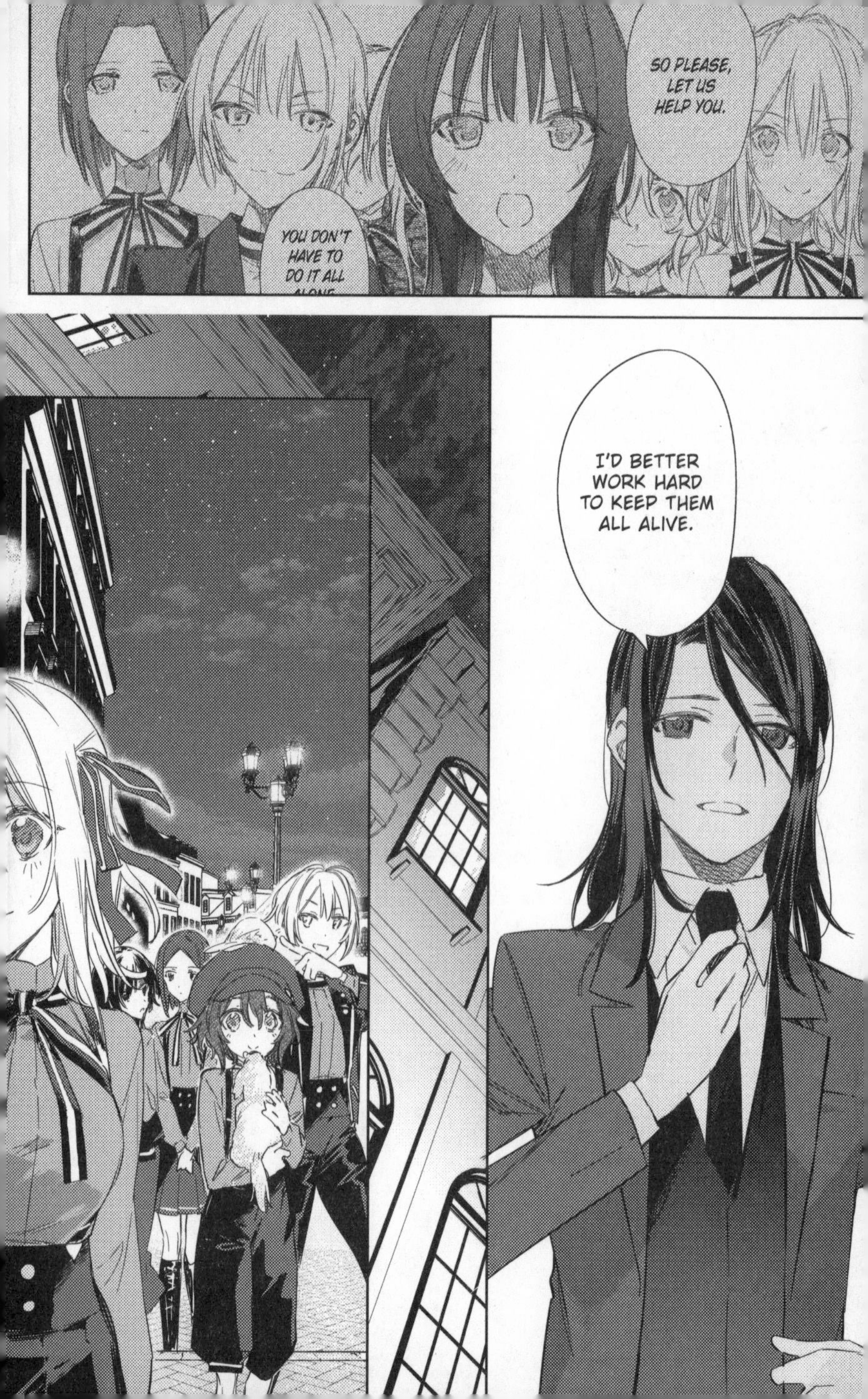
SO PLEASE, LET US HELP YOU.
YOU DON'T HAVE TO DO IT ALL
I'D BETTER WORK HARD TO KEEP THEM ALL ALIVE.

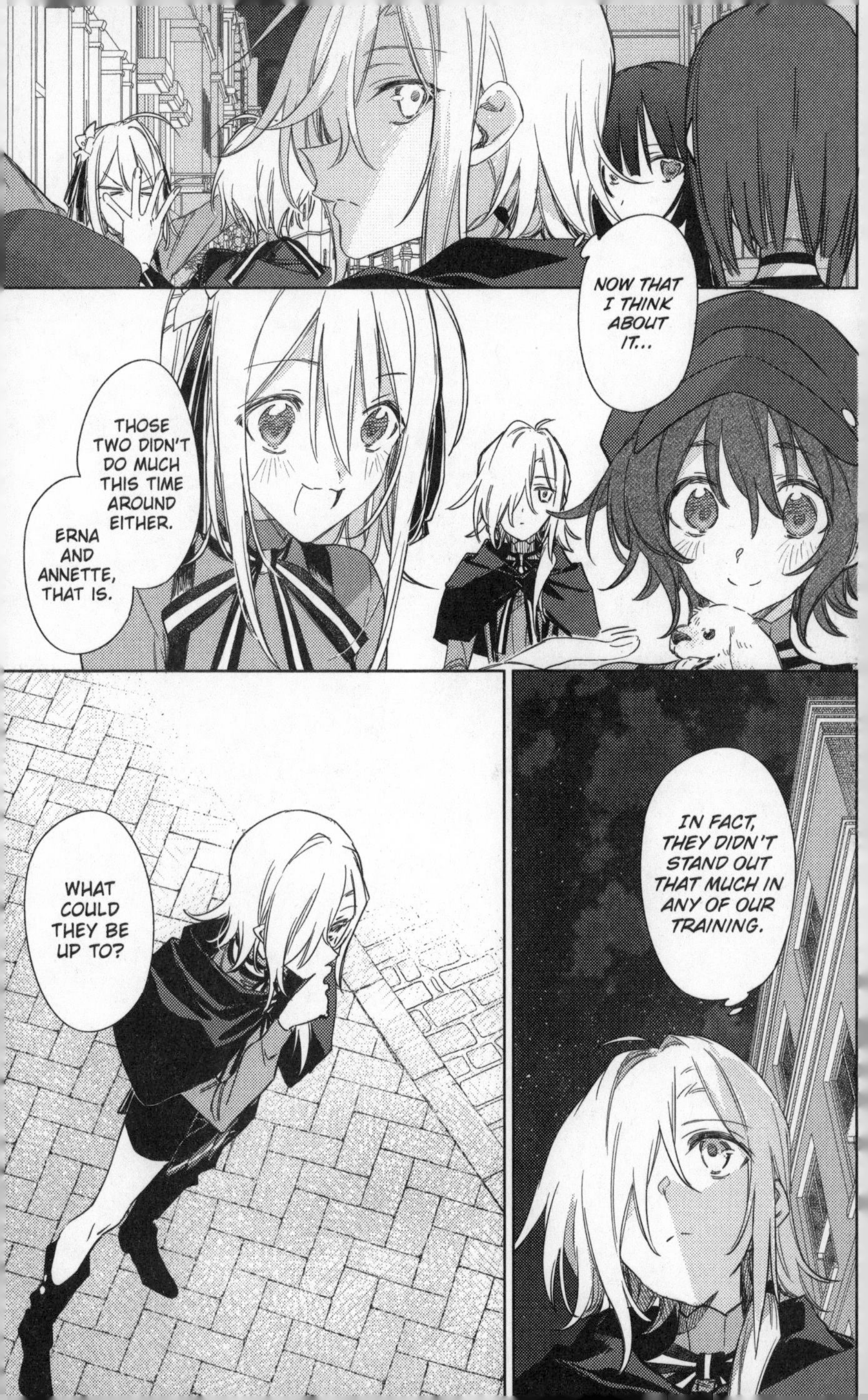
NOW THAT I THINK ABOUT IT...
THOSE TWO DIDN'T DO MUCH THIS TIME AROUND EITHER.
ERNA AND ANNETTE, THAT IS.
IN FACT, THEY DIDN'T STAND OUT THAT MUCH IN ANY OF OUR TRAINING.
WHAT COULD THEY BE UP TO?

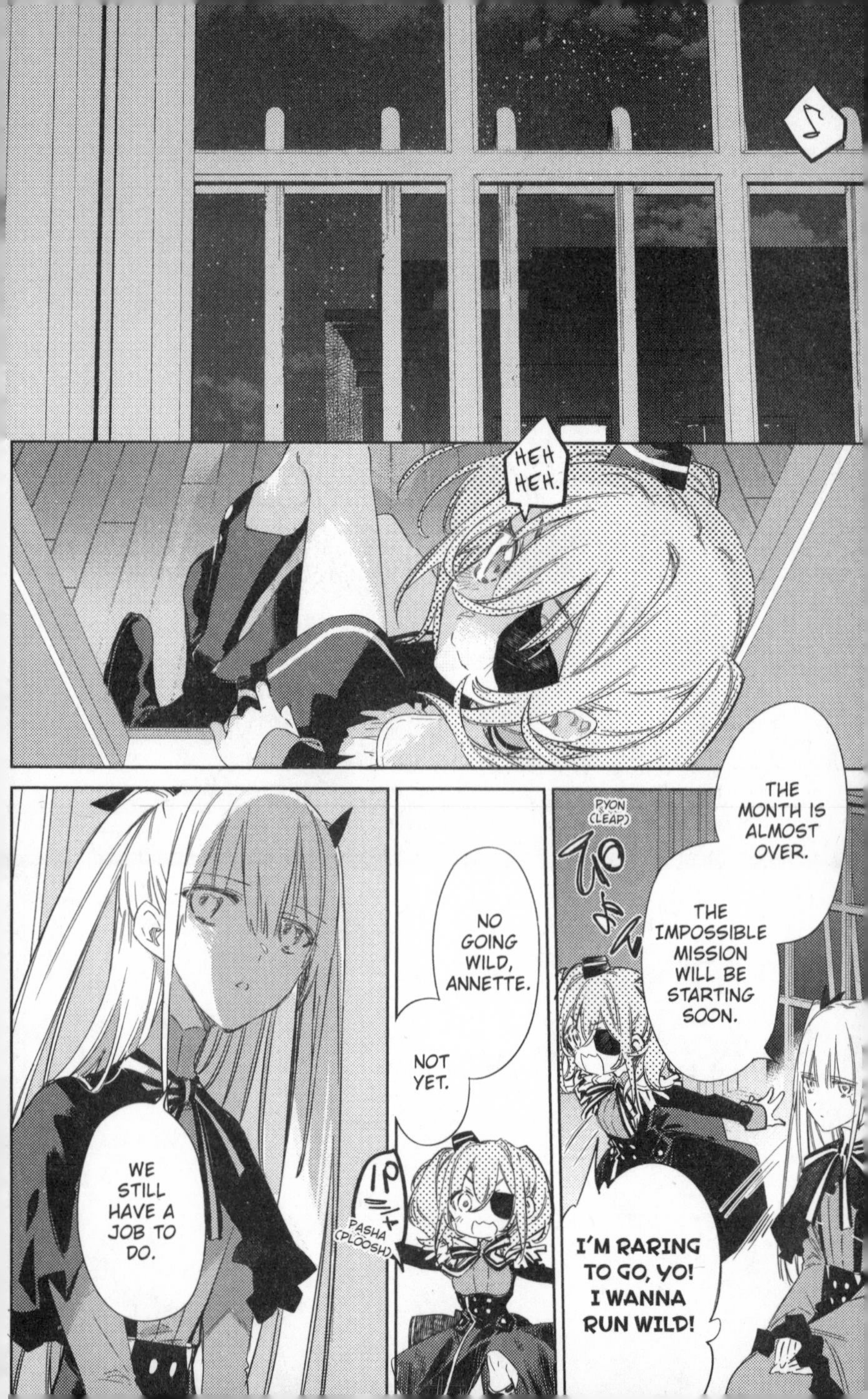
♪
HEH HEH.
PYON (LEAP)
THE MONTH IS ALMOST OVER.
THE IMPOSSIBLE MISSION WILL BE STARTING SOON.
I'M RARING TO GO, YO! I WANNA RUN WILD!
NO GOING WILD, ANNETTE.
NOT YET.
PASHA (PLOOSH)
WE STILL HAVE A JOB TO DO.

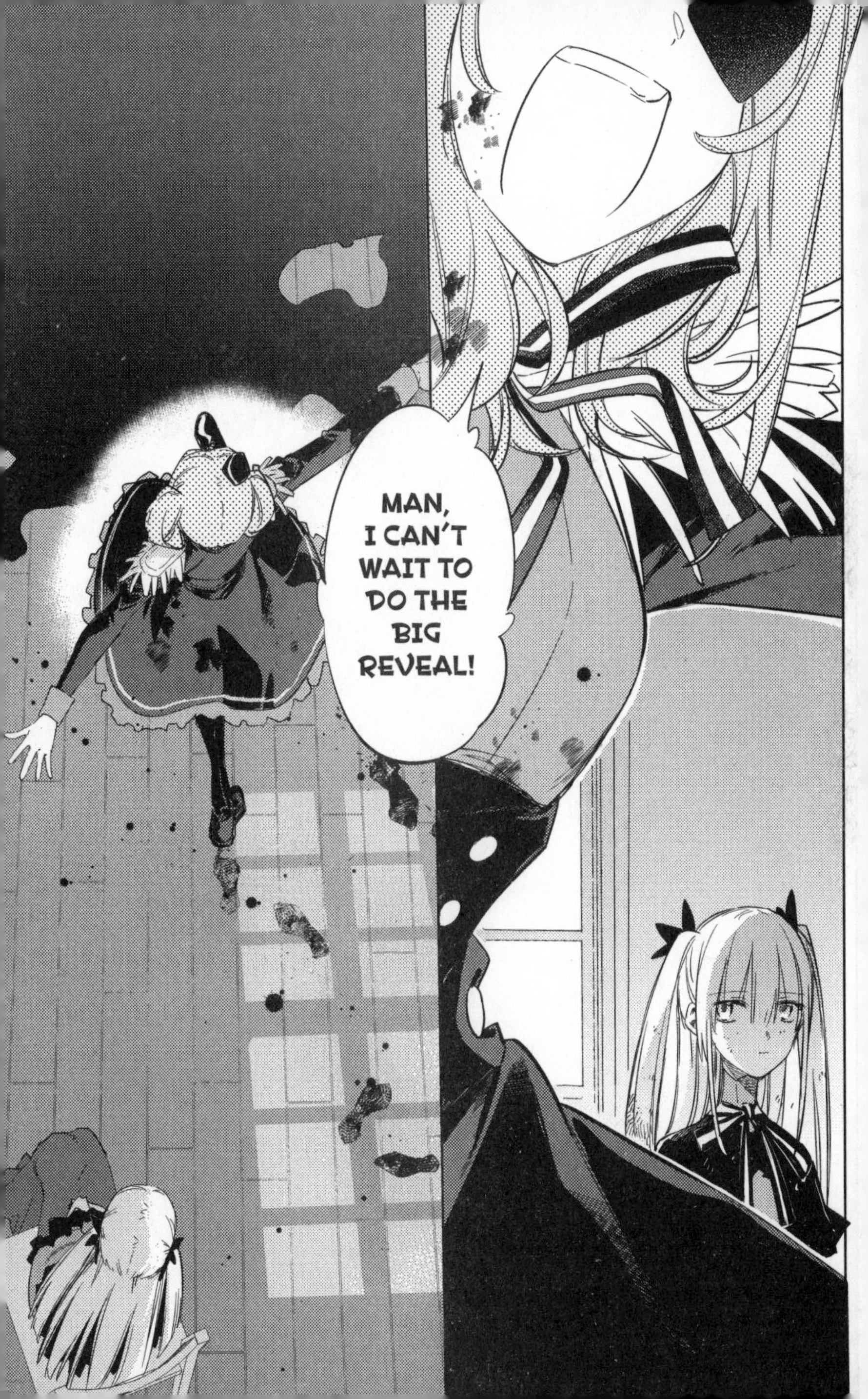
MAN, I CAN'T WAIT TO DO THE BIG REVEAL!

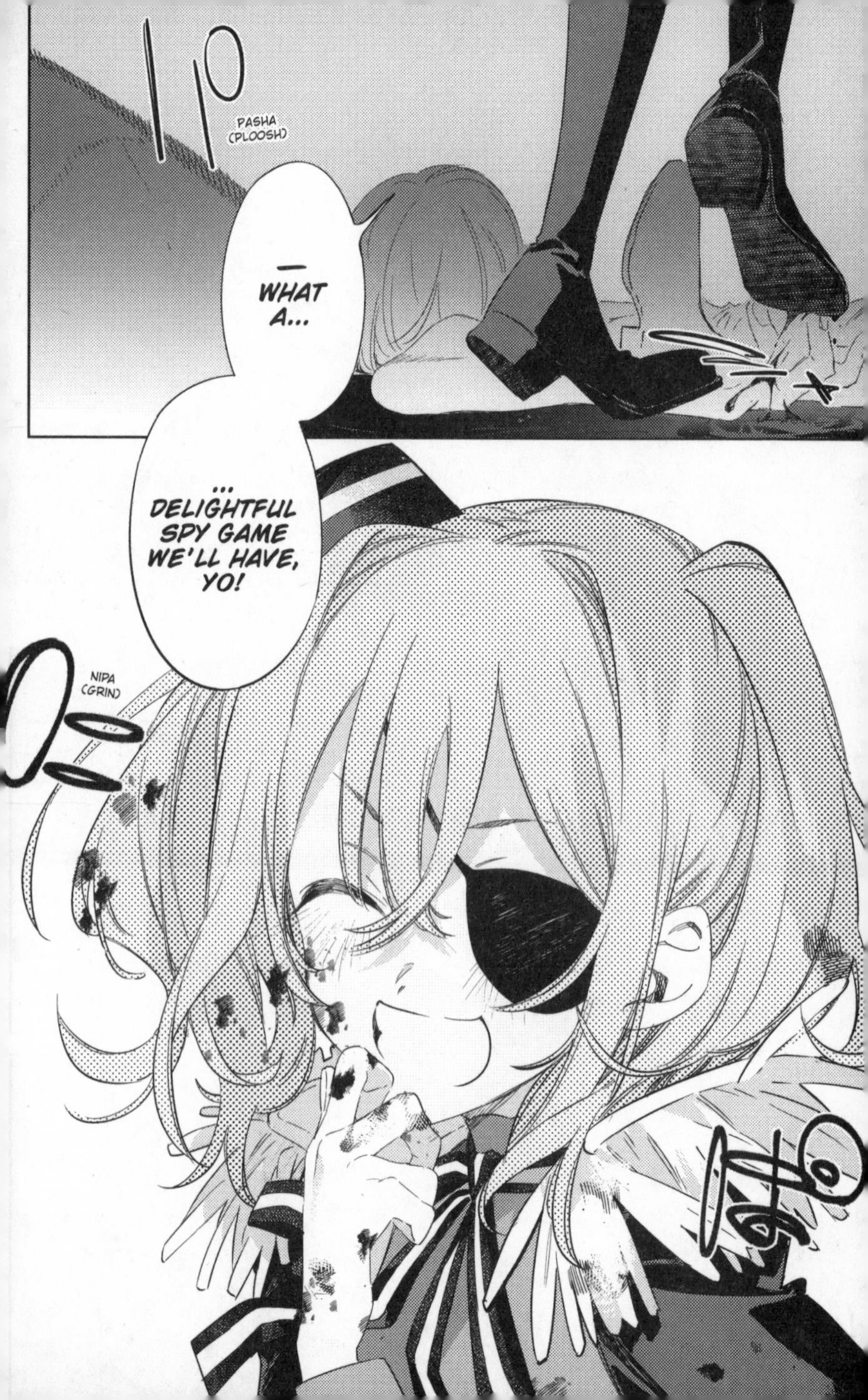
PASHA (PLOOSH)
—WHAT A...
...DELIGHTFUL SPY GAME WE'LL HAVE, YO!
NIPA (GRIN)

Chapter 10

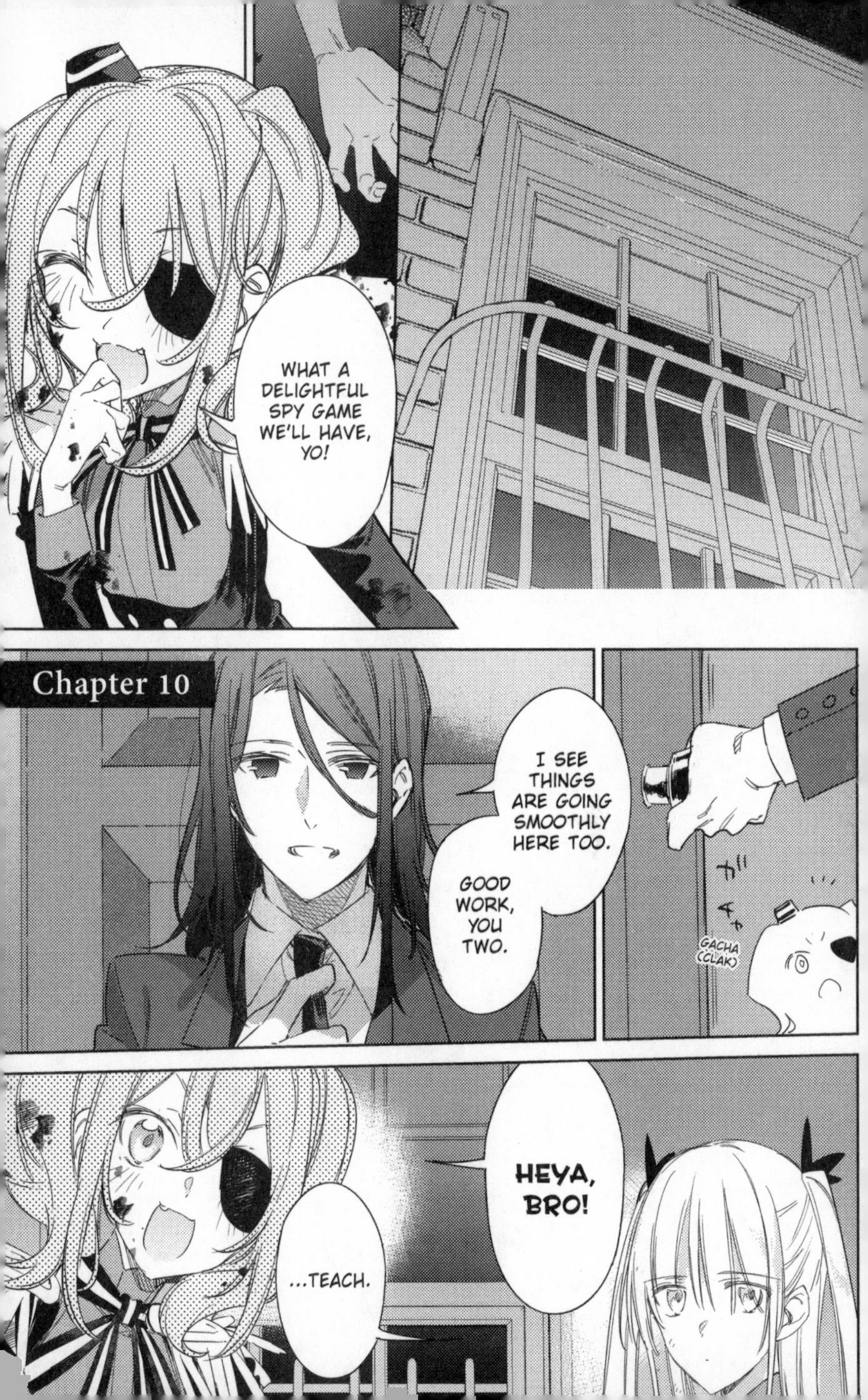
WHAT A DELIGHTFUL SPY GAME WE'LL HAVE, YO!
GACHA (CLAK)
I SEE THINGS ARE GOING SMOOTHLY HERE TOO.
GOOD WORK, YOU TWO.
HEYA, BRO!
...TEACH.

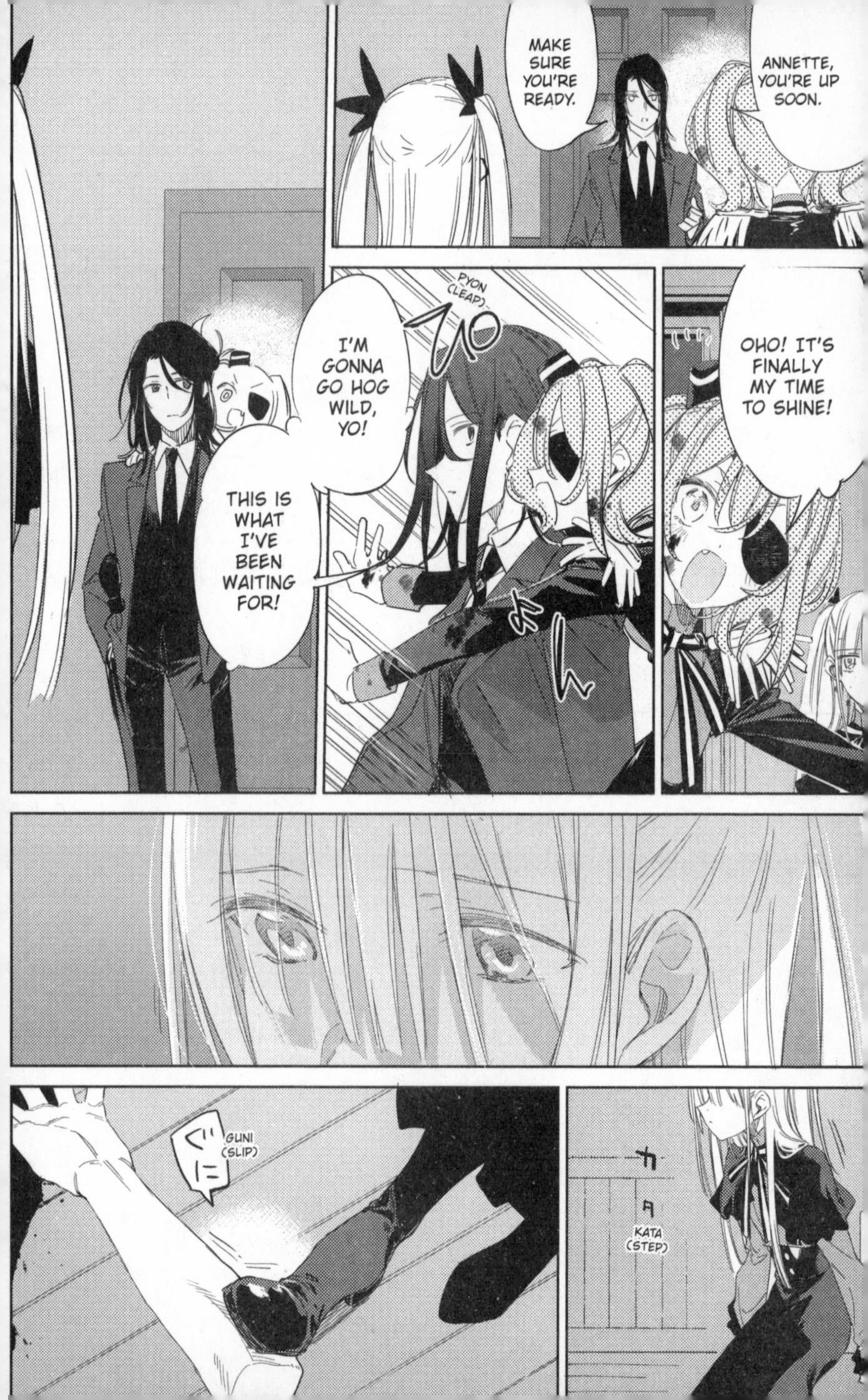
ANNETTE, YOU'RE UP SOON.
MAKE SURE YOU'RE READY.
OHO! IT'S FINALLY MY TIME TO SHINE!
PYON (LEAP)
I'M GONNA GO HOG WILD, YO!
THIS IS WHAT I'VE BEEN WAITING FOR!
KATA (STEP)
GUNI (SLIP)

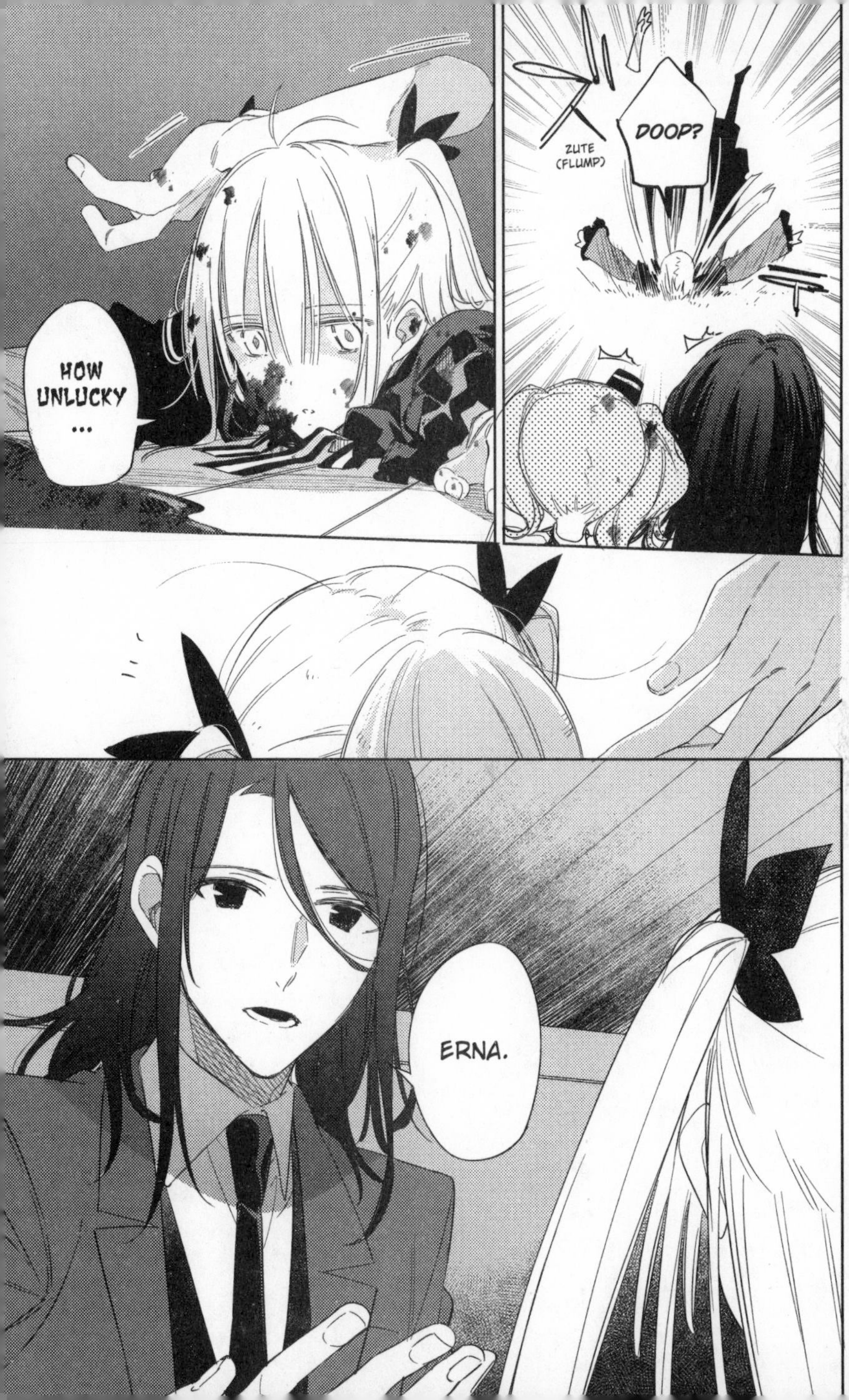
DOOP?
ZUTE (FLUMP)
HOW UNLUCKY ...
ERNA.

Chapter 10 — Departure

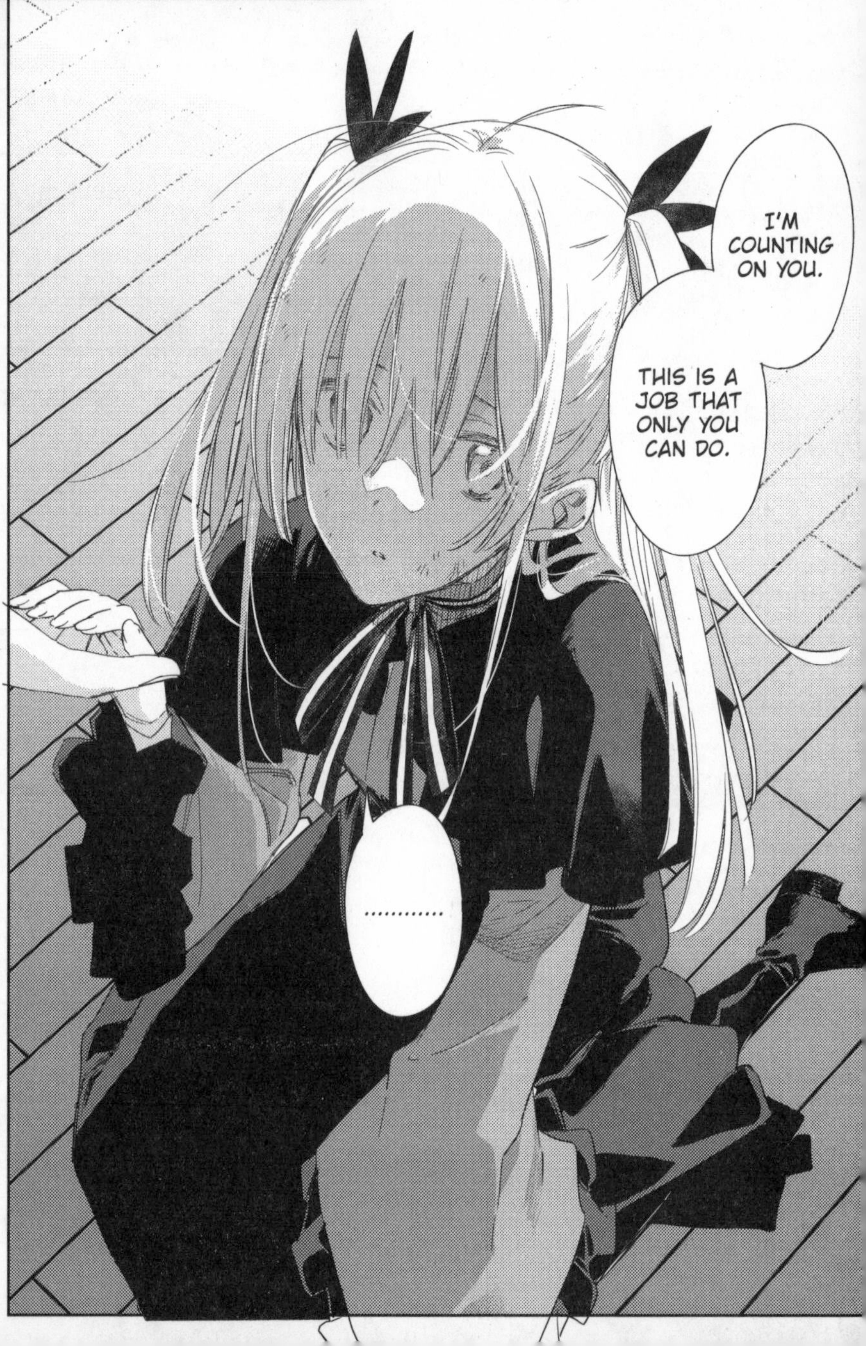
I'M COUNTING ON YOU.
THIS IS A JOB THAT ONLY YOU CAN DO.
....

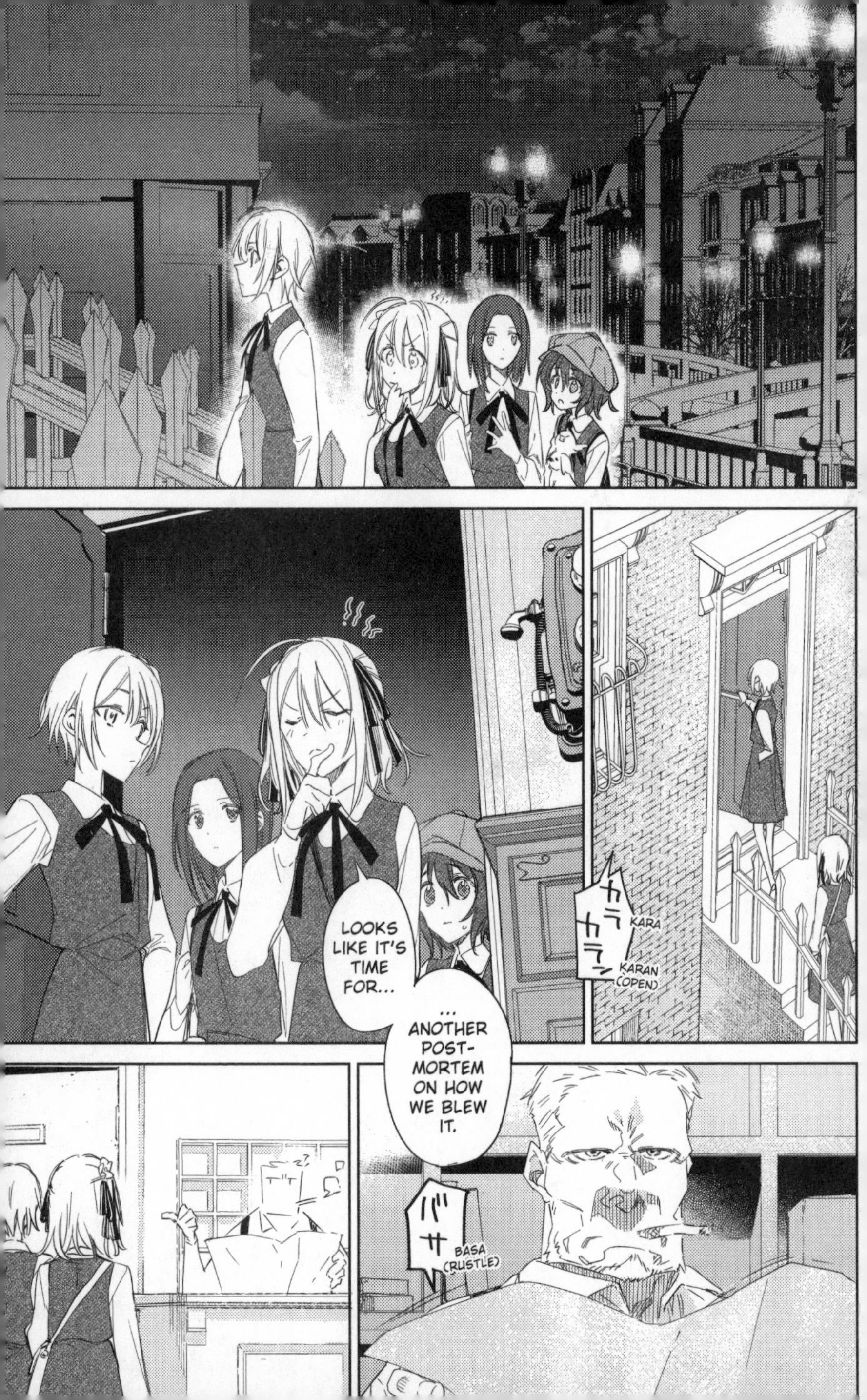

カラ
KARA
カラン
KARAN (OPEN)
LOOKS LIKE IT'S TIME FOR...
... ANOTHER POST-MORTEM ON HOW WE BLEW IT.
バサ
BASA (RUSTLE)

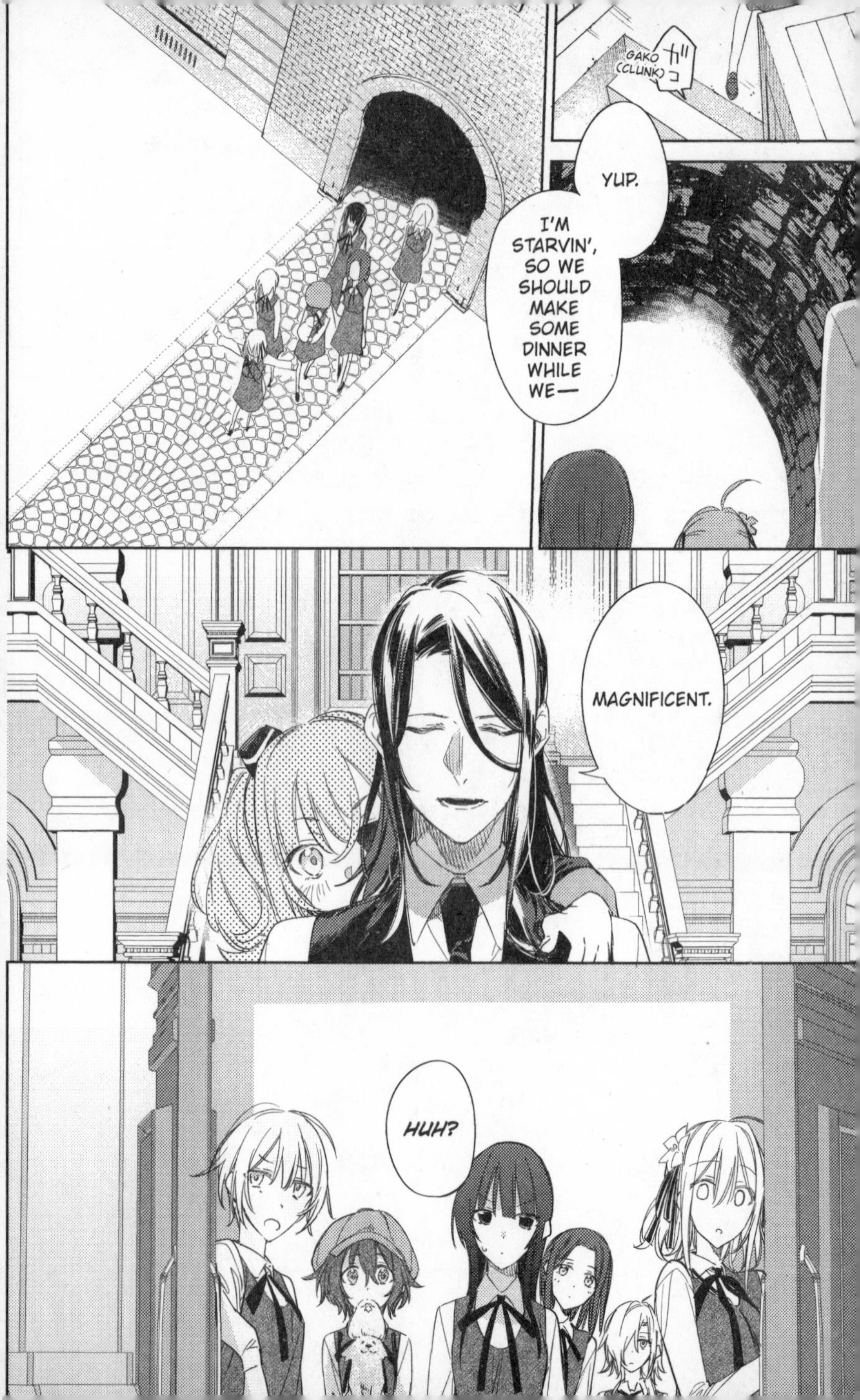
ガコ
GAKO (CLUNK)
YUP.
I'M STARVIN', SO WE SHOULD MAKE SOME DINNER WHILE WE—
MAGNIFICENT.
HUH?

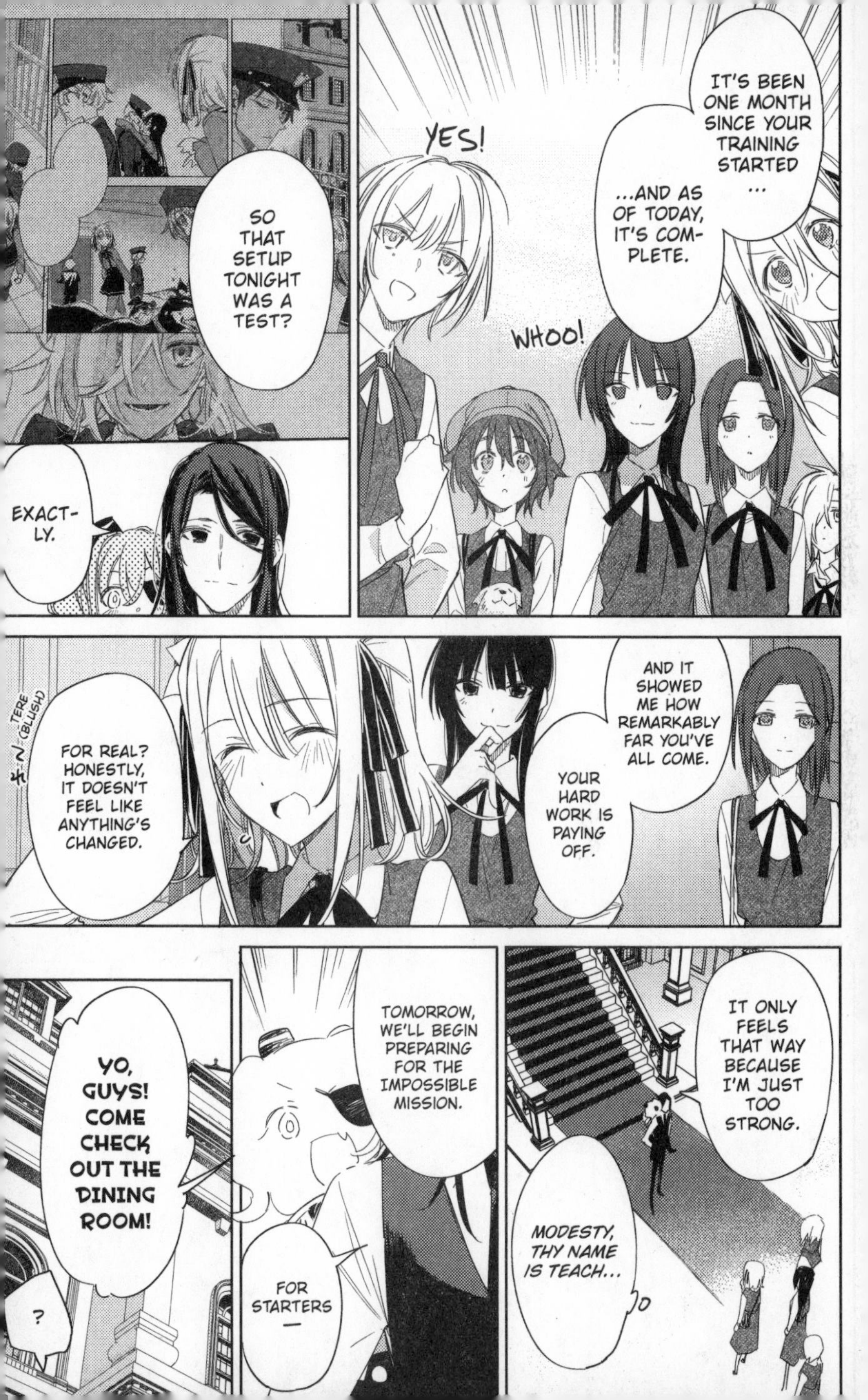
IT'S BEEN ONE MONTH SINCE YOUR TRAINING STARTED ...
...AND AS OF TODAY, IT'S COMPLETE.
YES!
WHOO!
SO THAT SETUP TONIGHT WAS A TEST?
EXACTLY.
AND IT SHOWED ME HOW REMARKABLY FAR YOU'VE ALL COME.
YOUR HARD WORK IS PAYING OFF.
TERE (BLUSH)
FOR REAL? HONESTLY, IT DOESN'T FEEL LIKE ANYTHING'S CHANGED.
IT ONLY FEELS THAT WAY BECAUSE I'M JUST TOO STRONG.
MODESTY, THY NAME IS TEACH...
TOMORROW, WE'LL BEGIN PREPARING FOR THE IMPOSSIBLE MISSION.
FOR STARTERS—
YO, GUYS! COME CHECK OUT THE DINING ROOM!
?

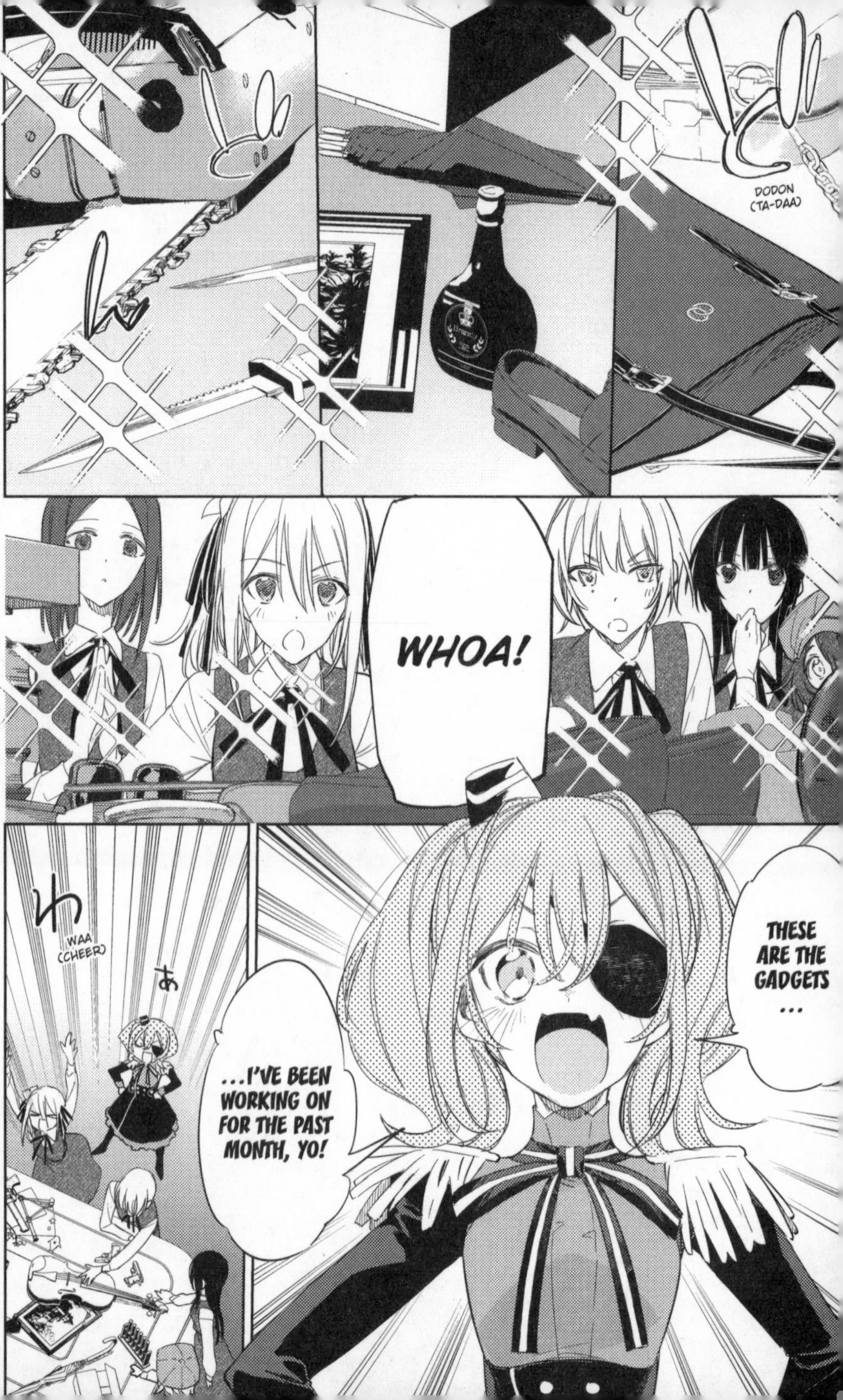

DODON (TA-DAA)
WHOA!
THESE ARE THE GADGETS...
...I'VE BEEN WORKING ON FOR THE PAST MONTH, YO!
WAA (CHEER)

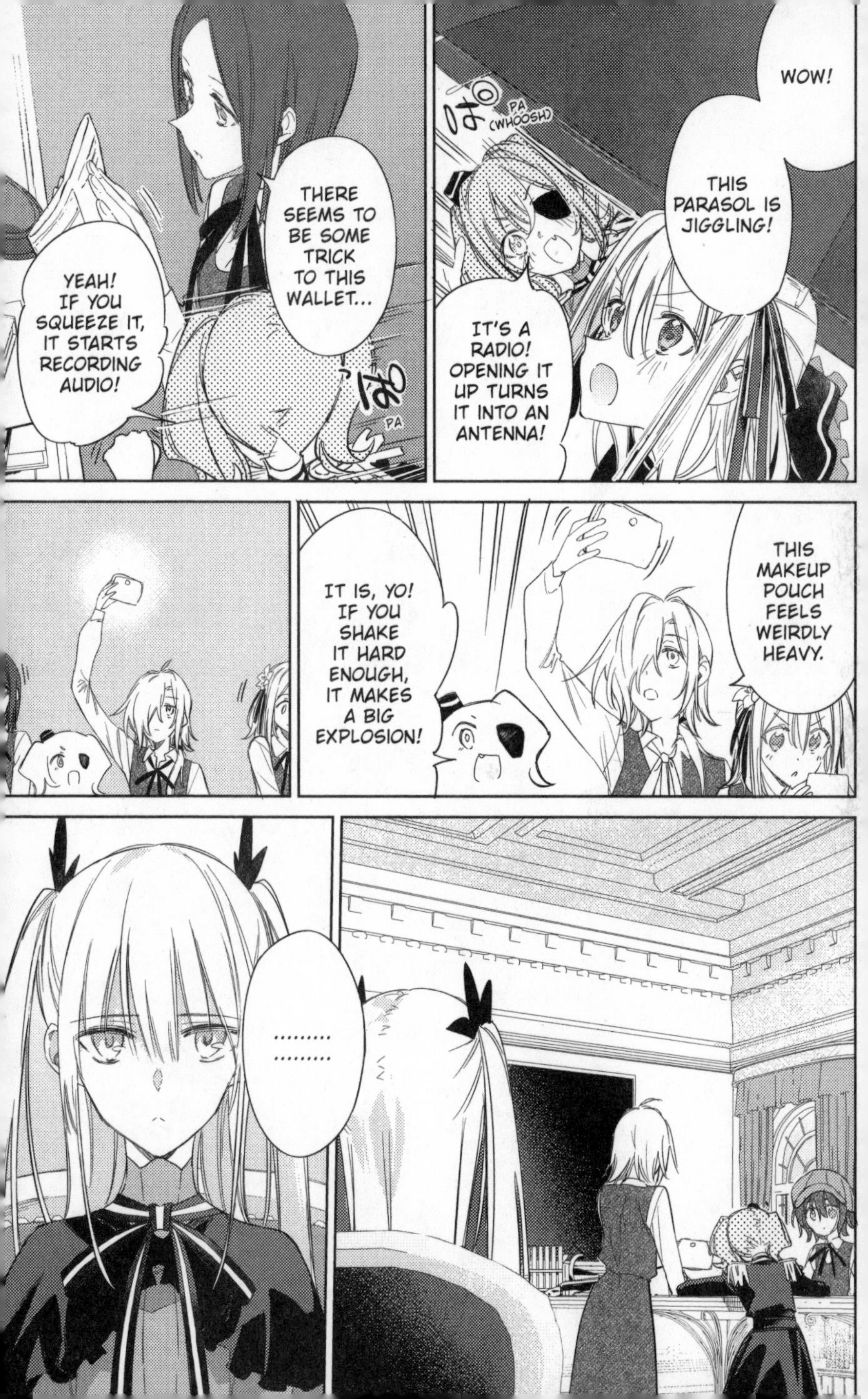
WOW!
THIS PARASOL IS JIGGLING!
PA (WHOOSH)
IT'S A RADIO! OPENING IT UP TURNS IT INTO AN ANTENNA!
THERE SEEMS TO BE SOME TRICK TO THIS WALLET...
PA
YEAH! IF YOU SQUEEZE IT, IT STARTS RECORDING AUDIO!
THIS MAKEUP POUCH FEELS WEIRDLY HEAVY.
IT IS, YO! IF YOU SHAKE IT HARD ENOUGH, IT MAKES A BIG EXPLOSION!
....
....

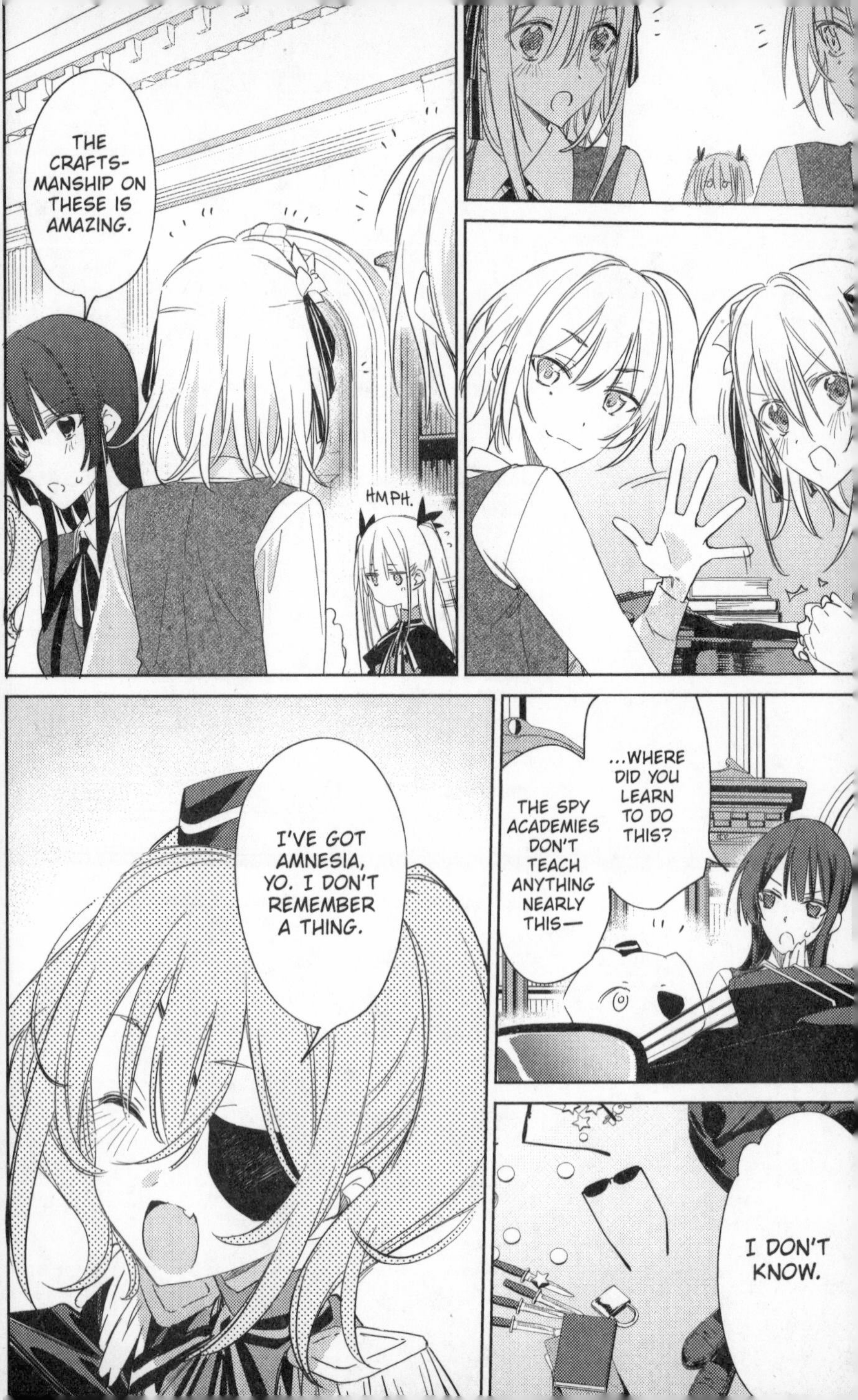
THE CRAFTSMANSHIP ON THESE IS AMAZING.
HMPH.
...WHERE DID YOU LEARN TO DO THIS?
THE SPY ACADEMIES DON'T TEACH ANYTHING NEARLY THIS—
I DON'T KNOW.
I'VE GOT AMNESIA, YO. I DON'T REMEMBER A THING.

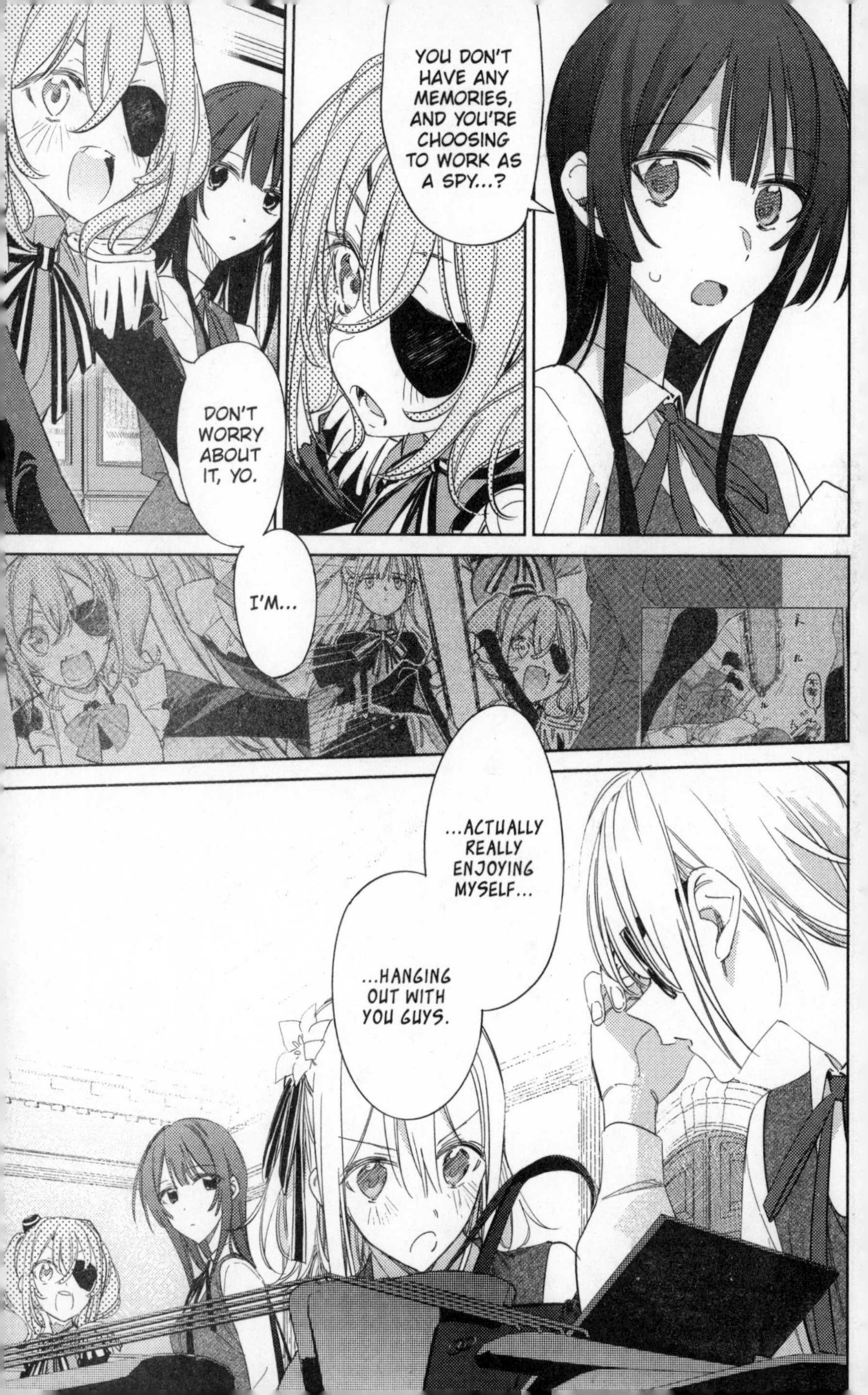
YOU DON'T HAVE ANY MEMORIES, AND YOU'RE CHOOSING TO WORK AS A SPY...?
DON'T WORRY ABOUT IT, YO.
I'M...
...ACTUALLY REALLY ENJOYING MYSELF...
...HANGING OUT WITH YOU GUYS.

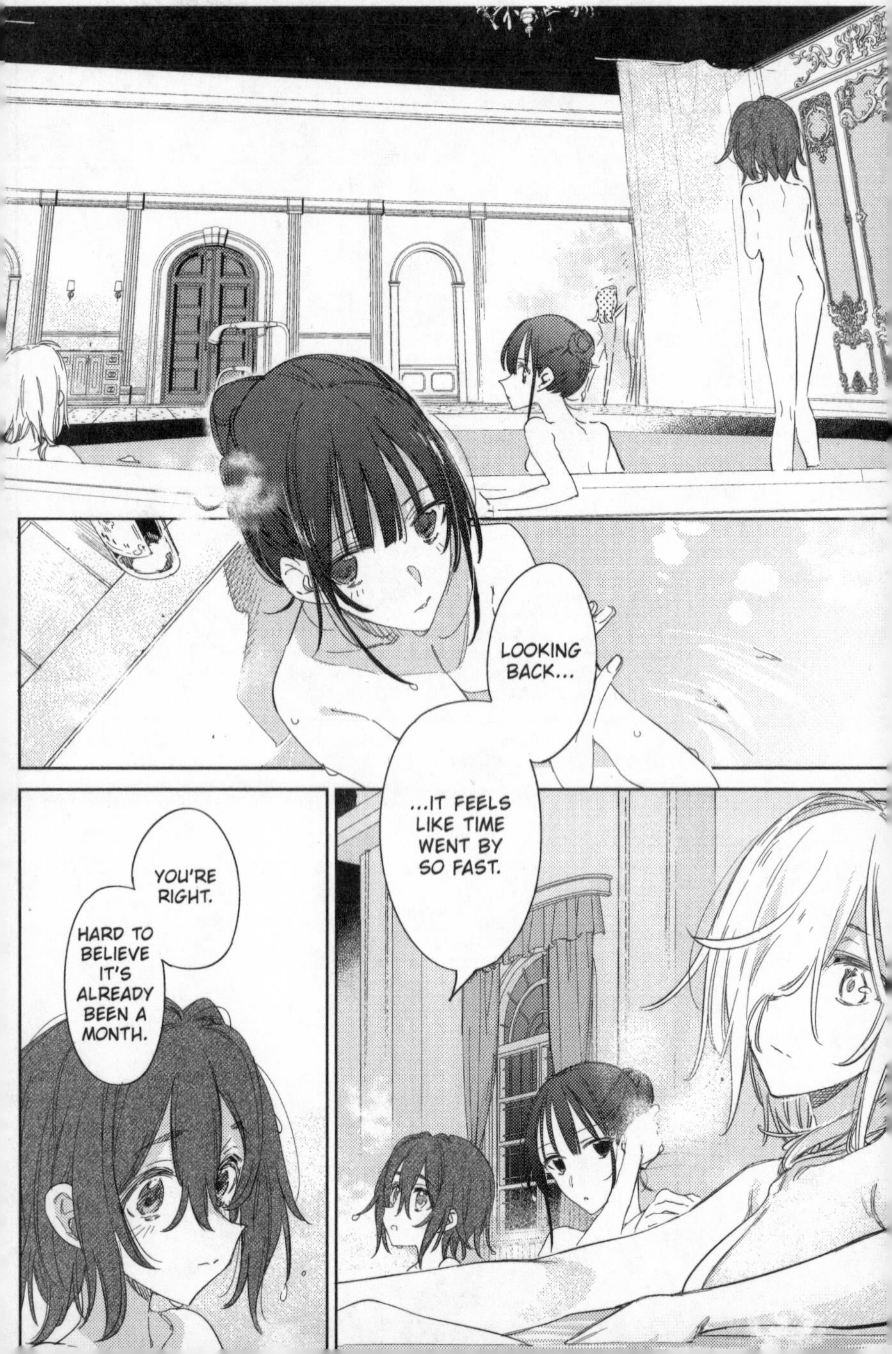
LOOKING BACK...
...IT FEELS LIKE TIME WENT BY SO FAST.
YOU'RE RIGHT.
HARD TO BELIEVE IT'S ALREADY BEEN A MONTH.

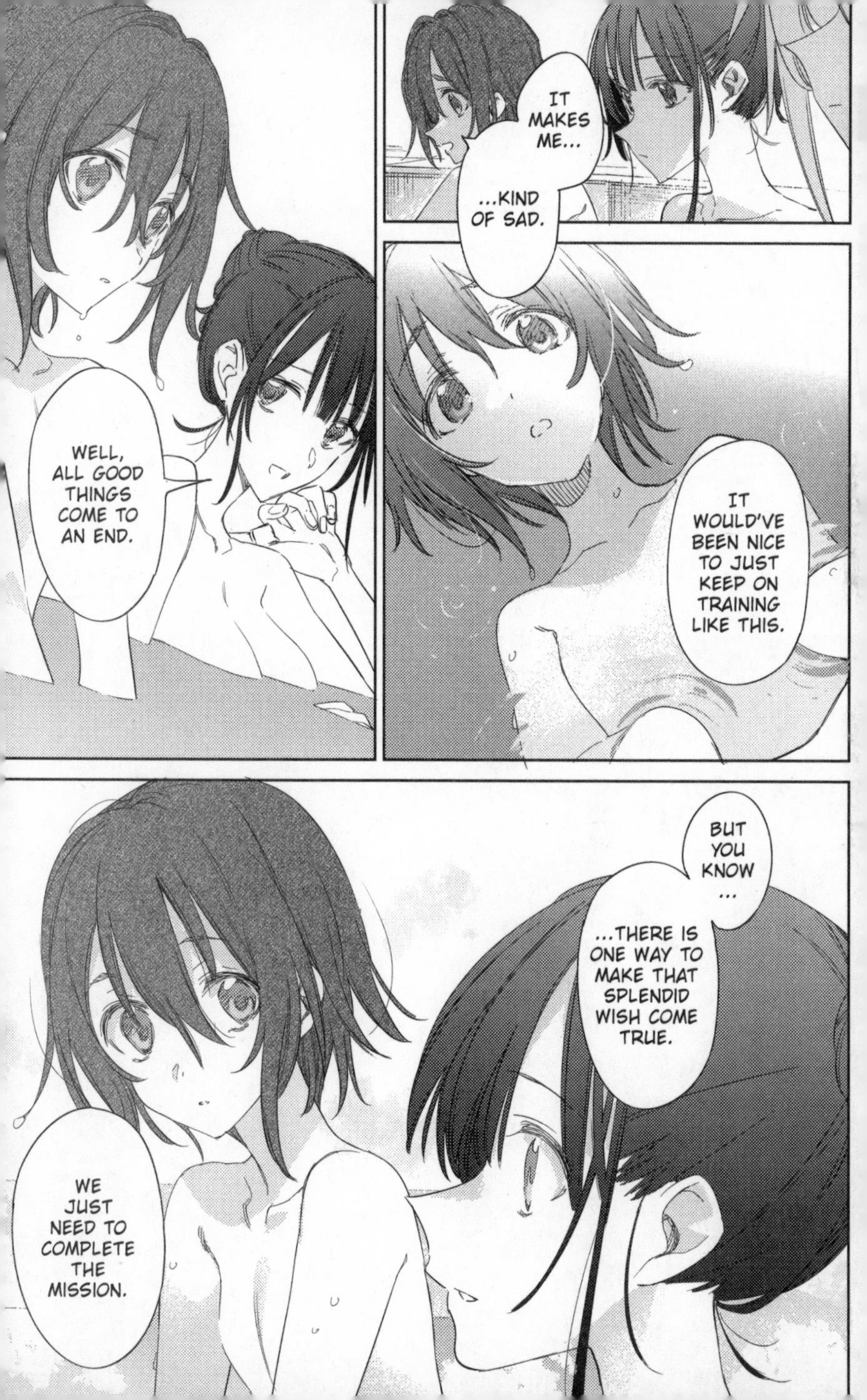
IT MAKES ME...
...KIND OF SAD.
IT WOULD'VE BEEN NICE TO JUST KEEP ON TRAINING LIKE THIS.
WELL, ALL GOOD THINGS COME TO AN END.
BUT YOU KNOW...
...THERE IS ONE WAY TO MAKE THAT SPLENDID WISH COME TRUE.
WE JUST NEED TO COMPLETE THE MISSION.

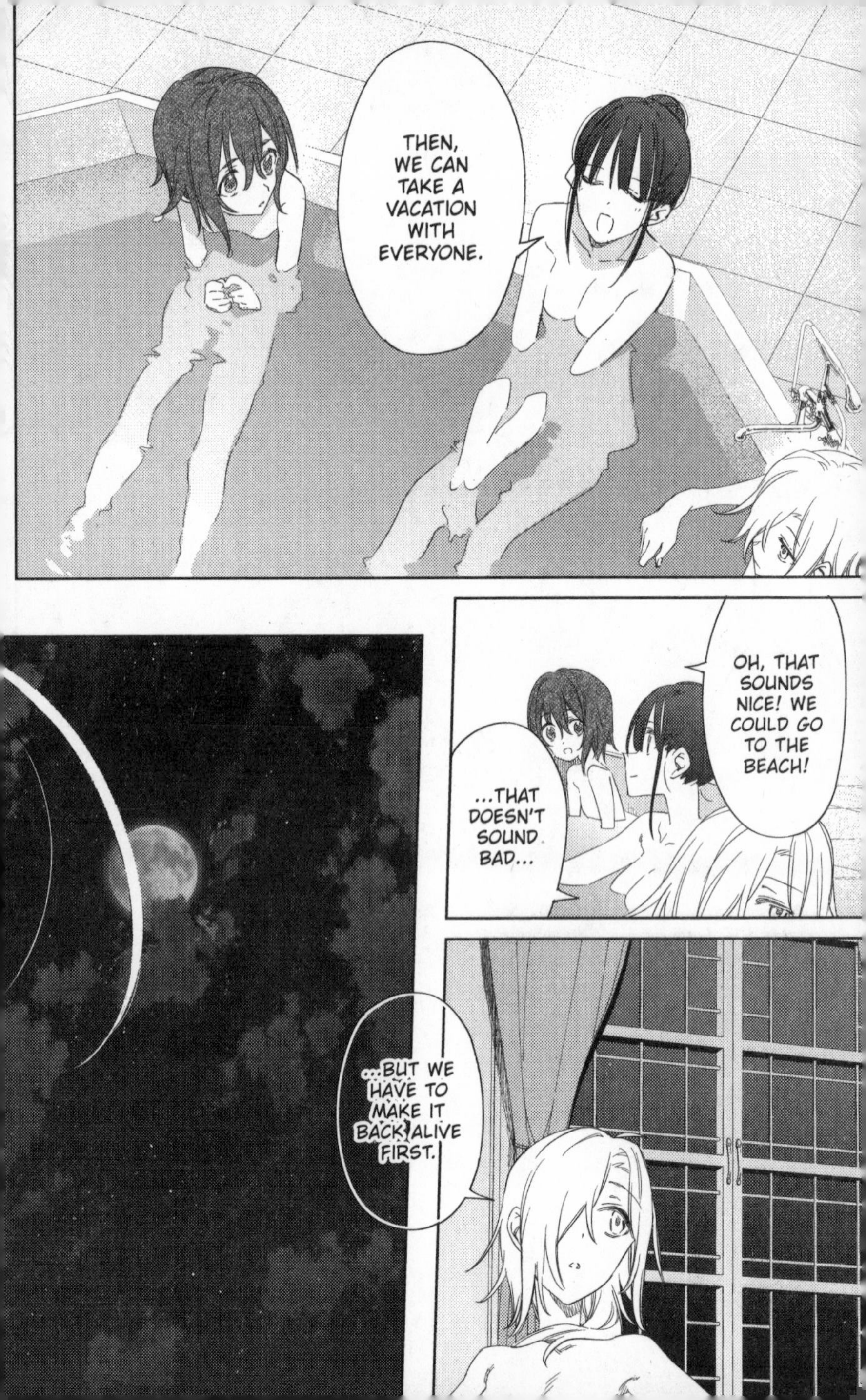
THEN, WE CAN TAKE A VACATION WITH EVERYONE.
OH, THAT SOUNDS NICE! WE COULD GO TO THE BEACH!
...THAT DOESN'T SOUND BAD...
...BUT WE HAVE TO MAKE IT BACK ALIVE FIRST.

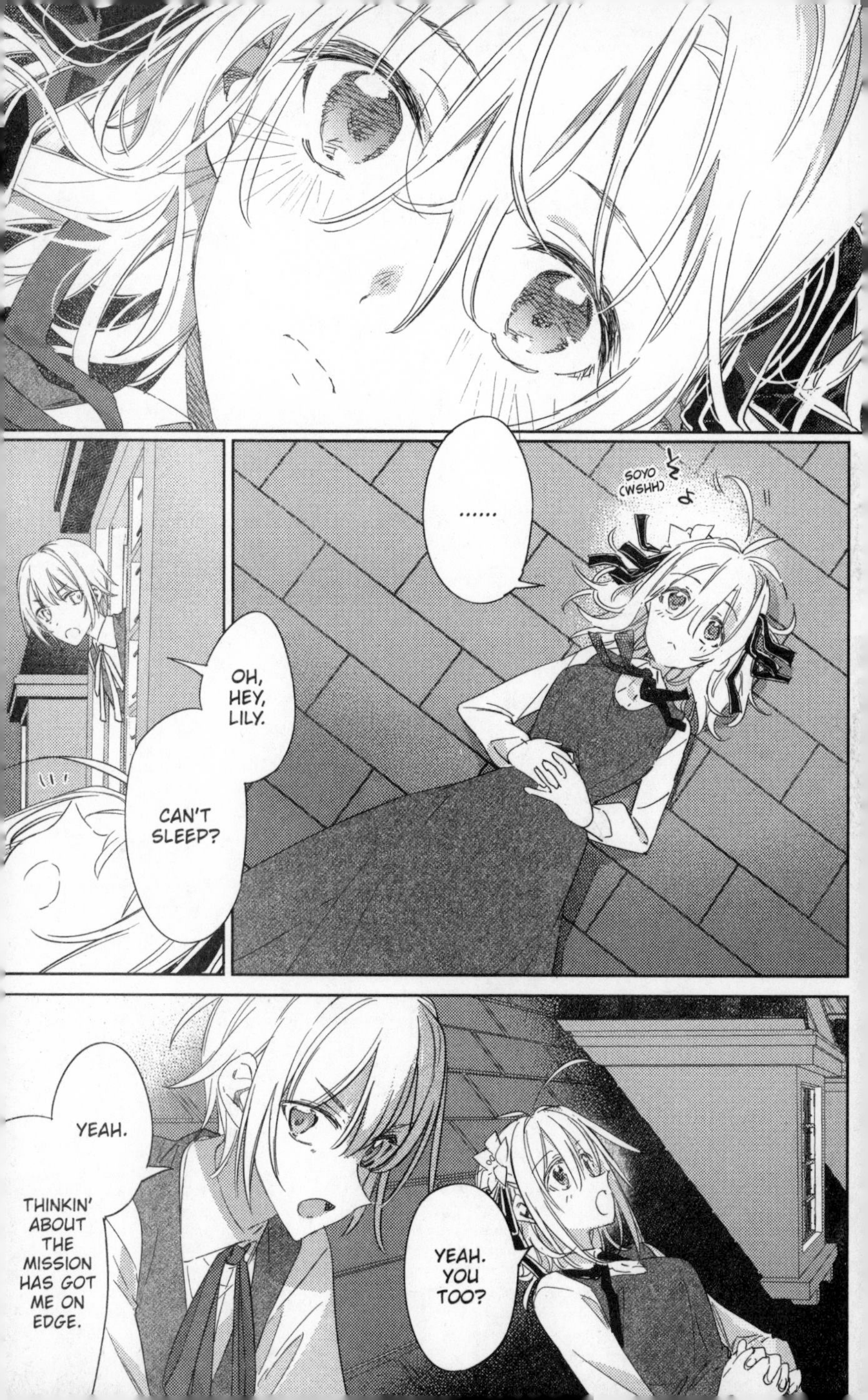
......
SOYO (WSHH)
OH, HEY, LILY.
CAN'T SLEEP?
YEAH. YOU TOO?
YEAH.
THINKIN' ABOUT THE MISSION HAS GOT ME ON EDGE.

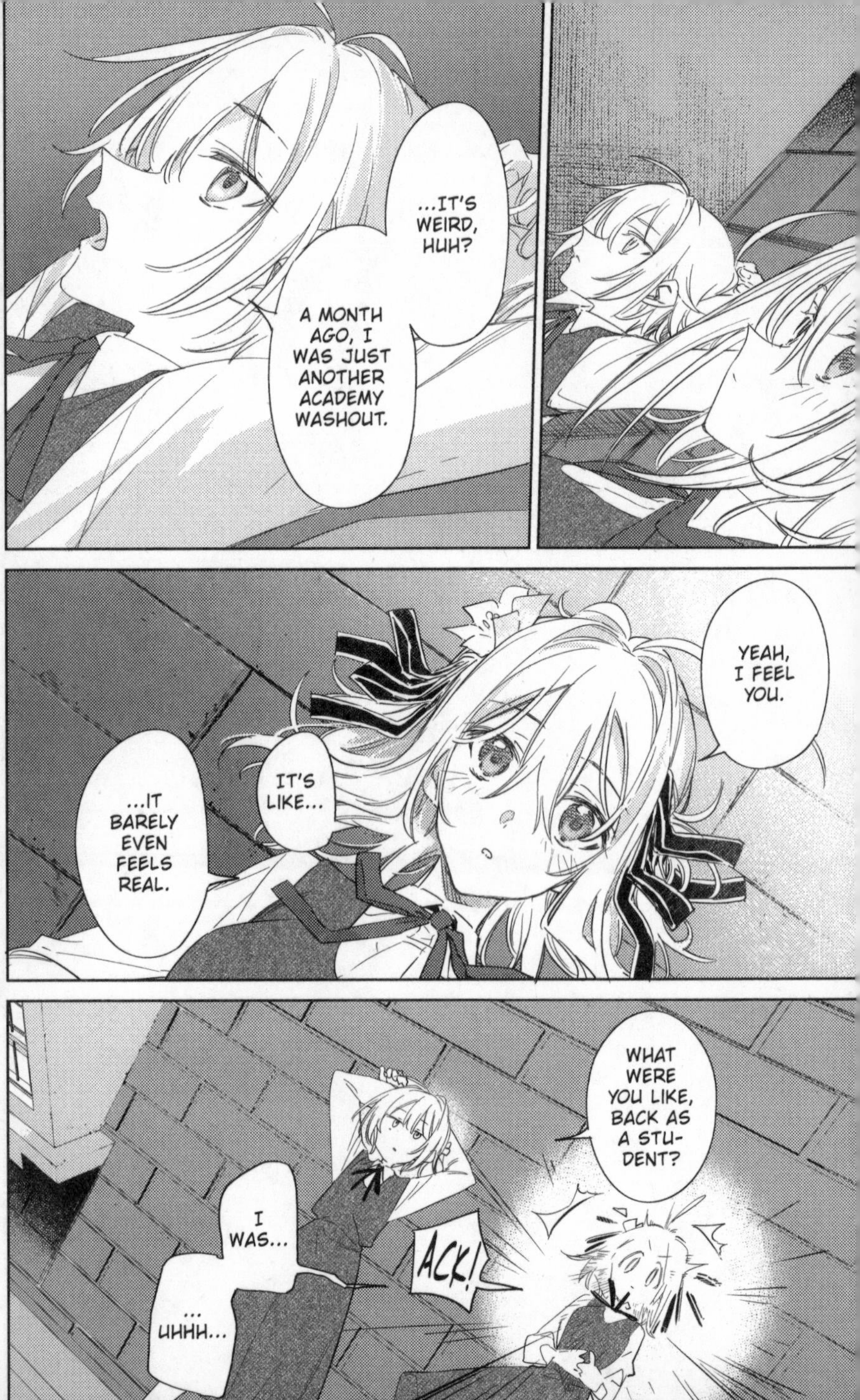
...IT'S WEIRD, HUH?
A MONTH AGO, I WAS JUST ANOTHER ACADEMY WASHOUT.
YEAH, I FEEL YOU.
IT'S LIKE...
...IT BARELY EVEN FEELS REAL.
WHAT WERE YOU LIKE, BACK AS A STU-DENT?
ACK!
I WAS...
... UHHH...

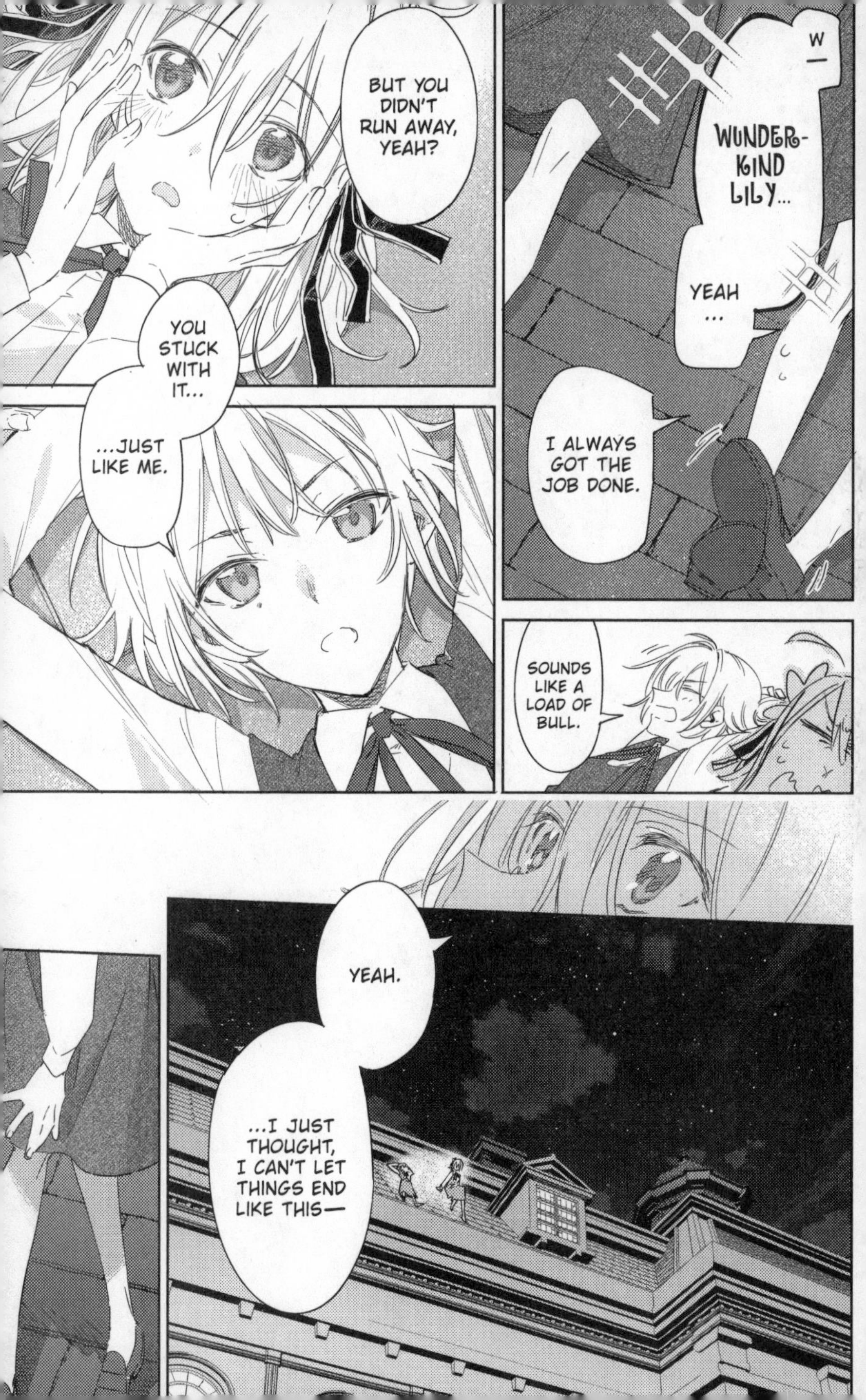
W—
WUNDER-KIND LILY...
YEAH...
I ALWAYS GOT THE JOB DONE.
SOUNDS LIKE A LOAD OF BULL.
BUT YOU DIDN'T RUN AWAY, YEAH?
YOU STUCK WITH IT...
...JUST LIKE ME.
YEAH.
...I JUST THOUGHT, I CAN'T LET THINGS END LIKE THIS—

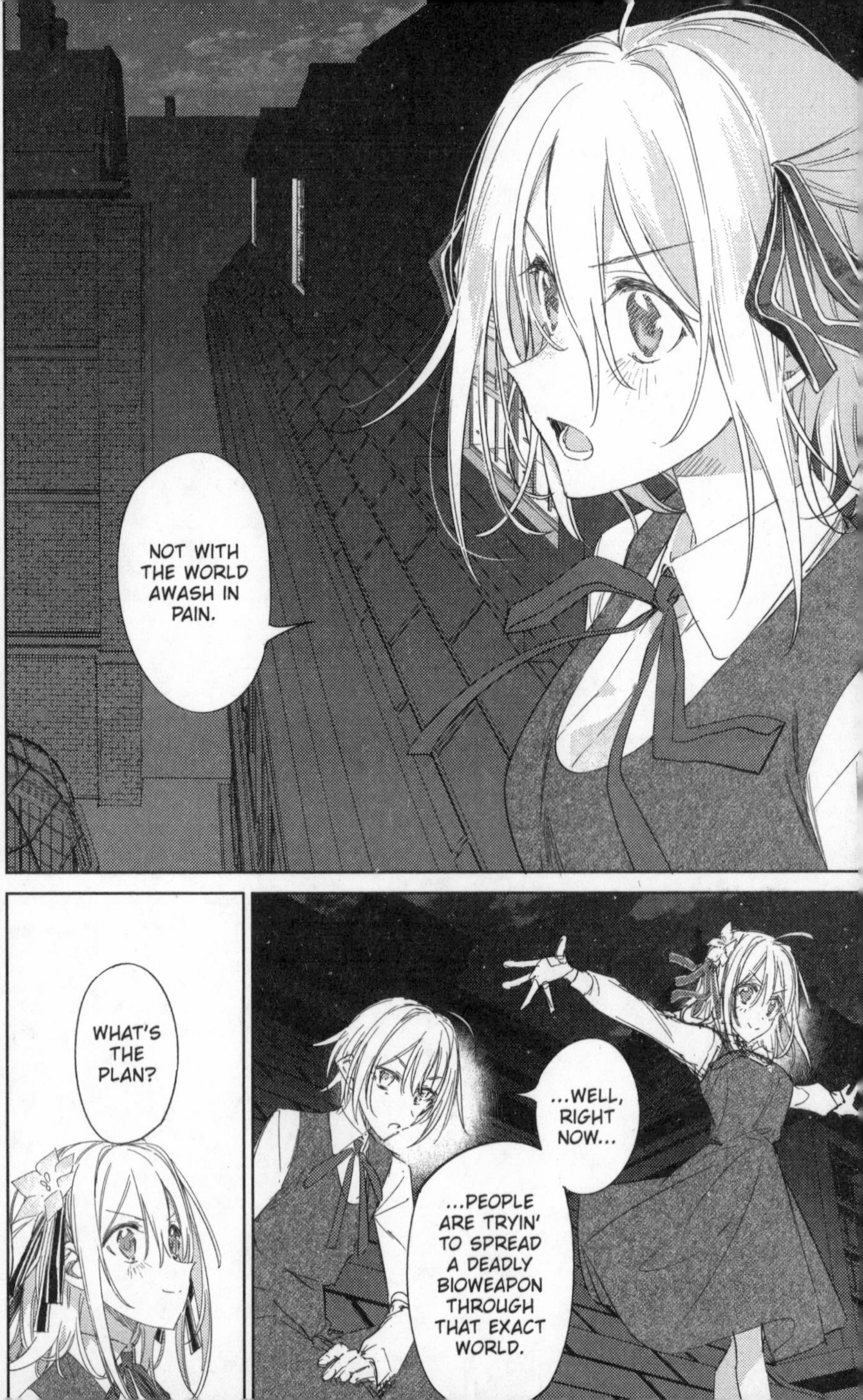
NOT WITH THE WORLD AWASH IN PAIN.
...WELL, RIGHT NOW...
...PEOPLE ARE TRYIN' TO SPREAD A DEADLY BIOWEAPON THROUGH THAT EXACT WORLD.
WHAT'S THE PLAN?

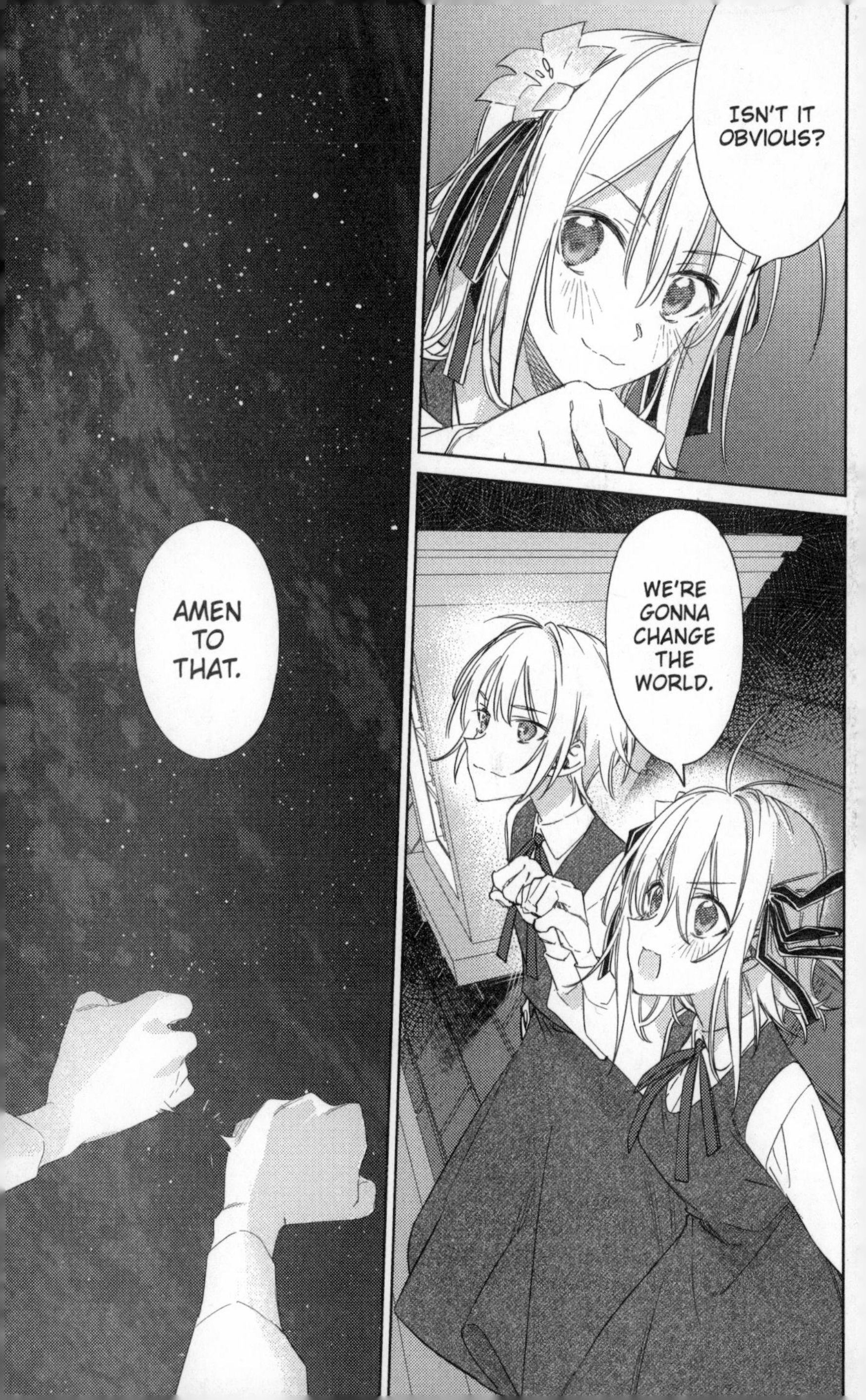
ISN'T IT OBVIOUS?
WE'RE GONNA CHANGE THE WORLD.
AMEN TO THAT.

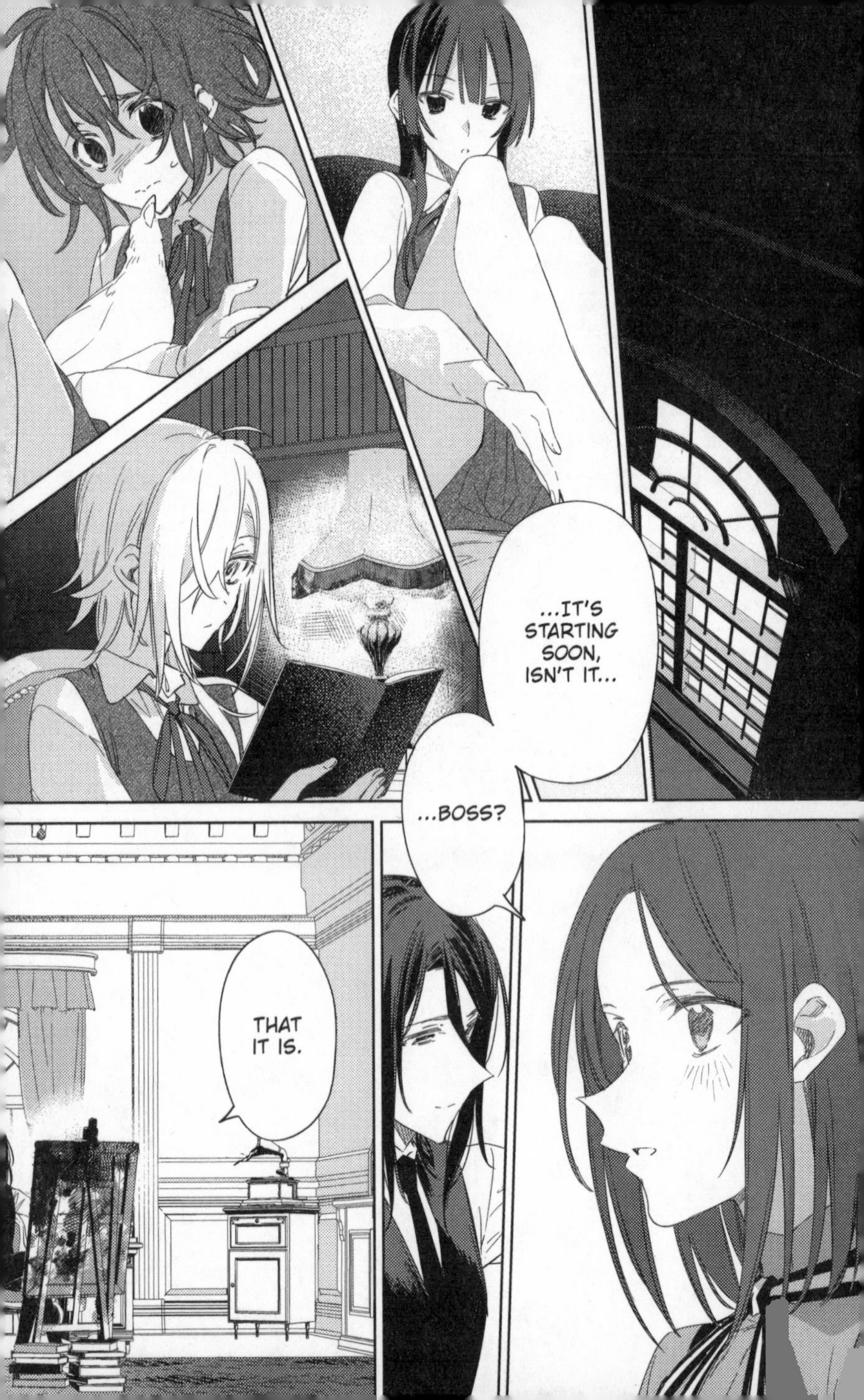
...IT'S STARTING SOON, ISN'T IT...
...BOSS?
THAT IT IS.

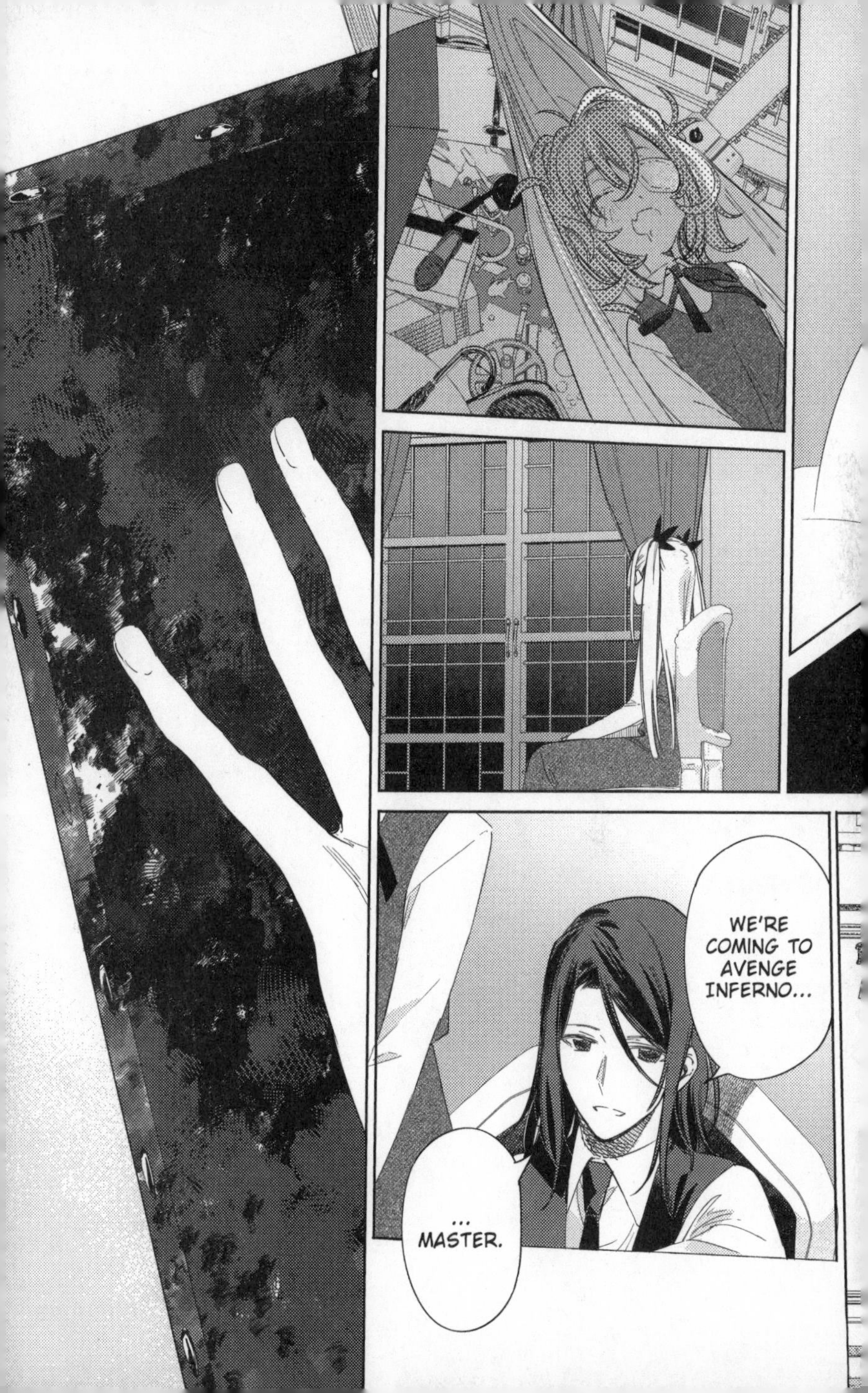
WE'RE COMING TO AVENGE INFERNO...
... MASTER.

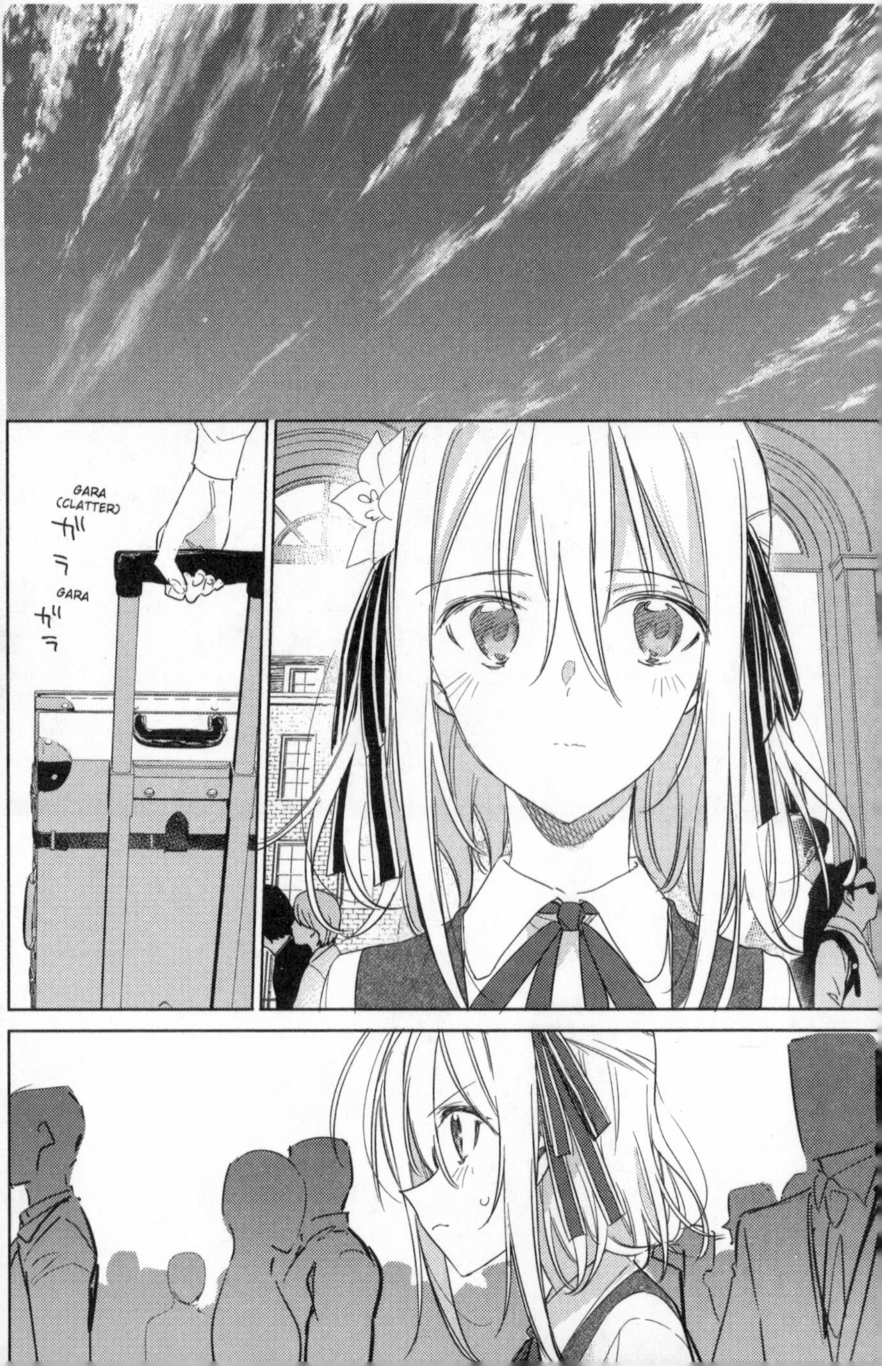
GARA (CLATTER)
ガラ
GARA
ガラ

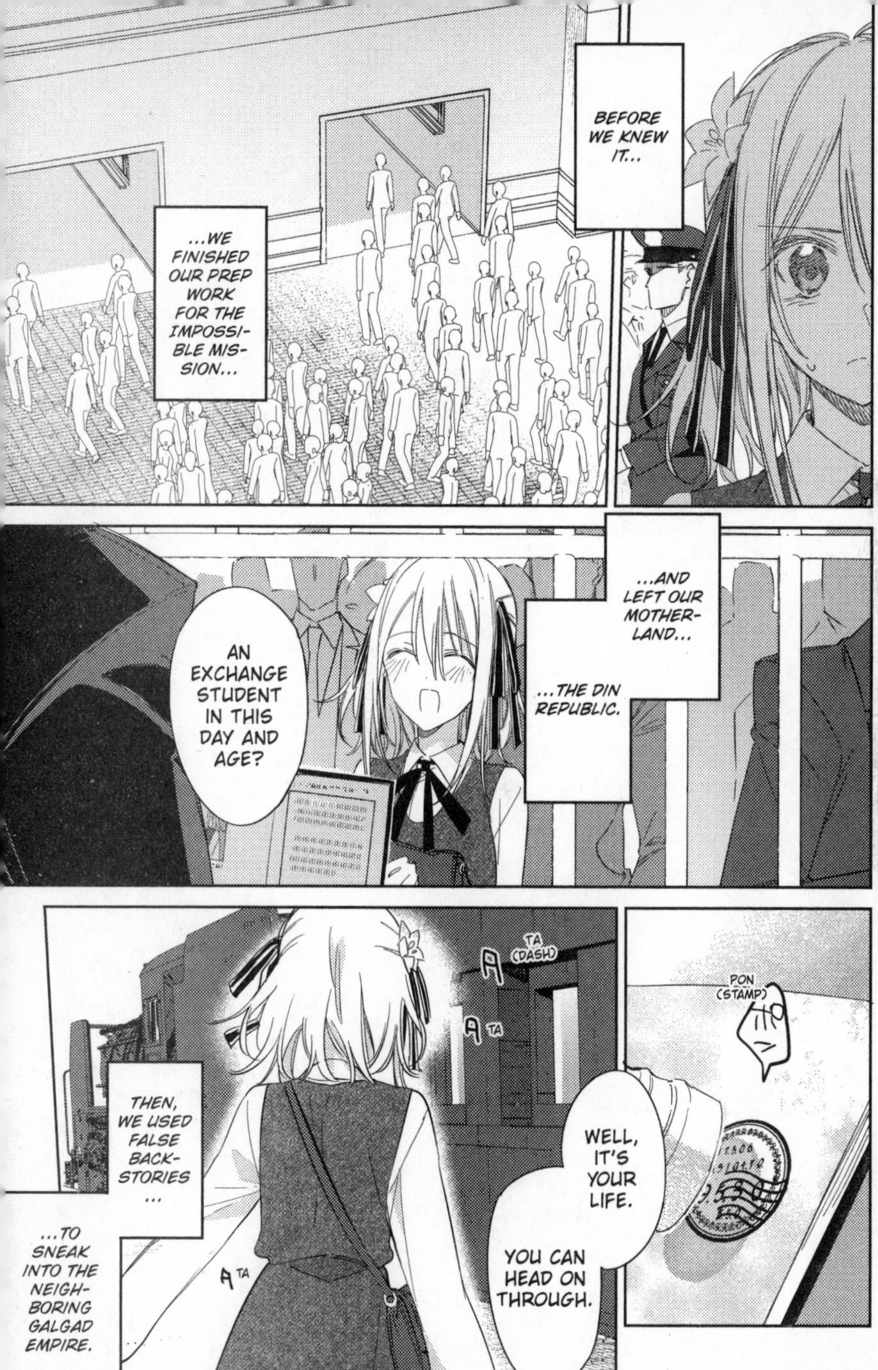
BEFORE WE KNEW IT...
...WE FINISHED OUR PREP WORK FOR THE IMPOSSIBLE MISSION...
...AND LEFT OUR MOTHERLAND...
...THE DIN REPUBLIC.
AN EXCHANGE STUDENT IN THIS DAY AND AGE?
PON (STAMP)
WELL, IT'S YOUR LIFE.
YOU CAN HEAD ON THROUGH.
TA (DASH)
TA
THEN, WE USED FALSE BACKSTORIES...
...TO SNEAK INTO THE NEIGHBORING GALGAD EMPIRE.
TA

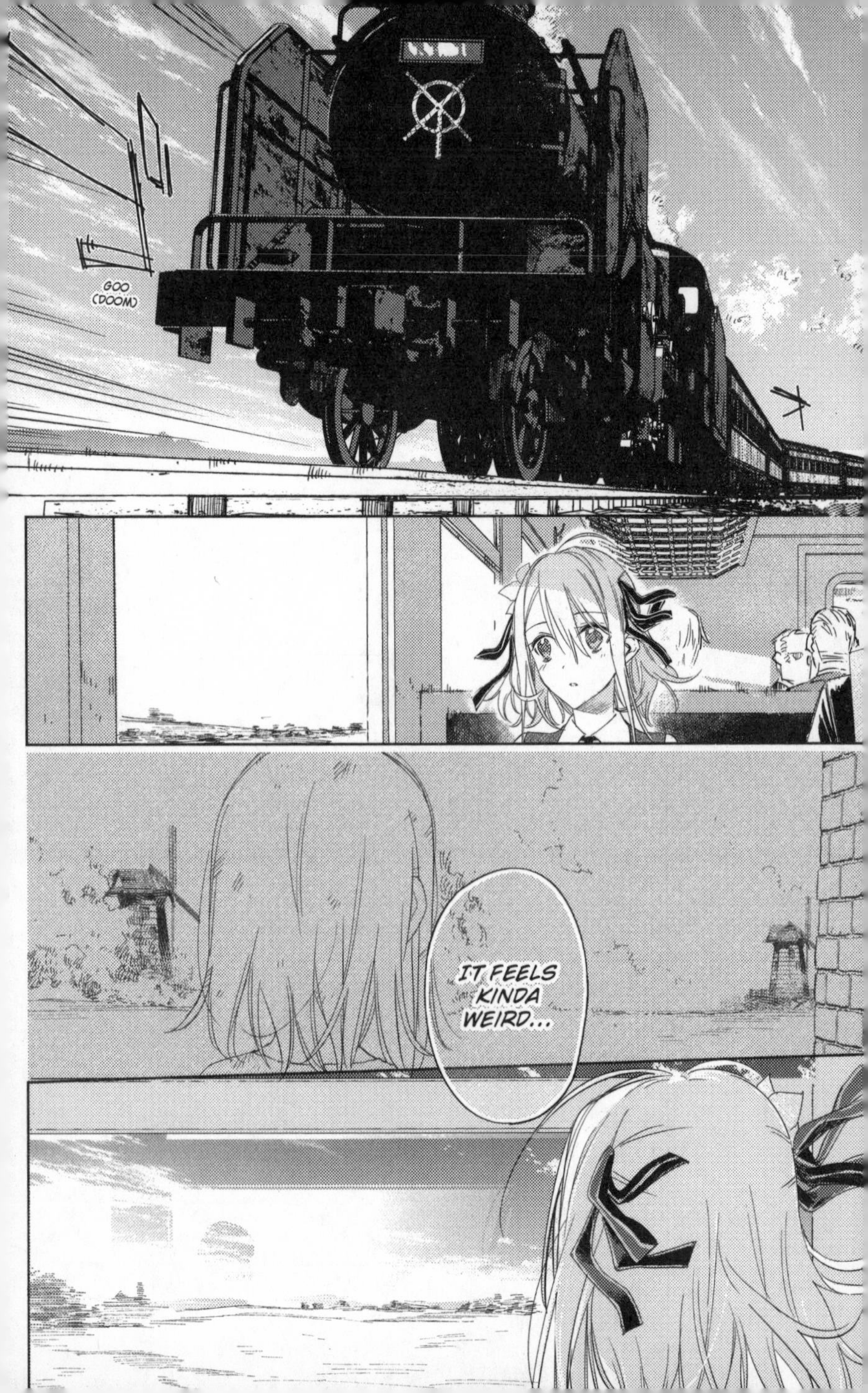
GOO
(DOOM)
IT FEELS KINDA WEIRD...

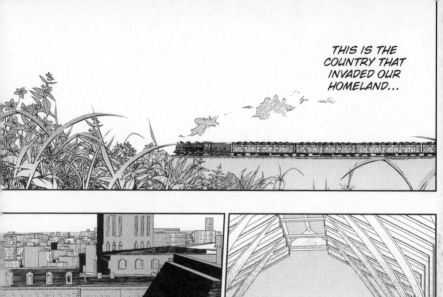

THIS IS THE
COUNTRY THAT
INVADED OUR
HOMELAND...

Darton

Capital
of the
Galgad
Empire

ギュ
(SQUEEZE)

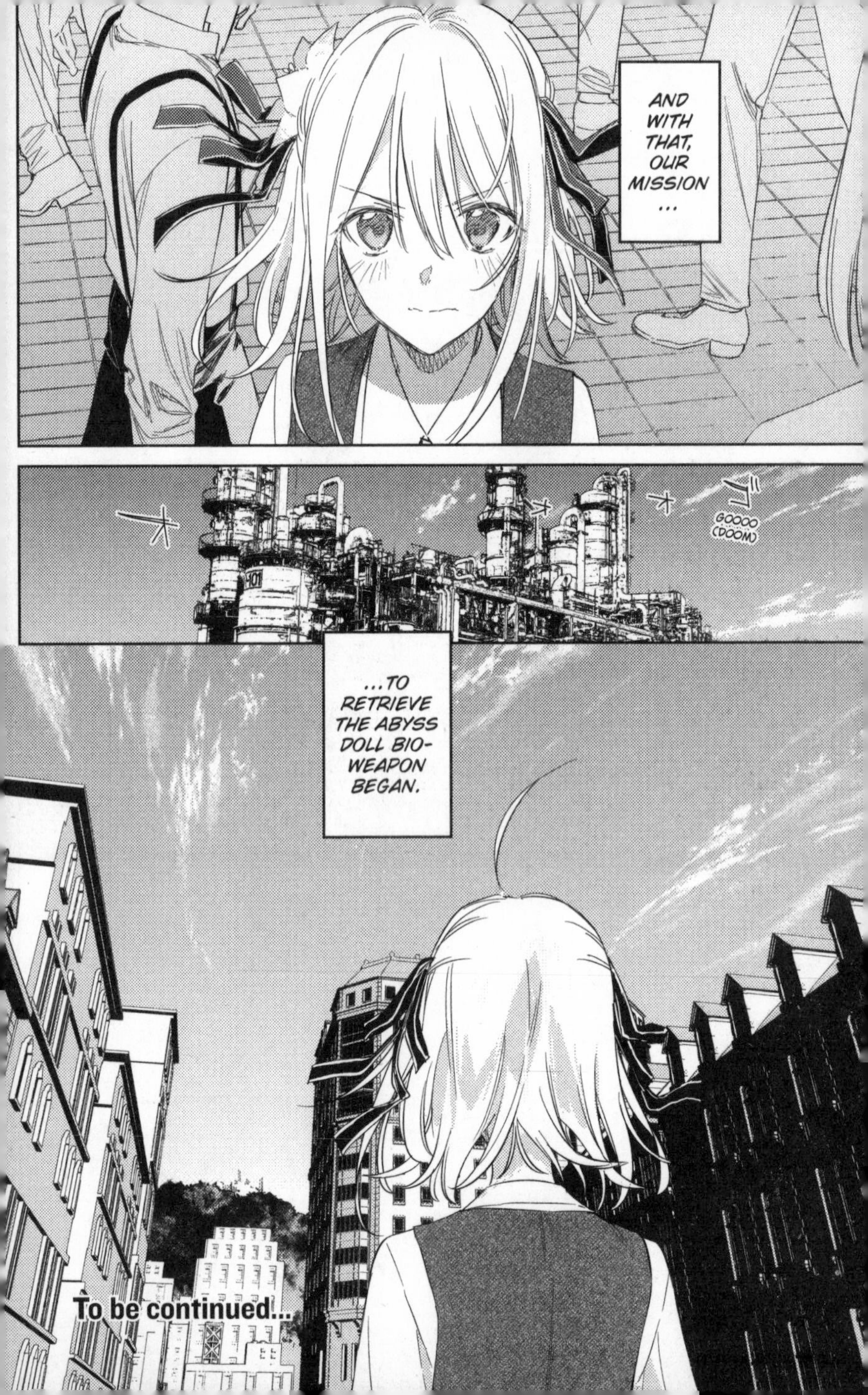
AND WITH THAT, OUR MISSION ...
GOOOO (DOOM)
...TO RETRIEVE THE ABYSS DOLL BIO-WEAPON BEGAN.
To be continued...

SPY
CLASSROOM

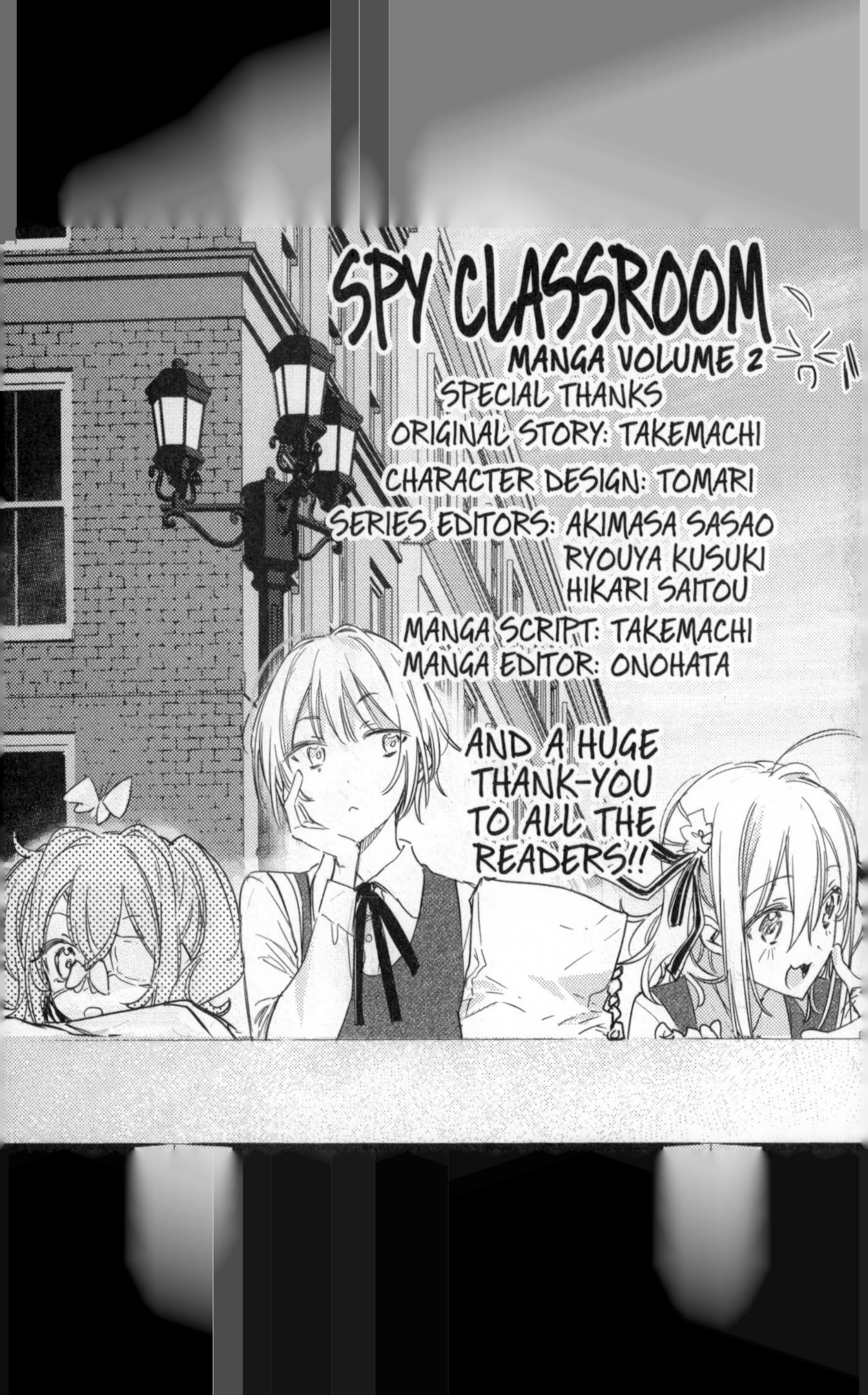
SPY CLASSROOM
MANGA VOLUME 2
SPECIAL THANKS
ORIGINAL STORY: TAKEMACHI
CHARACTER DESIGN: TOMARI
SERIES EDITORS: AKIMASA SASAO
RYOUYA KUSUKI
HIKARI SAITOU
MANGA SCRIPT: TAKEMACHI
MANGA EDITOR: ONOHATA
AND A HUGE THANK-YOU TO ALL THE READERS!!

The Detective Is Already Dead

When the story begins without its hero

Kimihiko Kimizuka has always been a magnet for trouble and intrigue. For as long as he can remember, he's been stumbling across murder scenes or receiving mysterious attaché cases to transport. When he met Siesta, a brilliant detective fighting a secret war against an organization of pseudohumans, he couldn't resist the call to become her assistant and join her on an epic journey across the world.

...Until a year ago, that is. Now he's returned to a relatively normal and tepid life, knowing the adventure must be over. After all, the detective is already dead.

Volume 2 available wherever books are sold!

 YEN ON

TANTEI HA MO, SHINDEIRU. Vol. 1
©nigozyu 2019
Illustration: Umibouzu
KADOKAWA CORPORATION

COMBATANTS WILL BE DISPATCHED!

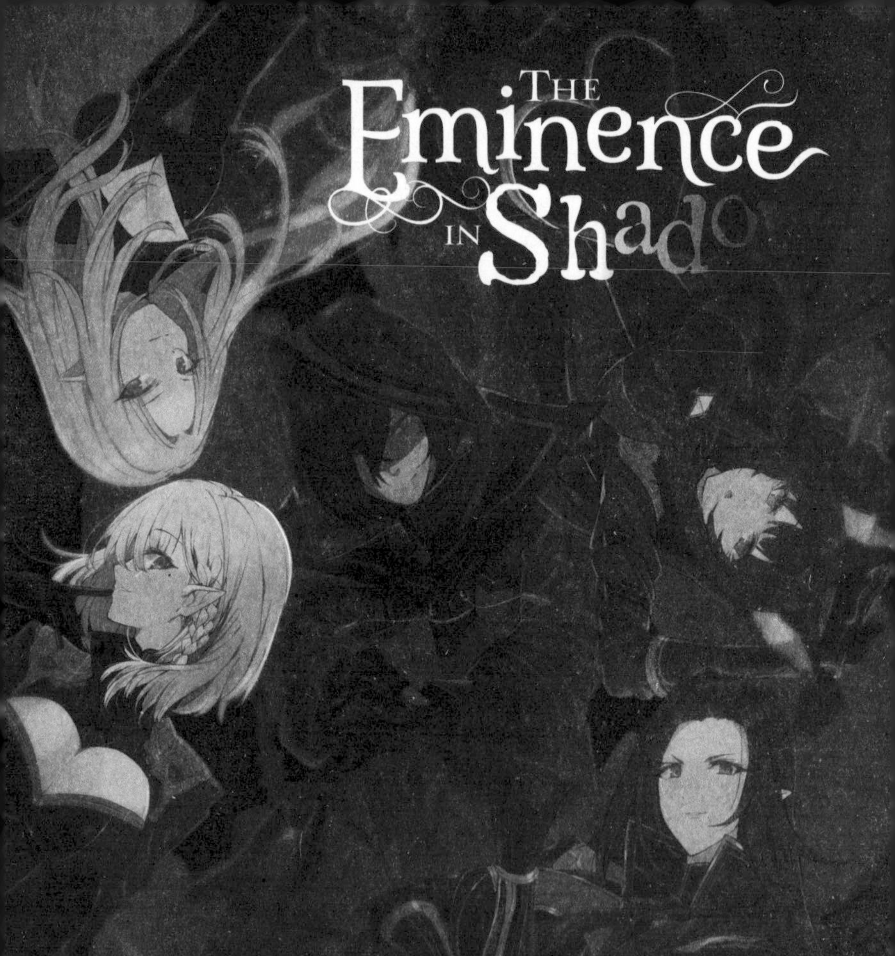
THE
Eminence
IN Shado

So I'm a Spider, So What?

MANGA VOL. 1-10

LIGHT NOVEL VOL. 1-13

AVAILABLE NOW!

I'M GONNA SURVIVE—JUST WATCH ME!

I was your average, everyday high school girl, but now I've been reborn in a magical world...as a spider?! How am I supposed to survive in this big, scary dungeon as one of the weakest monsters? I gotta figure out the rules to this QUICK, or I'll be kissing my short second life good-bye...

YOU CAN ALSO KEEP UP WITH THE MANGA SIMUL-PUB EVERY MONTH ONLINE!

Yen Press
YenPress.com

YEN ON

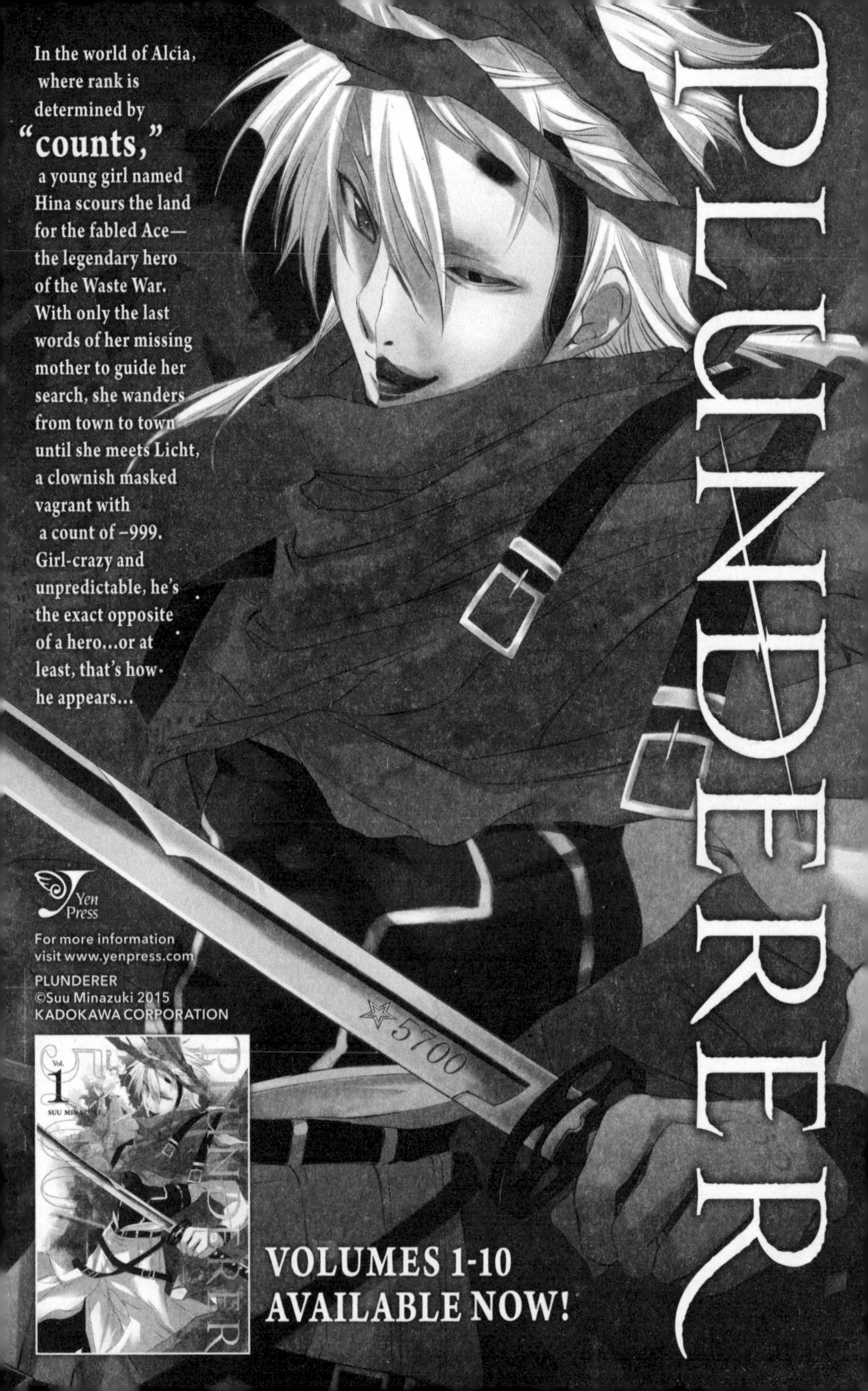
PLUNDERER
In the world of Alcia, where rank is determined by
"counts,"
a young girl named Hina scours the land for the fabled Ace—the legendary hero of the Waste War. With only the last words of her missing mother to guide her search, she wanders from town to town until she meets Licht, a clownish masked vagrant with a count of −999. Girl-crazy and unpredictable, he's the exact opposite of a hero...or at least, that's how he appears...
Yen Press
For more information visit www.yenpress.com
PLUNDERER
©Suu Minazuki 2015
KADOKAWA CORPORATION
5700
Vol. 1
VOLUMES 1-10
AVAILABLE NOW!

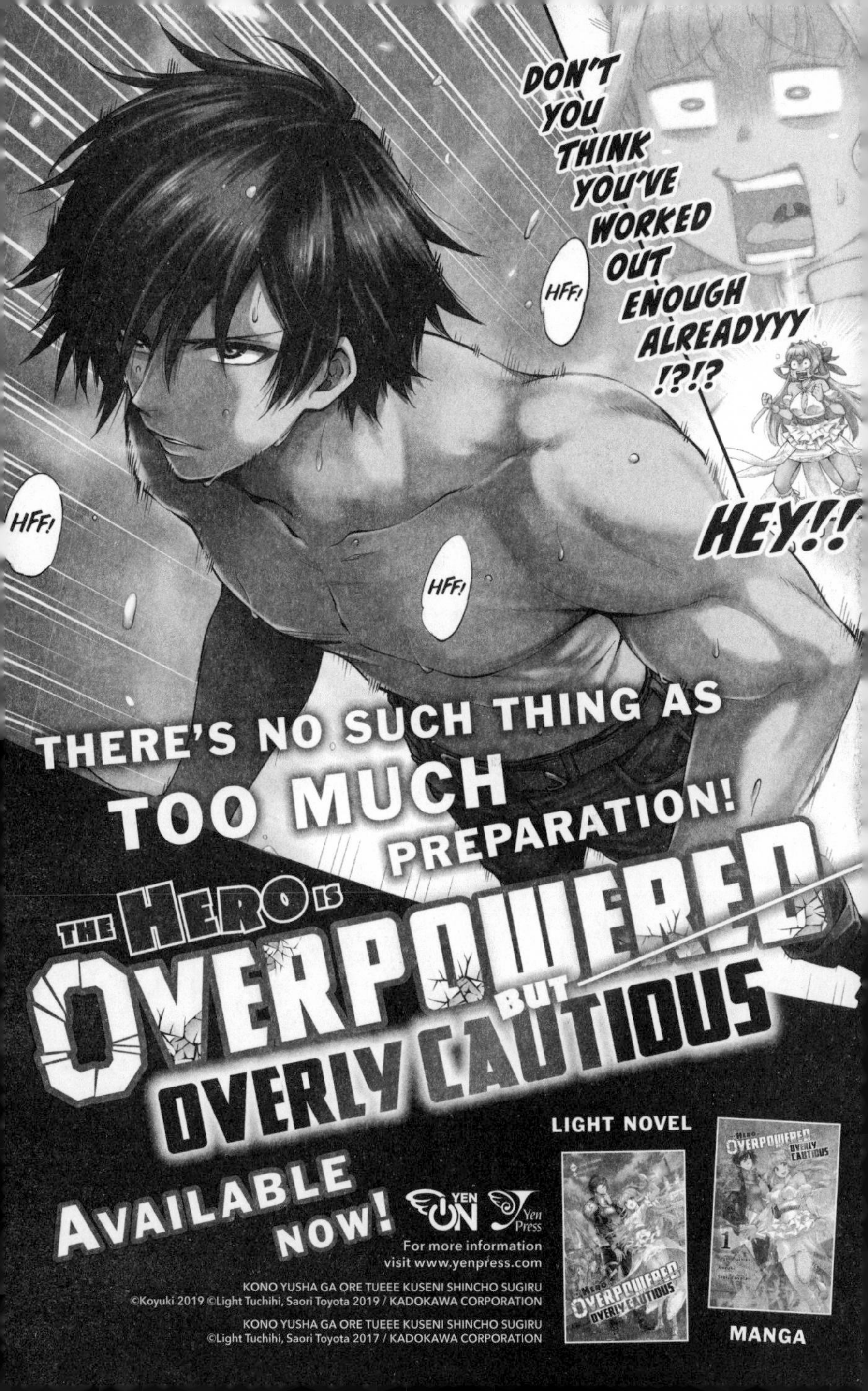
DON'T YOU THINK YOU'VE WORKED OUT ENOUGH ALREADYYY !?!?
HEY!!
HFF!
HFF!
HFF!
THERE'S NO SUCH THING AS TOO MUCH PREPARATION!
THE HERO IS OVERPOWERED BUT OVERLY CAUTIOUS
LIGHT NOVEL
MANGA
AVAILABLE NOW!
YEN ON
Yen Press
For more information visit www.yenpress.com
KONO YUSHA GA ORE TUEEE KUSENI SHINCHO SUGIRU ©Koyuki 2019 ©Light Tuchihi, Saori Toyota 2019 / KADOKAWA CORPORATION
KONO YUSHA GA ORE TUEEE KUSENI SHINCHO SUGIRU ©Light Tuchihi, Saori Toyota 2017 / KADOKAWA CORPORATION

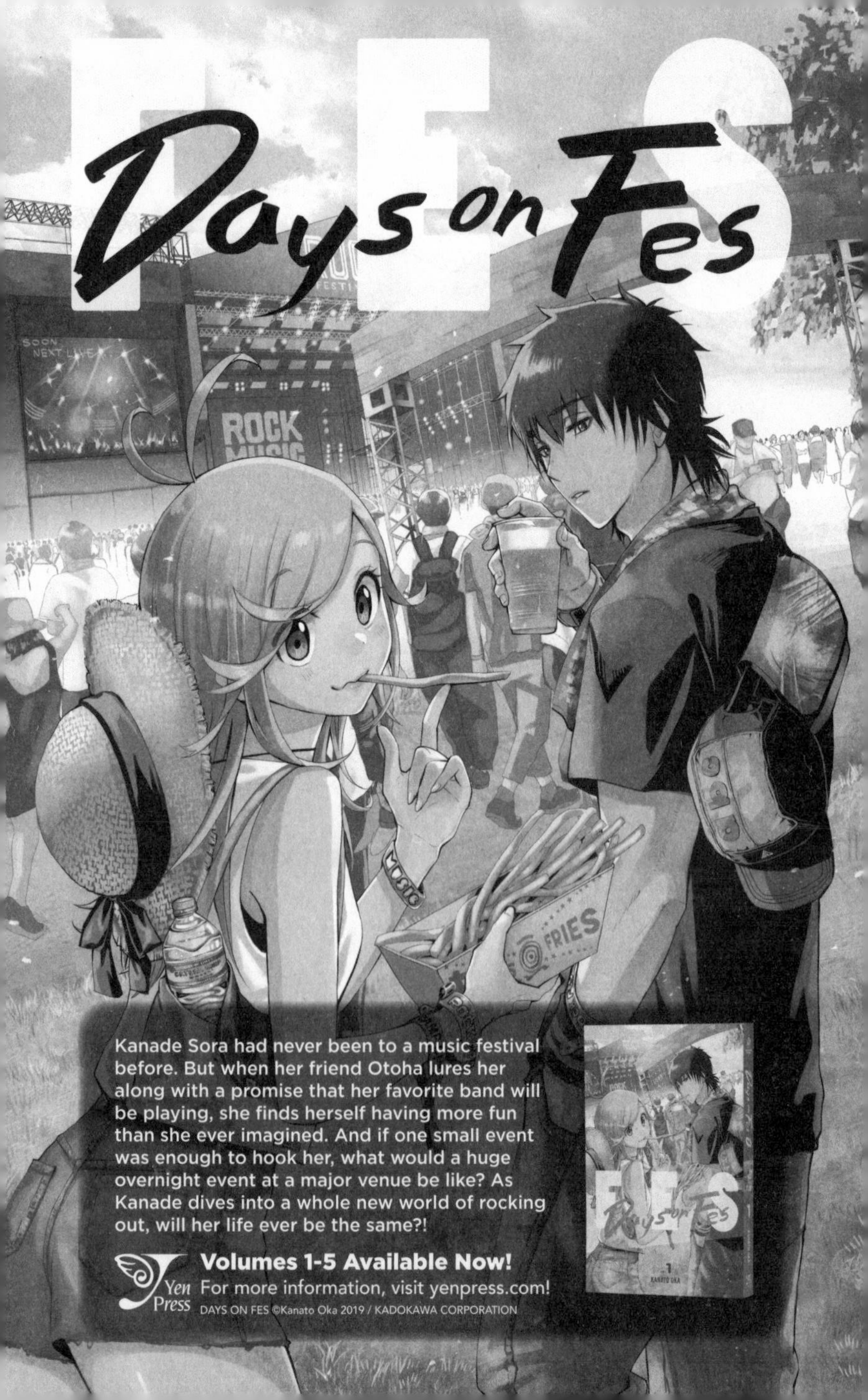
Days on Fes
Kanade Sora had never been to a music festival before. But when her friend Otoha lures her along with a promise that her favorite band will be playing, she finds herself having more fun than she ever imagined. And if one small event was enough to hook her, what would a huge overnight event at a major venue be like? As Kanade dives into a whole new world of rocking out, will her life ever be the same?!
Yen Press
Volumes 1-5 Available Now!
For more information, visit yenpress.com!
DAYS ON FES ©Kanato Oka 2019 / KADOKAWA CORPORATION

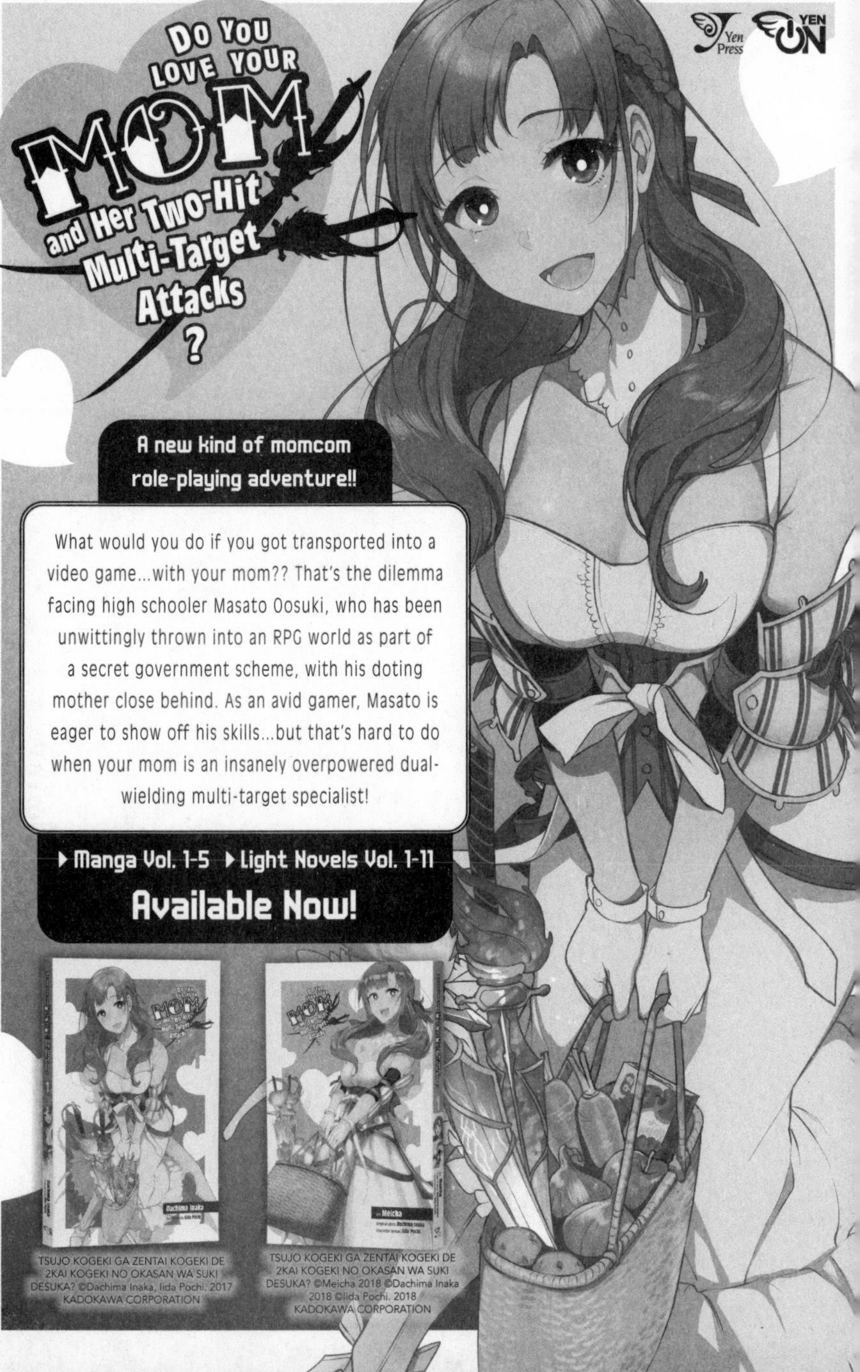
Yen Press
YEN ON
DO YOU LOVE YOUR MOM and Her Two-Hit Multi-Target Attacks?
A new kind of momcom role-playing adventure!!
What would you do if you got transported into a video game...with your mom?? That's the dilemma facing high schooler Masato Oosuki, who has been unwittingly thrown into an RPG world as part of a secret government scheme, with his doting mother close behind. As an avid gamer, Masato is eager to show off his skills...but that's hard to do when your mom is an insanely overpowered dual-wielding multi-target specialist!
▶ Manga Vol. 1-5 ▶ Light Novels Vol. 1-11
Available Now!
TSUJO KOGEKI GA ZENTAI KOGEKI DE 2KAI KOGEKI NO OKASAN WA SUKI DESUKA? ©Dachima Inaka, Iida Pochi. 2017 KADOKAWA CORPORATION
TSUJO KOGEKI GA ZENTAI KOGEKI DE 2KAI KOGEKI NO OKASAN WA SUKI DESUKA? ©Meicha 2018 ©Dachima Inaka 2018 ©Iida Pochi. 2018 KADOKAWA CORPORATION

SPY CLASSROOM 02

SeuKaname

- ORIGINAL STORY **Takemachi**
- CHARACTER DESIGN **Tomari**

- TRANSLATION **Nathaniel Hiroshi Thrasher**   - LETTERING **Arbash Mughal**

SPY KYOSHITSU Vol. 2
© SeuKaname 2021
© Takemachi, Tomari 2021
First published in Japan in 2021 by KADOKAWA CORPORATION, Tokyo.
English translation rights arranged with KADOKAWA CORPORATION, Tokyo and Yen Press, LLC through Tuttle-Mori Agency, Inc.

English translation © 2022 by Yen Press, LLC

Yen Press
150 West 30th Street, 19th Floor
New York, NY 10001

Visit us at yenpress.com
facebook.com/yenpress ■ twitter.com/yenpress
yenpress.tumblr.com ■ instagram.com/yenpress

First Yen Press Edition: June 2022
Edited by Yen Press Editorial: Won Young Seo
Designed by Yen Press Design: Jane Sohn, Andy Swist

Yen Press is an imprint of Yen Press, LLC.
The Yen Press name and logo are trademarks of Yen Press, LLC.

Library of Congress Control Number: 2021948867

ISBNs: 978-1-9753-4512-9 (paperback)
978-1-9753-4513-6 (ebook)

10 9 8 7 6 5 4 3 2 1

WOR

Printed in the United States of America